A Troubled Marriage

A Troubled Marriage

Domestic Violence and the Legal System

Leigh Goodmark

NEW YORK UNIVERSITY PRESS
New York and London

NEW YORK UNIVERSITY PRESS
New York and London
www.nyupress.org

References to Internet websites (URLs) were accurate at the time of writing.
Neither the author nor New York University Press is responsible for URLs
that may have expired or changed since the manuscript was prepared.

Library of Congress Cataloging-in-Publication Data

Goodmark, Leigh, 1969–
A troubled marriage : domestic violence and the legal system /
Leigh Goodmark.
p. cm.
Includes bibliographical references and index.
ISBN 978-0-8147-3222-9 (cl : alk. paper)
ISBN 978-0-8147-3343-1 (ebook)
ISBN 978-0-8147-3344-8 (ebook)
1. Family violence—Law and legislation—United States.
2. Justice, Administration of—United States. I. Title.
KF9322.G65   2011
345.73'02555—dc23   2011028189

New York University Press books are printed on acid-free paper,
and their binding materials are chosen for strength and durability.
We strive to use environmentally responsible suppliers and materials
to the greatest extent possible in publishing our books.

Manufactured in the United States of America
10 9 8 7 6 5 4 3 2 1

For Doug, Juliet, and Carter

Contents

Acknowledgments

For the past two years, I have had the luxury of thinking and writing about the issues that I care about passionately. I have a great many people to thank for that opportunity.

Deborah Gershenowitz, Gabrielle Begue, and NYU Press gave me the chance to do something I have always wanted to do. I am grateful for the opportunity and for their support of this project.

Dean Phil Closius and the University of Baltimore School of Law have consistently provided me with what I needed to complete this book: research assistance, time to write, and encouragement. Dean Closius's unstinting support for the University of Baltimore's Center on Applied Feminism has also given me a platform for engaging others who are thinking and writing about these issues. I am lucky to teach at a school with a gifted faculty that cares deeply about feminism. Special thanks to Professors Michele Gilman, Jane Murphy, Dionne Koller, Nancy Modesitt, Amy Dillard, Rachel Camp, Kim Brown, Michael Meyerson, and Garrett Epps, who consistently encouraged me as I wrote. Professor Margaret E. Johnson is the best friend, collaborator, and colleague a person could have. I am grateful for her enthusiasm, her belief in me and in this book, her tireless work on behalf of women subjected to abuse, and her willingness to share her thoughts about that work with me.

Professors Melissa Breger, Margaret Drew, Catherine Klein, Tamara Kuennen, Kelly Browe Olson, and Robin Runge all read drafts of chapters (and in some cases, drafts of the whole book) and gave me the benefit of their expertise and their invaluable insights. Professor Nancy Levit is a wonderful mentor. I cannot thank her enough for her support, her line-editing skills, her pointed questions, and her willingness to share her publishing experience.

Thanks to Washington University Law School, the University of Cincinnati School of Law, the Southeastern Association of Law Schools, Northeastern University School of Law, the New England School of Law, and LatCrit for giving me opportunities to present portions of the book and to benefit from participants' feedback. Portions of articles appearing in the *Florida*

State University Law Review, the Yale Journal of Law and Feminism, and the Washington University Journal of Law and Policy were adapted for the book; I thank the staffs of those journals for their work.

My research assistants—Tamara Sanders Dowd, Kate Kiemle Buckley, Jennifer Salyers, Kristen Ross, Kate Hummel, and particularly Evan Koslow and Peggy Chu—have all contributed enormously to this book. I thank them for their tireless work, their unending good humor, and their willingness to decipher my cryptic requests at all hours of the day and night. Bijal Shah tracked down every book and obscure article I requested. My administrative assistant, Shannon Wrenn, makes my life run so seamlessly that I have no idea what goes wrong.

My mother, Marsha Wahrman, taught me to be a feminist; my father, Jerry Goodmark, taught me that a lawyer's job is to help make people's lives better. Their influences are clear in this work. Thanks to my brother Craig, who always helps me keep things in perspective. I might give you a free copy after all.

My children, Juliet and Carter, decorated my research boxes when I was writing and could not play with them. My husband, Doug, has listened to me howl about the injustices my clients experience for more than 15 years. Their support, encouragement, and love are unmatched. They are the reason that I am able to do the work that I do, and for that, and everything else, I thank them.

Introduction

The telephone rings. Your daughter—or sister, or friend—is on the other end, describing how her partner abused her and asking for your advice. What would you tell her? To call the police, press charges, seek a protective order or divorce? The chances are good that one of the options that immediately came to mind involved the legal system. Even if your initial response was not legal, it is virtually certain that if your daughter or sister or friend chose to disclose the abuse to anyone else, she would come into contact with the legal system at some point. While shelter, counseling, and other services are available for women subjected to abuse, no other intervention is as frequently invoked as the law—indeed, access to other services may only be available if a woman subjected to abuse¹ pursues some sort of legal remedy against her partner. Women subjected to abuse are steered toward the legal system, assured that the system will keep them safe, offered a proscribed set of choices reflecting prevalent notions of what an appropriate intervention in a case involving domestic violence should be, and expected to choose one of those options.

That there is a legal response to domestic violence at all is, for some, a victory in and of itself. Historically, domestic violence was treated as a private affair, an extension of the husband's right to control the behavior of his wife, to be handled within the confines of the home. Only in the last 40 years or so has American society—pushed by the feminists, activists, and women subjected to abuse who made up the early battered women's movement—acknowledged that public systems and institutions have a responsibility to address abuse, and chosen the legal system as the primary vehicle for doing so.

Convinced that the state should intervene on behalf of women subjected to abuse, advocates urged the state to assume responsibility for policing and prosecuting domestic violence. The drive to criminalize domestic violence, the focus on police response, and the development of civil and criminal laws specifically designed to address domestic violence were policy choices proposed and endorsed by many, although not all, within the battered women's movement. These policy initiatives dovetailed with a growing societal desire to get "tough on crime" and attracted backers interested in channeling resources into police and prosecution. The Violence Against Women Act of 1994 articulated the state's priorities in addressing domestic violence: law-related services, particularly within the criminal justice system, received exponentially greater funding than counseling, shelters, transitional housing, or other non-legal assistance for women subjected to abuse.

This turn to the law was consistent with the worldview of the women advocating for state involvement in combating domestic violence. The early battered women's movement was a feminist movement, and feminism has long relied on the law to redress women's subordination. The equality feminists of the 1970s turned to the courts to fight laws and policies that treated men and women differently in a variety of contexts, including receipt of alimony, administering estates, serving on juries, and eligibility for public benefits. Feminists fought for equality in the workforce and education, giving teeth to Title VII of the Civil Rights Act of 1964's ban on discrimination in employment on the basis of sex and the requirement in Title IX of the Education Amendments of 1972 that men and women have equal access to a range of educational opportunities, from university admissions to high school athletics. While there has certainly been criticism of feminism's reliance on the law, it is undeniable that using the law to fight discrimination brought huge gains for women throughout the 1970s and 1980s. That feminists would again turn to the law to address abuse in the home, therefore, was not terribly surprising.

The particular bent of domestic violence law, however, is attributable not to equality feminism, but to the prevailing feminist ideology of the 1980s and 1990s, when many of these laws were enacted: dominance feminism. Dominance feminists, led by law professor Catharine MacKinnon, contended that male domination of women in the sexual sphere was the primary vehicle for women's continued subordination. MacKinnon argued that "our male-dominated society, aided by male-dominated laws, had constructed women as sexual objects for the use of men."[2] Dominance feminists cast the unwillingness of the law to confront issues of sexual harassment, rape, and domestic violence as a manifestation of men's assertion of dominion over the sexuality of women. But for all of its discourse around law as a reflection of male desires, norms, priorities, and mores, dominance feminists were surprisingly willing to rely on the law and on the men charged with enforcing the law—police, prosecutors, lawyers, and judges—to protect women from societal expressions of male domination. Dominance feminists seemed to assume that state intervention on behalf of women would yield a net positive result, and, in keeping with that belief, turned to the state to fight women's subordination.

To justify the need for a state response, dominance feminists argued that women were victims of patriarchal authority within the home, an authority frequently asserted through the use of physical, psychological, and sexual violence without societal sanction or repercussions. Domestic violence was seen as part of a system of societal norms that granted men dominion over their homes and everything within them, including their families, norms that tacitly gave men the ability, if not the right, to use physical violence to maintain control over their possessions. Deeply held beliefs about the state's powerlessness to intervene in private family matters enabled men to abuse their wives with impunity. To break a man's hegemony over his abused spouse, dominance feminists argued, required the state to pierce the veil of privacy, to challenge men's presumptive authority to "discipline" their wives, and ultimately, to intervene in the life of the family using the power of the legal system to send the message that the continued domination and control of women through abuse would not be permitted by the state. These arguments have been spectacularly persuasive in erecting a criminal and civil legal response to domestic violence. Today, every state has both criminal and civil laws that enable the state to intervene on behalf of women subjected to abuse, provide women subjected to abuse with protection, punish men who abuse their partners, and consider domestic violence in a variety of legal settings.

The feminists who fought for laws and policies to address domestic violence looked at domestic violence through the lens of dominance feminism. That lens colored the advocacy choices that they made. Domestic violence law and policy reflects the influence of dominance feminism in its definitions of domestic violence, its images of "victims" and "perpetrators," its preference for separating women subjected to abuse from their partners, and its emphasis on the role of the state in righting power imbalances between women subjected to abuse and their partners. Legal definitions of domestic violence, informed by dominance feminism's conception of women as subordinated through force and the threat of force, focus disproportionately on physical abuse. Stereotypes of women subjected to abuse as passive, weak, and powerless grew from dominance feminism's theoretical construct of women as (potential or actual) victims. Within the domestic violence literature, the portrait of a subordinated woman in need of salvation anchored laws and policies that assumed that all women subjected to abuse do want or should want separation from their partners. That belief in the passivity of women subjected to abuse and the state's responsibility to intervene to save subordinated women has been used to justify mandatory interventions that deprive women subjected to abuse of autonomy and agency in the name of protection. These theories, and the policy choices that stem from them, have shaped the legal response to domestic violence: excessively focused on physical violence rather than the totality of a woman's experience of abuse, concerned primarily with separating women from their partners, regardless of the effectiveness of such policies or the desires of individual women, and bound to stereotypes of women subjected to abuse that take power from individual women and validate intrusions on women's autonomy.

The belief that the legal system is best placed to respond to domestic violence has become a cultural norm. That norm, in turn, has created expectations that women will use the legal system and that the system will provide women with the protection and support that they need. Both of those premises are open to challenge, however. The willingness of women subjected to abuse to use the legal system turns on a number of contextual variables, including race, class, sexual orientation, immigration status, relationship status, disability, geographic location, and previous experience with the law. Openness to engaging the system also varies by which part of the system is at issue—the criminal or civil justice system. The law is simply not a one size fits all solution. Moreover, legal remedies are sometimes insufficient to protect women subjected to abuse. The media are replete with stories of women who called the police, obtained protective orders, assisted with the criminal prosecution of their partners, or sought the assistance of the family courts, only to be further abused, sometimes fatally. Worse still, in seeking the assistance of the legal system, many women are forced to endure the scorn and skepticism of the police, prosecutors, lawyers, and judges they believed were there to help them.

The time has come to reevaluate the legal system's responsiveness to the complex and variable needs of women subjected to abuse. One way to engage in such a reexamination is to shift the theoretical lens through which domestic violence law and policy is viewed. The dominance feminist perspective has been challenged by feminist theorists who argue that the experiences of individual women, rather than a stereotyped universal woman—the subordinated victim—must be at the center of feminist theorizing and policymaking. Anti-essentialist feminists argue that there is no unitary women's experience; how women of color experience domestic violence may be vastly different from white women, or poor women different from those with greater means. The attempt to shoehorn all women's experiences into that of the über-woman, anti-essentialist feminists contend, has privileged the experiences of white, middle-class, heterosexual women over those of others. Instead, anti-essentialists argue, women stand at the intersection of the various identities that construct them: race, sexual orientation, socioeconomic class, disability, and other defining characteristics. Laws and policies must be attentive to this intersectionality; only then can those policies meet women's needs. Although anti-essentialist feminism has taken root among feminist legal theorists, it has yet to permeate the legal structures, laws, and policies that make up the legal response to domestic violence.

Examining domestic violence law and policy through an anti-essentialist lens surfaces its underlying dominance feminist roots. Anti-essentialist feminist theory prompts questions about why the law defines domestic violence as it does and whose interests are protected (and whose ignored) by domestic violence law and policy. Anti-essentialism rejects the notion that one set of solutions is appropriate for every woman subjected to abuse, requiring instead that efforts to address domestic violence create space for individual women to express their own needs, goals, and values and make their own choices. Anti-essentialist feminism brings the voices of underrepresented women to the fore. Using this lens makes it difficult to defend a system that operates under a restrictive definition of domestic violence, sees all women subjected to abuse as the same, assumes that they all want the same things, and embraces a set of policies intended to serve these presumptive goals. After its dominance feminist assumptions have been unearthed and critiqued, anti-essentialist feminism provides a theoretical framework for reconstructing domestic violence law and policy and for seeking solutions beyond the legal system.

The question of whose goals the legal system serves is a crucial one. Even those women who find a modicum of safety through the legal system may find that the pursuit of those remedies comes at a very real price. The legal system's response is structured around society's goals in addressing domestic violence—immediate deterrence and punishment of abusers and separation of abusers from their partners. But the goals of a woman subjected to abuse may be very different, and whether her interaction with the legal system is a positive one depends, in large part, on what her goals for the interaction are. In a 1997 article entitled "Arrest: What's the Big Deal?" Barbara Hart, one of the founders of the battered women's movement, articulated six goals for intervention by the legal system in cases involving domestic violence. Those goals were safety, first and foremost; followed by stopping the violence; holding perpetrators accountable; challenging the perpetrator's belief in his right to control his partner; restoration of women subjected to abuse—economically as well as to health, to life without fear, to relationships severed by the perpetrator; and enhancing the agency of women subjected to abuse.[3] Those goals certainly make sense from the societal perspective, given that the legal system is charged with maintaining public order and ensuring that citizens comply with its laws. Indeed, most advocates for women subjected to abuse would likely agree with those goals, perhaps even in that order. A different question, though, is whether women themselves would agree with these priorities. Women subjected to abuse might not rank safety first among their goals, and different women would almost certainly make different choices at different times, which can make policymaking difficult, given the need to create laws that govern behavior throughout society. Women subjected to abuse might also suggest that a number of goals are missing, including the desire to maintain a relationship with a partner despite the abuse and the desire to co-parent with an abusive partner.

The battered women's movement has ceded control over the responses to domestic violence, enabling the state, through the legal system, to take primary responsibility for addressing domestic violence and to determine the objectives of that response. Developing that legal response to domestic violence has profoundly shaped domestic violence policy. Millions of dollars have been poured into police and prosecution, parole and probation, and legal services. Funding has also flowed to research on the effectiveness of these interventions, research which questions just how well this money has been spent. In a zero-sum world of dollars for responses to domestic violence, overreliance on the legal system has stunted the development of other options.

This book will explore how the legal response to domestic violence evolved in the United States, why that response has proven problematic for many women, and what a better system might look like. Chapter 1 documents the growth of the legal response to domestic violence in the United States. The chapter begins with a discussion of dominance feminism and traces the dominance feminist influence on the evolution of domestic violence law and policy. The chapter also introduces the concept of governance feminism, explaining how feminists were able to so significantly influence the direction of domestic violence law and policy. The chapter then turns to a consideration of the disproportionate support for legal, particularly criminal, interventions to address domestic violence among feminists and politicians, leading to the passage of the Violence Against Women Act in 1994. The influence of the Violence Against Women Act's funding priorities on the societal response to domestic violence is explored, as are troubling issues created or exacerbated by the government response: the embrace of an essentialist vision of women subjected to abuse and the professionalization of the battered women's movement.

Chapters 2 through 5 critique various aspects of the current legal response to domestic violence. Chapter 2 focuses on the definition of domestic violence in the law, examining how the groundbreaking work of psychologist Lenore Walker influenced the legal definition of domestic violence and grounded that definition in women's experiences of physical abuse, an influence that continues today. The chapter then turns to more recent social science research defining domestic violence and examines why the law has been slow to incorporate these new understandings of domestic violence. The chapter argues that domestic violence law and policy could better reflect the lived experiences of women subjected to abuse by redefining abuse within the law and suggests a new definition. Chapter 3 turns to the stereotypes of women that currently infect the legal system and the ramifications of those stereotypes for women subjected to abuse who seek the system's assistance. Chapter 3 maps the construction of the paradigmatic victim, a construction informed by Walker's theory of learned helplessness and enshrined in the law through battered woman syndrome. The chapter ends with a discussion of the consequences of the failure to conform to this stereotype for women subjected to abuse. Chapter 4 explores the normative preference for separation-based domestic violence law and policy—the assumption that women should and do want to separate from their abusive partners and that they will separate from their partners given the opportunity to do so. The chapter highlights the risks of separation, details and examines the effectiveness of various separation-based remedies, and notes the paucity of assistance available to women who choose to remain in relationships with men who abuse. Finally, chapter 5 considers how mandatory policies, including mandatory arrest, no-drop prosecution, and mediation bans, operate to deprive women subjected to abuse of autonomy and agency when they come into contact with the legal system. The chapter concludes that these policies undermine a fundamental principle of the early battered women's movement—the empowerment of women subjected to abuse—and details the ways in which women experience these policies as disempowering. These chapters all highlight the influence of the dominance feminist perspective on various aspects of the development of domestic violence law and policy, arguing that that orientation is in part to blame for the problems some women face when they turn to the legal system and that it explains why others choose not to use the system at all.

The final three chapters of the book advocate for a shift in our theoretical frame of reference from dominance to anti-essentialist feminism, and reconstruct domestic violence law and policy using that lens. Chapter 6 posits a set of anti-essentialist principles to guide the reconstruction of domestic violence law and policy, arguing for a system that is woman centered and attentive to the diversity among women subjected to abuse and that humanizes men who abuse, maximizes the options available for women subjected to abuse, and looks beyond the law both to aid women subjected to abuse and to address domestic violence. Chapter 7 imagines how a hypothetical case might move through an anti-essentialist legal system. Chapter 8 envisions an extra-legal response to domestic violence, one that provides women with opportunities to seek justice without employing the state-run justice system, creates opportunities for women's economic empowerment, engages meaningfully with men who abuse their partners without subjecting them to state sanction, and enlists the wider community in establishing accountability for domestic violence.

The current legal response to domestic violence serves some women well. But it serves many women poorly, and some women not at all. Shifting the theoretical frame highlights problems within the system, provides a different vantage point for considering these issues, and spurs thinking about how to address them. If our goal is to create a system that is more responsive to women subjected to abuse, shifting perspectives is a good place to start.

1

Developing the Legal Response

In 1970, if your husband slapped, punched, kicked, or otherwise hurt you in some way, you had little recourse. You could call the police, but if they responded, they were likely to tell your spouse to take a walk around the block to cool down. Arrest was rare, particularly in the absence of life-threatening injury or if the assault happened out of the sight of the responding officers (as it usually did). In the unlikely event that your husband was, in fact, arrested, the chances that he would be prosecuted for his actions were also quite slim. If he was prosecuted, that case would be based on a violation of the general criminal laws of assault or battery rather than for the specific crime of assaulting or battering a spouse. In the even unlikelier event that your husband was convicted, it was unheard of to expect that he would serve time in jail for his crime.

If you looked to the civil justice system, your choices were similarly limited. If you lived in a state that permitted divorce on the basis of cruelty of treatment and could surmount the significant evidentiary and definitional hurdles required to establish those grounds, you might be able to divorce your spouse. A court order keeping your spouse away might be available as a condition of the divorce, but was by no means guaranteed. If your boyfriend assaulted you, police and prosecutors were even less likely to be helpful, and no civil relief at all was available. Similarly, if your husband or boyfriend threatened you, degraded you, or forced you to conform to his rules, you had no legal remedy—that was simply how relations between men and women were structured.

Today, police in every state have the ability to make an arrest in a domestic violence case and are either encouraged or required to make that arrest. Police collect the kind of evidence at the scene that will enable prosecutors to establish a viable case even if the woman chooses not to cooperate with the prosecution. Prosecutors routinely charge domestic violence crimes and bring cases with or without victim assistance, and judges can sentence men found to be abusive to jail time and participation in specialized services like batterer intervention programs designed to address their violence. Probation units monitor the behavior of men who have been abusive when they are released into their communities; batterer intervention programs report the results of their work to sentencing courts. Women can seek civil protective orders against husbands, boyfriends, and in some states, dates, safeguarding them against abuse, harassment, threats, and unwanted contact and granting them financial assistance, custody of children, use and possession of family homes or vehicles, and other relief intended to keep them safe. Women can seek divorces based on domestic violence and have courts consider that abuse in making alimony and property distribution determinations. The vast majority of states now consider domestic violence in custody and visitation determinations as well. Over the course of the last 40 years, the mushrooming response to domestic violence has transformed the legal landscape for women seeking relief from abuse.

The coalescence of theory and the ability to translate that theory into law and practice accounts for this stunning transformation of the American legal system's response to domestic violence. Feminist legal theory provided the framework for constructing the legal response, while feminist political power enabled advocates to persuade lawmakers to adopt new laws and policies on domestic violence. Both the theoretical framework and the tactics used to ensure the passage of these laws and policies had profound implications for the shape of the legal response to domestic violence. Those theoretical and political choices provided women with previously unimaginable opportunities to use the legal system to address abuse—but also gave rise to many of the problems that women subjected to abuse grapple with today.

The Theoretical Framework—Dominance Feminism

Rejecting feminist legal theories that advocated for women's equality with men (equality feminism) or highlighted women's innate differences from men (cultural feminism), dominance feminism contended that the legal system's central concern should be remedying women's subjugation, a subjugation created and reinforced by women's sexual subordination to men. As dominance feminism's most prominent theorist, law professor Catharine MacKinnon, explained in her groundbreaking 1982 article, "Feminism, Marxism, Method, and the State: An Agenda for Theory," "feminism fundamentally identifies sexuality as the primary social sphere of male power . . . The substantive principle governing the authentic politics of women's personal lives is pervasive powerlessness to men, expressed and reconstituted daily *as* sexuality."[1] Subjugation to men defines what it is to be a woman; the gender female is constructed by woman's relative sexual powerlessness, through what MacKinnon calls "the eroticization of the dominance and submission."[2] Male dominance is reinforced through sexual violence and the threat of sexual violence, practiced as rape, sexual assault, sexual harassment, prostitution, pornography, and domestic violence. As MacKinnon writes,

> [Y]ou see that a woman is socially defined as a person who, whether or not she is or has been, can be treated in these ways by men at any time, and little, if anything, will be done about it. This is what it means when feminists say that maleness is a form of power and femaleness a form of powerlessness.[3]

In dominance feminism, men are actors, women acted upon; men are subjects, women are objects.

Dominance feminists see the state as "male jurisprudentially";[4] that is, MacKinnon explains, "the law sees and treats women the way men see and treat women."[5] The state promotes dominance and protects male power by ignoring the use of violence against women and codifying the male perspective in law. Because the male experience is "the dominant point of view and defines rationality, women are pushed to see reality in its terms, although this denies their vantage point as women in that it contradicts at least some of their lived experience, particularly the experience of violation through sex."[6] What the state should do, however, is alleviate women's subjugation by recognizing "that male forms of power over women are affirmatively embodied as individual rights in law,"[7] and replacing existing law with a jurisprudence embodying the woman's point of view. As MacKinnon argued during a 1987 debate, "We are looking to empower women. We have the audacity to think that we might be able to use the state to help do it."[8]

MacKinnon cites the qualified success of sexual harassment law to support her argument that a jurisprudence based on the woman's point of view could help women escape subordination. Harnessing the expressive power of the law made "events of sexual harassment illegitimate socially as well as legally for the first time. Let me know if you figure out a better way to do that."[9] MacKinnon concludes,

For feminist jurisprudence, the sexual harassment attempt suggests that if a legal initiative is set up right from the beginning, meaning if it is designed from women's real experience of violation, it can make some difference. To a degree women's experience can be written into law, even in some tension with the current doctrinal framework. Women who want to resist their victimization with legal terms that imagine it is not inevitable can be given some chance, which is more than they had before. Law is not everything in this respect, but it is not nothing either. Perhaps the most important lesson is that the mountain can be moved. . . . Sometimes even the law does something for the first time.[10]

Dominance feminism profoundly influenced the legal feminism of the 1980s and early 1990s. By 1995, law professor Kathryn Abrams would argue that "dominance feminism has become the ascendant feminist legal theory, shaping the socially transformative legal claim for sexual harassment and helping women see the systematic oppression cloaked and perpetuated under the guise of legal neutrality."[11] Though its role would be less heralded, it would shape the legal response to domestic violence as well.

Critiquing Dominance Feminism

Notwithstanding the undeniable power of MacKinnon's writings and the influence of dominance feminism among legal feminists, MacKinnon's work drew pointed criticism for its portrayal of women as victims, its diminution of women's agency, its tendency toward essentialism, and its reliance on the state to redress women's powerlessness.

Dominance feminism's insistence on the centrality of women's subordination led some critics to redub it "victim feminism." MacKinnon's response reflects the importance of the notion of victimization to the theory: "To those who think 'it isn't good for women to think of themselves as victims,' and thus seek to deny the reality of their victimization, how can it be good for women to deny what is happening to them? Since when is politics therapy?"[12] Despite her defense, critics cautioned that the excessive focus on victimization could have negative consequences for women, arguing that such a perspective perpetuates harmful stereotypes of women as passive and weak. One particularly problematic outgrowth of the characterization of women as victims is the undercutting of women's agency. As law professor Martha Mahoney writes, "Defining gender by what is done to women makes it hard to see the many ways in which women act in our own lives and in the world."[13] In its insistence on women as subordinated, subject to the sexual victimization of men, dominance feminism largely ignores women's acts of strength and resistance and capacity for self-governance and self-direction.

Dominance feminism's tendency to assume the sameness of all women's experiences provoked critique as well. Critics charged that dominance feminism was grounded in gender essentialism, "the notion that a unitary, 'essential' woman's experience can be isolated and described independently of race, class, sexual orientation and other realities of experience."[14] Notwithstanding MacKinnon's assertion that men, rather than dominance feminists, were responsible for essentialism, because "we are all measured by a male standard for women, a standard that is not ours,"[15] critics argued that MacKinnon's theory left little room for considering how women's differing identities affected their experiences of subordination and power. Moreover, essentializing women normalizes the experiences of relatively more powerful white, middle-class women at the expense of those without power. As law professor Angela Harris writes,

> MacKinnon assumes, as does the dominant culture, that there is an essential "woman" beneath the realities of differences between women—that in describing the experiences of "women" issues of race, class, and sexual orientation can therefore be safely ignored or relegated to the footnotes. In her search for what is essential womanhood, however, MacKinnon rediscovers white womanhood and introduces it as universal truth.[16]

The notion of redeploying the state on behalf of women invited additional skepticism. The idea that women should turn to a state run for and by men to undo the subordination wrought by men seemed a dubious proposition to some critics. Political science professor Wendy Brown notes, "[T]o be 'protected' by the same power whose violation one fears perpetuates the very modality of dependence and powerlessness marking much of women's experiences across widely diverse cultures and epochs."[17] Some saw the turn to the state as simply trading regulation by one set of men with individual power for regulation by another set of men with institutional power and wondered about the consequences of that choice.[18]

Despite these criticisms, however, dominance feminism flourished within the legal academy and, indeed, throughout the feminist world. The impact of dominance feminism would be profound in the realm of domestic violence law and policy.

Dominance Feminism and Domestic Violence

Catharine MacKinnon never theorized domestic violence as rigorously as she did rape, pornography, or sexual harassment. She categorized battering as a subset of the sexual victimization of women, writing, "A feminist analysis suggests that assault by a man's fist is not so different from assault by a penis, not because both are violent but because both are sexual."[19] But MacKinnon's ideas permeated the battered women's movement and the legal response to domestic violence. The domestic violence movement of the 1970s and '80s embraced the dominance feminist conception of domestic violence as rooted in a system of patriarchy; men's violence was, as MacKinnon had argued, yet another manifestation of men's subordination of women. The early battered women's movement sought to protect these victimized subjects of men's oppression using the power of the state to rewrite the relationships between husbands and wives. While some questioned these choices at the time, the dominance feminist underpinnings of the work of the early battered women's movement are unmistakable.

Battered women's advocates argued that domestic violence sprang not from the problems or pathologies of individual families, but from a patriarchal system that encouraged men to use violence to control their wives and failed to punish them meaningfully (if at all) for doing so. Social conventions and structures created the context within which men could subordinate women; legal structures developed and peopled by men supported and reinforced that domination. Sociologist Kersti Yllo explains:

> Violence grows out of inequality within marriage (and other intimate relations that are modeled on marriage) and reinforces male dominance and female subordination within the home and outside it. In other words, violence against women . . . is a part of male control. It is not gender neutral any more than the economic division of labor or the institution of marriage is gender neutral.[20]

Subordination under the patriarchal rule of a partner transformed women into passive, reactive victims. In response to male aggression, MacKinnon argued, "women are socialized to passive receptivity; may have or perceive no alternative to acquiescence; may prefer it to the escalated risk of injury and the humiliation of a lost fight; submit to survive."[21] This notion of women as weak, meek, and unable to act to protect themselves was echoed in the work of Dr. Lenore Walker, the psychologist whose theories permeated the legal response to domestic violence. Her "dominance-informed theory of 'learned helplessness'"[22] shaped the public's perception of women subjected to abuse and profoundly affected domestic violence law and policy. Her work, and its impact on the legal system, will be explored at length in chapters 2 and 3.

Like dominance feminists, advocates in the early battered women's movement believed in the necessity of harnessing the power of the state on behalf of women. Sociologists Ellen Pence and Melanie Shepard recall, "Within the battered women's movement, there was little disagreement that it was the role of advocacy programs to challenge institutional practices that prevented women from getting the full protection of the legal system."[23] There was, however, heated disagreement about the extent to which the movement should be involved in advocating for policies that would increase the reach of the state into the lives of women and their partners, particularly when those women were not interested in having the state intervene. As one advocate explained:

> It was one of those you're damned if you do and you're damned if you don't things. When we started talking about arrest, I knew it was going to be used against Black men for reasons other than hitting a Black woman. It was things like the Birmingham police arresting 10 Black men to every White man that made me argue against it, but then I didn't want police walking away when a Black woman was beaten either. So in the end, I supported a policy which meant in most cases the man would be arrested and Black women would be down there to get him out. That's the way it is.[24]

Ultimately, advocates arguing for state intervention triumphed, and the response they designed to address domestic violence relied heavily on the use of both the civil and criminal justice systems. How state intervention operates in the lives of women subjected to abuse will be examined in chapters 4 and 5.

Translating Theory into Practice—Governance Feminism

Influenced by dominance feminist ideas about how domestic violence operated and how the state should intervene, battered women's advocates sought to translate those ideas into law, policy, and practice. Governance feminism explains the enormous success of their efforts.

Law professor Janet Halley has argued that despite their insistence on their relative powerlessness, feminists have actually had tremendous success in infusing legal and institutional governance structures with their ideas. In her book, *Split Decisions: How and Why to Take a Break from Feminism*, Halley argues,

If you look around the United States, Canada, the European Union, the human rights establishment, even the World Bank, you see plenty of places where feminism, far from operating from underground, is running things. . . . In some important senses . . . feminism rules. Governance feminism. Not only that, it *wants* to rule. It has a will to power.[25]

This will to power drove feminists to seek legislative and legal remedies for a variety of issues. Halley points to dominance feminist (what she terms "power feminist") victories in the 1980s and '90s as proof of the existence of governance feminism:

[P]ower feminists and cultural feminists began in the early 1980s to identify some fairly specific targets of activism—rape and other forms of direct violence . . . as leverage points for the desubordination of women. They formed important alliances with social and religious conservatives morally opposed to those practices, and made significant progress in articulating and enforcing legal sanctions against them.[26]

In the realm of domestic violence, law professor Aya Gruber notes, battered women's advocates forged partnerships with victim's rights advocates, law and order conservatives, and the state—strange bedfellows for a feminist movement—to institutionalize changes to both law and the legal system designed to deploy the legal system on behalf of women subjected to abuse.[27] While, as Halley concedes, feminists may not have achieved all of their goals, the feminists of the 1980s and '90s were enormously successful in restructuring the legal response to domestic violence, a feat made possible only by virtue of their political power and their willingness both to assert that power and to seek partnerships with others that would maximize that power—even if it meant ignoring the ambivalence of some within the movement and working toward a common goal for very different reasons.

Constructing the Legal Response

Feminists had long seen legal intervention as essential to the protection of women subjected to abuse, both to safeguard individual women and to harness the expressive function of the law. Making domestic violence illegal and actionable sent the message that such abuse was not socially sanctioned and would, in fact, invite the coercive power of the state on behalf of the woman subjected to abuse. The coalescence of dominance feminism and governance feminism made the construction of the legal response to domestic violence possible and transformed the context within which women subjected to abuse interacted with the state.

The first legal responses to domestic violence were implemented in the civil justice system. Using the injunctive relief available to civil courts, advocates created the civil protection order, a court order prohibiting an abusive partner from continuing to assault, threaten, harass, or otherwise abuse and compelling him to stay away from his partner. The earliest orders contained only these most basic terms, but for the first time gave women a remedy that they could access without (in some jurisdictions) having to rely on police or prosecutors for assistance. Women controlled these orders, asking only for the terms that they believed necessary to counteract their abuse. Civil protective orders provided women subjected to abuse with a judicially enforceable right to have their partners kept away from them.

Seeing a range of other problems facing their clients, however, advocates continued to seek additional remedies, looking for ways to establish financial stability for women subjected to abuse, settle custody and visitation issues, and ensure that weapons were removed from abusive partners. Moreover, advocates fought to expand the definition of domestic violence beyond physical abuse, make orders available to women in non-marital relationships, extend the time that orders remained effective, and provide for enforcement of those orders through civil and criminal contempt. Many states passed civil protective order laws in the late 1970s and early 1980s, and by 1989, every state had a civil remedy, but those laws have been amended repeatedly over the last 20 years to address these additional concerns. While advocates may not have achieved all that they would like with respect to protective orders (in Maryland, for example, advocates have repeatedly attempted to expand the definition of domestic violence and to lower the burden of proof for obtaining protective orders, to little avail), by and large they have been remarkably successful in persuading legislatures to expand civil protection order laws. The impact of these laws is examined in chapter 4. The battered women's movement also secured significant changes in custody and visitation law. Most states now take domestic violence into account in some way when making custody and visitation decisions; many state laws include presumptions against awarding custody and/or unsupervised visitation to parents who have abused their partners.

Advocates successfully sought to criminalize domestic violence as well. The 1984 report of the Attorney General's Task Force on Family Violence strongly recommended strengthening the criminal justice response to domestic violence, characterizing domestic violence as primarily a criminal justice issue. As task force member and former prosecutor Jeanine Pirro argued at the time, "We believe [domestic violence] is a criminal problem and the way to handle it is with criminal justice intervention."[28] Changes to the criminal justice system were both substantive and procedural. States enacted laws specifically criminalizing certain behaviors when those behaviors targeted intimate partners and increased sentences for crimes committed against intimate partners; the impact of redefining domestic violence through the criminal law is the subject of chapter 2. States also mandated, through law and policy, that police make arrests in cases involving domestic violence and that prosecutors bring cases whenever sufficient evidence existed to do so. The ramifications of these policies for women subjected to abuse are discussed at length in chapter 5.

By the late 1980s, the extraordinary achievement of the battered women's movement in constructing a legal response to domestic violence was manifest. But advocates reported that notwithstanding these legislative victories, problems persisted in getting the legal system to respond to the plight of women subjected to abuse. To that end, they sought increased federal funding for police, prosecutors, and civil legal assistance. The Violence Against Women Act (VAWA), the result of these efforts, cemented the position of the legal system as the primary responder to domestic violence in the United States. Like the legal innovations that preceded it, VAWA reflected the influence of dominance feminism, with its view of subordinated women and the state's responsibility for acting to end that subordination.

Prioritizing the Legal Response: The Violence Against Women Act

Federal support for law-related domestic violence programs began in the 1970s, when the Law Enforcement Assistance Administration (LEAA) provided funding for 28 local and three national demonstration projects designed to clarify the role of the criminal justice system in preventing and controlling domestic violence. Those grants were not necessarily intended to increase the involvement of the criminal justice system in domestic violence cases; rather, the congressional mandate was to define how the criminal justice system should interact with community organizations and social service agencies in handling domestic violence cases. While the Family Violence Program administered only a small portion of LEAA's overall funding, it was the first federal response to domestic violence, if not the most useful one. Law professor G. Kristian Miccio argues that the program, which funded the development of police protocols for responding to domestic violence calls and training manuals, only solidified previously held conceptions that domestic violence was a private problem created by the bad behavior of individuals and justified poor police response to women subjected to abuse.[29]

Although LEAA's funding for domestic violence programs increased steadily throughout the 1970s, the program was completely defunded in 1980 after Congress denied President Jimmy Carter's budget request. New federal funding for domestic violence programs would come four years later. Despite the outcry from congressional conservatives over what they saw as a federal imposition into what traditionally had been the province of individual families and state laws (Senator Gordon Humphrey of New Hampshire argued, "The federal government should not fund missionaries who would war on the traditional family or on local values"[30]), Congress approved funding for the Family Violence Prevention and Services Act in 1984. That money, designed to increase public awareness of domestic violence and to provide education and training on the issue, went primarily to shelters and social service programs and did not appreciably benefit the legal system.

By 1994, the legal landscape had changed substantially. Feminist victories in state legislatures had revolutionized the legal system's response to domestic violence. Battered women's advocates played a major role in crafting VAWA, deciding what the legislative priorities should be and, in so doing, setting the policy agenda for the next generation federal response to domestic violence. Their priority was using federal funds to reinvent the legal system, to make police, prosecutors, and judges responsive to the needs of women subjected to abuse, using the incentive of significant federal grants. Where before there had been laws, now there were laws and money, and battered women's advocates hoped that the combination of the two would finally make the legal system react.

Enacted as part of the Violent Crime Control and Law Enforcement Act of 1994, VAWA created a set of new grant programs that devoted federal funds to improving the legal system's response to domestic violence. The STOP (Services for Training Officers and Prosecutors) Grant, the single largest pool of money appropriated under VAWA, was designed to strengthen the law enforcement response to violence against women by enabling states and localities to hire and train personnel, receive technical assistance, collect data, and purchase equipment. While victim services agencies must by law receive a share of STOP grant monies, the grant is specifically intended to "increase the apprehension, prosecution, and adjudication of persons committing violent crimes against women."[31] Originally authorized at $26 million for fiscal year 1995, the fiscal year 2010 budget allocated $189 million for STOP grants. The STOP program also received $140 million in the economic stimulus package passed by Congress in 2009; by way of contrast, transitional housing programs for women subjected to abuse received only $43 million through that legislation.[32]

Another large pool of money available to law enforcement is channeled through the Grants to Encourage Arrest Policies program, intended to "assist state governments, Indian tribal governments, and units of local government in treating domestic violence as a serious violation of the criminal law" by promoting and providing guidance to law enforcement agencies employing pro-arrest policies.[33] Prior to 2005, states and localities had to verify that they had implemented mandatory arrest laws or policies to receive funds through the Grants to Encourage Arrest Policies program, prompting jurisdictions that had not already adopted mandatory arrest policies to make such changes to police practice. The 2005 reauthorization of VAWA allowed states to affirm that they had enacted either mandatory or pro-arrest laws or policies, a significant change in federal policy. Authorized at $28 million in fiscal year 1996, the Grants to Encourage Arrest Policies program made $60 million available in fiscal year 2010.

VAWA includes a number of other grants as well, and even when those grants are not made directly to the criminal justice system, they frequently provide benefits to law enforcement. Grant programs targeting women in rural communities, older individuals, individuals with disabilities, and youth all permit grant funds to be used for training law enforcement and funding collaboration between law enforcement, prosecutors, and other community partners. VAWA grants are not the only funds available to the criminal justice system to combat domestic violence; other programs, like the Byrne grant program, also provide states with money to fight crime and to provide services to crime victims, including women subjected to abuse. VAWA also confers non-monetary benefits on law enforcement. The remedies made available to battered immigrant women through VAWA, for example, include the U Visa, which makes legal immigrant status available to women subjected to abuse who cooperate with law enforcement in the arrest and prosecution of their abusive partners. That program, and the benefit it provides to law enforcement, is discussed in detail in chapter 4.

VAWA also channels money into the civil justice system. VAWA provides funding for training judges and court personnel on domestic violence and child custody and visitation. VAWA funds a network of civil attorneys providing assistance to women subjected to abuse in family, immigration, administrative, housing, and protective order matters. Originally funded at $12 million in fiscal year 1998, the Civil Legal Assistance for Victims program received $41 million in the fiscal year 2010 federal budget.

According to the United States Department of Justice's Office on Violence Against Women (OVW), the results of 16 years of spending on police, prosecutors, and courts "are encouraging. OVW-funded grantees experienced increased arrest and prosecution of perpetrators both through new programs and the extensive training of law enforcement personnel, prosecutors, judges, probation officers, magistrates, and related court personnel."[34] Reporting of domestic violence has increased; the rate of intimate partner violence is down (although it is worth noting that the decrease in intimate partner assaults tracks the general decrease in crime rates over the past decade). What has not declined, however, is the rate at which women are killed by their intimate male partners, which decreased less than the rates of other homicides between 1976 and 2004. In 2006, reflecting on the effectiveness of the VAWA programs it administers, the Office on Violence Against Women explained to Congress:

> There are no magic cures when it comes to stopping violence against women. . . . it takes time and effort for communities to establish the comprehensive coordinated community responses necessary for all of these agencies, officials, and practitioners to maximize their individual and collective efforts to reach the goal of ending violence against women. The VAWA grant programs are moving the country in that direction.[35]

VAWA reflects a dominance feminist approach to addressing domestic violence. VAWA not only harnesses the power of the state to relieve the subordination of women, but does so in a way that seeks to shift the balance of power between women and their partners by leveraging state power on the woman's behalf. By devoting the vast majority of VAWA funding to the legal system, particularly the criminal justice system, the law makes a policy statement about VAWA supporters' confidence in the ability of the legal system to redress violence against women. VAWA intentionally brings the power of the state to bear against abusive partners, intervening in relationships, making the private public, and using state coercion to punish men who abuse their partners. In so doing, VAWA attempts to eradicate subordinating behavior.

Placing the original VAWA in the Omnibus Crime Act of 1994 framed domestic violence as a criminal justice problem. Sponsors and supporters of VAWA sold the measure as "a comprehensive approach that is both tough on criminals and smart about crime prevention"[36] and stressed that "[s]tates and local governments can use these funds to hire new police officers and prosecutors, or to train existing cops and prosecutors, not social workers."[37] The bill was intended to fundamentally alter what was seen as society's insufficiently punitive response to domestic violence. As Democratic Congresswoman Carolyn Maloney of New York explained, "Right now, if you assault a stranger, you go to jail. If you assault your spouse, you get therapy. The Violence Against Women Act brings an end to this backward system."[38]

Given that kind of rhetoric, it is hardly surprising that the vast majority of the monies made available through VAWA went, either directly or indirectly, to the criminal justice system. But the intense focus on the criminal justice system crowded out other potential strategies for addressing domestic violence. Invoking the power of the criminal justice system should have been one strategy, not the lone strategy, for combating abuse; in the zero-sum game of funding, monies spent on law enforcement are not spent on other crucial services for women subjected to abuse, like housing, job training, education, or economic development. The limited focus of VAWA funding is problematic because it assumes that abuse is simply a function of lax or insufficient law enforcement, ignoring other potential causes and explanations; as law professor G. Kristian Miccio argues, "[B]y focusing solely on the criminal justice system and criminal sanctions, other aspects of communal life that contribute to the perpetuation of male intimate violence remain unexamined—and unaccountable."[39]

Relying on the criminal justice system also ignored the possibility that the goals of the state and the goals of individual women subjected to abuse could diverge. Social work professor Susan Schechter discussed this problem in the context of the LEAA funding of the 1970s:

> The most fundamental critique pointed out that LEAA's interests lay in making the criminal justice system operate more smoothly and in improving police weaponry and training, whereas the feminist anti-rape and battered women's movements' interests were in preserving victims' rights to self-determination as well as ending violence against women. . . . LEAA brushed aside the fact that improving prosecution rates and helping victims are not always compatible, especially for those women who do not want to prosecute.[40]

VAWA raises identical issues; the dilemma created by such divergent goals will be addressed in chapters 4 and 5.

Essentialism and the Politics of the Battered Women's Movement

Activism around VAWA also prompted questions about who spoke for the battered women's movement. Although law professor Katharine Bartlett asserts in her description of VAWA that "[t]he unity of women's groups on issues of domestic violence has been unequivocal and unambivalent,"[41] some women, particularly women of color, were profoundly ambivalent about and frankly uncomfortable with the direction that the movement was taking.

The battered women's movement has long struggled with issues of race. Although women of color have been involved in the movement from its beginnings, the face of the battered women's movement has been that of a white, middle-class, heterosexual woman. The early women's movement's desire to propound a unified women's experience—a "We the Women" position—ignored or silenced differences in favor of presenting one voice. As law professor Angela Harris notes, the gender essentialism written in to this type of rhetoric worked to silence the voices of women of color. "Not surprisingly, the story they tell about 'women,' despite its claim to universality, seems to black women to be peculiar to women who are white, straight, and socioeconomically privileged."[42] Differences were deemed unimportant, and the experiences of white women became the standard around which law and policy were crafted.

Feminists brought gender essentialism with them into the battered women's movement. Attempting to universalize the experience of being abused, advocates for women subjected to abuse argued that abuse was a pervasive societal problem. As psychologist Lenore Walker wrote in *The Battered Woman*, "Battered women are found in all age groups, races, ethnic and religious groups, educational levels, and socioeconomic groups. Who are the battered women? If you are a woman, there is a 50 percent chance it could be you!"[43] The result of this campaign was to bring to the forefront the one characteristic shared by all of these women—that they were women. Variation in women's experiences of abuse was suppressed behind the face of the dominant culture, the face of a white woman. Unsurprisingly, with white women as the movement's focus, the particular problems facing women of color were largely ignored. While there is little doubt that domestic violence does, in fact, affect women of all ages, races, ethnicities, religions, educational levels, and socioeconomic classes, it is equally true that all of these groups experience abuse differently. Women of color, poor women, and lesbians face a number of obstacles not encountered by straight, white, middle-class women, obstacles that may cause them to respond differently to abuse. The decision to universalize women's victimization in the home, manifested in the movement's "every woman could be a victim" rhetoric, pushed the concerns of marginalized women further to the sidelines of debates about how to address domestic violence.

Putting a white face on the battered woman had a political dimension. To increase funding to assist and legal protections for women subjected to abuse, advocates needed the support of state and federal politicians and policymakers. While politicians may not have been terribly interested in the problems of poor black women, it was easier to sell them on the need to protect their own mothers, sisters, and daughters. In the 1970s, the leaders of the battered women's movement opted to universalize the experience of being abused in order to move the issue of domestic violence onto the national agenda. Battered women's advocates recast the image of the woman subjected to abuse to reflect society's most powerful voices, a choice designed to send the message that because domestic violence affected white women, it was worthy of the attention of those in power. This recasting, though, had perverse consequences. As sociologist Beth Richie points out, "In the end, the assumed race and class neutrality of gender violence led to the erasure of low-income women and women of color from the dominant view."[44]

The passage of VAWA is attributable in part to the success of the battered women's movement in persuading policymakers of the universality—whiteness—of domestic violence. Law professor Barbara Fedders argues:

> The ability of the movement to win legislative victories such as the VAWA . . . seems premised on its capacity to convince legislators that domestic violence affects middle-class and white women as much or more than low-income women and women of color. . . . The conspicuous presence of white, middle-class women sent an unspoken but unmistakable message to legislators: Although domestic violence is a universal problem, it gains political significance primarily because it affects white, middle-class women such as those in this movement, those you know, and those who vote.[45]

During the floor debates on VAWA, legislators referred frequently to the murder of a white woman, Nicole Brown Simpson, by her African American ex-husband, former football player O.J. Simpson, as justification for the legislation.

VAWA's dedication of resources to the legal system reflects assumptions by the white women at the forefront of the movement about the desirability of increasing state intervention into the lives of women subjected to abuse. Looking back on the movement, sociologists Ellen Pence and Melanie Shepard (who embraced the legal response to domestic violence) concede,

[W]omen of color have been far more cautious in mapping out strategies for reform that would involve an expanded role for police and the courts in women's lives. Much of the early work of legal reform efforts was marked by a certain naïveté on the part of the White middle-class leadership about the role of the legal system in maintaining existing relations of ruling.[46]

Women of color, even those who worked as legal advocates, were skeptical of the legal system's ability to help women subjected to abuse: "I think White women talked more as if the courts belonged to us [all women] and therefore should work for us where we [women of color] always saw it as belonging to someone else and talked more about how to keep it from hurting us."[47]

VAWA and the Transformation of the Battered Women's Movement

VAWA also hastened a trend that some in the battered women's movement viewed with alarm from the moment that the first infusions of federal money arrived: the professionalization of the movement in response to government funding. Feminists drove the early battered women's movement, and service agencies reflected those roots. Women who had been subjected to abuse frequently staffed shelters and other organizations. They believed that male violence was a symptom of patriarchy within the home, reinforced by patriarchy in society. Many shelters and service agencies were egalitarian and non-hierarchical, dedicated to empowering women subjected to abuse through self-help. Asserting women's rights to bodily integrity and self-determination were essential components of agency strategy.

The infusion of government money into the battered women's movement brought an increasing number of professionals and professional organizations into service provider roles. Historian Elizabeth Pleck notes that LEAA's preference for shelters founded by established charities over those begun by feminists created competition for finite resources and enabled public and private funders to channel money away from feminist-identified organizations.[48] Government funders wanted to see staff expertise beyond the experience of having been abused; as law professor G. Kristian Miccio writes,

Shelters were required to demonstrate that staff were credentialed in specialized areas, and "credentialed" was often synonymous with having a professional degree. Knowledge and expertise gained through life, work experience, or both often failed to satisfy this requirement. Consequently, formerly battered women, without degrees but with work experience at shelters, were noncredentialed and marginalized.[49]

Increasing professionalization changed not only agencies' organizational structure, but also their sense of mission. Where staff had once felt that they were part of a social movement to combat the abuse of women, professionalization created silos that confined staff to their individual jobs, impairing their ability to see themselves as part of a larger struggle.

Government funding also brought bureaucracy, as shelters and service organizations were forced to change policies and procedures to comply with grant requirements. The need to answer inquiries about provision of services in language that echoed the vocabulary of government programs shaped the ways in which organizations interacted with users of services. Women who had been "sisters" became "clients" for the purposes of government reports, and those who worked with women adopted a more clinical language. These requirements were not designed to change feminist organizational practices, as social work professor Susan Schechter recounts; funders "simply expected battered women's programs to respond like every other social service organization."[50]

Government funding essentially altered the way in which shelters and service providers approached their work with women subjected to abuse. Professionals frequently characterized domestic violence as a criminal justice or mental health problem rather than as a reflection of a patriarchal society. The political dimension of the work of many service organizations was lost. Cathryn Curley, the co-founder of the Safe Haven Shelter in Duluth, Minnesota, acknowledges the tension between engaging in political work and meeting grant-driven expectations: "We were much more activists back in the beginning, and now we're more service providers. We still participate as much as we can in systems change, but we have . . . these grants that we have to fulfill our obligation for. Serve so many people, provide so many services."[51] Women were no longer seen as responsible for developing and able to formulate responses to the abuse in their lives; services became "patronizing" and "pathologizing."[52] Women's options narrowed as professionals urged women to leave their relationships. This change in philosophy highlighted a shift toward assuming individual women should take responsibility for ending abuse, rather than ascribing the existence of abuse to the patriarchy.

Moreover, it departed from the early movement's ethos of helping women to maximize their alternatives for addressing domestic violence by preferring and advocating one option—separation—over all others.

Some service providers voice frustration with the ways in which government mandates shape their work; in the words of one rural Kentucky shelter director, "Once they've funded us I want them to get the fuck out of the way. On our worst day we do a much better job of serving and listening to women than the people at social services or mental health."[53] Nonetheless, their reliance on government money has forced service providers to accede to government requirements, and the pressure to professionalize has suppressed the resistance of many shelters and service providers.

The influence of government funding on shelters and service providers has been well documented. Less discussed is the impact of increased government funding on legal services providers within the battered women's movement. Government funding for legal services, particularly the funding that became available under VAWA, carried with it the same pressures toward professionalism and need for standardization other parts of the movement experienced. Legal advocates, too, have become bureaucratized and professionalized, and those tendencies have undermined their effectiveness in their work with women subjected to abuse, suggests sociologist Angela Moe Wan.[54] Linguist Shonna Trinch documented this impact on legal advocates working with women seeking protective orders in a prosecutor's office in the Southwest. She writes,

> Many people in my field sites confided to me that the term *advocate* is a misnomer, because the work that institutional professionals must do is more amenable to their institutions than it is to the needs of their clients. . . . Put simply, it seems nearly impossible to have advocates located within the very system that they are supposed to struggle against.[55]

Reliance on government funding co-opted the battered women's movement. While "[n]o social movement survives the process of community acceptance with all of its radical ideas intact," historian Elizabeth Pleck observes, "The battered women's cause had been considerably tamed by the coalitions and compromises it made in order to receive state and federal funding."[56] Advocates felt that co-optation as they interacted with other legal system actors. One advocate explained, "[Y]ou don't bite the hand that feeds you. If the state's attorney is signing your paycheck, you're not gonna' stand up in a public meeting and say that prosecutors are failing to do their job."[57]

Advocates lost their ability to serve as an external check on system accountability once they moved inside of the systems that they had once critiqued.

In an attempt to explain why the current state of the battered women's movement is "morally and politically adrift," law professor G. Kristian Miccio points first to the transformation of the movement through government funding into a network of social service agencies.[58] Government funding changed a political movement dedicated to eradicating the patriarchy and ensuring women's empowerment and autonomy into a player within the "nonprofit industrial complex . . . increasingly depoliticized centers focused on a sanitized version of recovery, with no politics allowed if you want to keep your funding."[59]

The battered women's movement envisioned a society where the legal system would be responsive to women's needs, intervene to prevent their subordination and in so doing, subvert patriarchal power. With dominance feminism as a guiding philosophy and the power of governance feminism, the movement fought for and won legislative victories that allowed it to reconstruct the legal landscape, creating criminal and civil justice remedies and funding the development of those systems. But those victories came at a price. The movement went from being woman-centered to victim-centered, from self-help to saving, from working with women to generate the options that best met their needs to preferring one option, separation, facilitated by the intervention of the legal system, from being suspicious of and cautious about state intervention to mandating such intervention. The question is whether, for women subjected to abuse, that price has been worth paying.

Defining Domestic Violence

Patricia Connors[1] was a vibrant, assertive, confident woman when she met and married Bruce Connors. In the early years of their relationship, Patricia and Bruce worked together to achieve the financial stability that would allow them to start a family, pooling their money in a joint checking account. They cooked together and socialized together. After their two children were born, however, Bruce's behavior toward his wife began to change. He required his wife to turn over all of the income from her home-based business, putting the proceeds first into a joint checking account to which she had no access and later into an account in his name alone. Bruce refused to give Patricia money for necessities, mandating that she submit any request for funds in advance. Requests were approved or denied within five days; requests were sometimes denied because, Patricia was told, she had "been a bitch." When Patricia asked to circumvent the process in an emergency, she was told that she should have planned in advance. Later, Bruce gave Patricia just enough money to travel to and from work each day and demanded receipts to prove how the money had been spent.

Bruce placed locks on the interior doors in their home, locking away food, cleaning supplies, towels, and toiletries. He locked the laundry room, denying Patricia the ability to wash clothes for herself or the children. Patricia smelled her clothes to ensure that they were not too dirty and wore the clothes she could not wash until they were threadbare. Bruce required his wife to ask him for a clean towel, a request that he could and did deny, forcing her to use the same one for weeks. He locked away the toilet paper, insisting that Patricia bring him an empty spindle before she could have a new roll. He allowed his young children to unlock the doors for their mother on occasion, but Patricia was never permitted to handle the keys. He would not allow her to shop, because she spent too much money on food, and would not allow her to cook, because he insisted he was a better cook. Bruce told Patricia to shower at night; when she dared to shower in the morning before work, he turned the water off mid-shower, forcing her to ask friends to use their bathrooms to get the shampoo out of her hair.

Bruce belittled and demeaned Patricia incessantly—she was stupid, a bitch, a terrible mother, a pathetic excuse for a person. He routinely cursed at her in front of their children. After the birth of their younger child, Bruce evicted Patricia from their bedroom, forcing her to sleep on a couch and telling her that her side of the bed now belonged to their pet. Eventually, he forbade Patricia from eating with or talking to the family, asking the children, "We're not interested in what Mom has to say, are we?" and "We don't want Mom to eat with us, do we?" Patricia ate the family's leftovers while standing in the kitchen, and her relationship with her children crumbled. By the end of their marriage, Patricia was a shell of the woman she had been 20 years earlier: depressed, anxious, disorganized, insecure, and angry with, yet still deferential to, her husband.

Certainly what Patricia Connors lived with for close to 20 years was abuse. Whether what Patricia Connors experienced was domestic violence in the eyes of the law, however, depends in large part on the state where she lives and the system to which she turns for help. While many women describe the kind of abuse Patricia endured as the worst of what they experience, state criminal and civil laws do not always recognize this type of behavior as domestic violence. The legal definition of domestic violence has largely been focused on physical assaults and threats to commit physical assaults. For the purposes of criminal prosecution or the issuance of a civil protective order, one hit, however minor, often carries greater weight than a daily barrage of emotional, economic, and other non-physical abuse.

The solution to this problem seems simple: change the law to incorporate the myriad forms of abuse that women experience. But convincing legislatures and courts of the need to recognize and remedy abuse beyond physical violence has been difficult. As a result, the law has not kept pace with evolving social science conceptions of abuse, leaving countless women without a legal remedy.

Social Science Definitions of Domestic Violence

In the 1970s and '80s, legal definitions of domestic violence tracked social science theories on abuse, focusing, as those theories did, on physical violence. Theories like the cycle of violence and, to a lesser extent, the Power and Control Wheel, shaped the law's understanding of abuse. In the early days of the battered women's movement, defining domestic violence primarily around physical abuse made sense, argues law professor Elizabeth Schneider. She writes,

[E]mphasizing the physical dimension of the abuse was critically important because society was more willing to redress real, physical hurt. Moreover, physical harm was an easier route to establishing and legitimating the notion that women were the subjects of abuse and that physical battering was something particular, serious, and unique that happened to women.[2]

More recently, however, social science has evolved past the law. Although the social science understanding of abuse now encompasses a range of behaviors and tactics beyond physical violence, the law generally maintains its myopic focus on actual and threatened incidents of physical harm.

Cycle of Violence

Psychologist Lenore Walker introduced the cycle of violence theory in her book, *The Battered Woman*. Walker identified three distinct phases in the abusive relationships of the women with whom she worked: a tension-building phase, the acute battering incident, and a contrite, remorseful "honeymoon" phase. The tension-building phase is characterized by minor physical abuse, as well as verbal and emotional abuse. During this phase, women attempt to delay and minimize the ferocity of the acute battering phase. While the effort to deflect the acute battering phase may be successful for a time, ultimately the woman will lose her ability to hold the man's violence at bay, culminating in an acute battering incident: "the uncontrollable discharge of the tensions that have built up during phase one."[3] The acute battering incident is marked by serious assaults and severe injury.

A period of loving contrition follows the acute battering incident. The abusive partner recognizes that he has acted unacceptably, confesses, begs for forgiveness, and attempts to woo his partner back with promises, declarations of love, gifts, and grand gestures. The third phase of the cycle entraps women in abusive relationships, reminding them of why they initially fell in love with their partners and blinding them to the repetition of the cycle. But, Walker contended, that repetition was inevitable, with the time between the phases growing shorter and the violence more intense, ending only with the death of one of the parties or the woman's decision to leave the relationship.

The legal system was quick to incorporate Walker's theory into its understanding of domestic violence. Actors within the legal system were (and still are) instructed to look for Walker's characteristic phases to determine whether a woman was actually experiencing abuse. The cycle of violence was an integral component of battered woman syndrome; expert testimony stressed the centrality of the cycle in explaining why women subjected to abuse failed to leave their relationships. The cycle was cited in state case law, statute, and practice.

Walker's cycle theory of violence was compelling for a number of reasons. Given the centrality of the acute battering incident in the cycle, the cycle theory squared nicely with the law's assumption that domestic violence meant serious, injury-causing physical assault. The theory's simple narrative comported with the stories of some women subjected to abuse, occurring frequently enough for judges to recognize it and vest it with credibility. The narrative had a clear villain and victim, which allowed for easy categorization of the parties to the action, suggested a solution (interrupt the cycle and the violence will stop), and cast the judge in the role of the hero who could, in fact, stop the violence by separating the parties and breaking the cycle. The cycle reflects the dominance feminist view of victims as passive non-actors—cycles are inevitable, something that people are sucked into and cannot easily escape. The cycle, like a force of nature, is more powerful than the individual caught up in it.

Shortly after Walker published *The Battered Woman*, however, scholars and experts began to question the validity of the cycle theory of violence. While a law student, David Faigman, now a law professor, found a number of methodological flaws in Walker's research and argued that Walker's own data did not support the ubiquity of the cycle of violence, even among the population of women she studied. Faigman contended that although Walker found evidence of each phase of the cycle among a significant number of her patients, she failed to aggregate the data to determine the proportion of women who actually experienced all of the phases of the cycle.[4] In her book, *Empowering and Healing the Battered Woman: A Model for Assessment and Intervention*, psychologist Mary Ann Dutton affirmed that not all violent relationships conformed to the cycle of violence. Later researchers have found that violence does not necessarily increase in frequency or severity over time; in fact, studies show that violence ceases in a large number of relationships, influenced by variables like age, legal marriage, and length of relationship.[5]

Other scholars maintained that the cycle theory failed to capture the complexity of domestic violence. As law professor Melanie Randall argued,

[T]he "cycle of violence" postulated by Walker misses the ongoing relational aspects of women's subordination in their relationships with violent male partners, as well as the patterns of domination and subordination which do not evaporate in any so-called "honeymoon phase" and which extend beyond the immediate consequences of men's discrete acts of violence to powerfully restrain women's freedom and autonomy.[6]

Particularly, the cycle theory discounts the damage done by emotional, psychological, economic, and other non-physical forms of abuse by focusing disproportionately on physical violence—the acute battering phase—as the trough of the woman's experience.

Although the cycle theory is no longer widely embraced by domestic violence professionals, it continues to influence the legal system. Legal system actors are still advised to look for the cycle of violence in relationships involving abuse, albeit in a more nuanced way.[7] Expert witnesses continue to advise courts and juries to look for the cycle of violence to explain a woman's reluctance to disclose abuse, for example, or her recantation of earlier allegations of abuse.[8] In New Jersey, judges considering a plaintiff's request to vacate a protective order are required to ensure that the plaintiff understands the cycle of violence before dismissing the order.[9] Case law in some states requires a finding that the woman has experienced multiple cycles of violence before she can introduce evidence of battered woman syndrome.[10] Expert testimony on domestic violence can be excluded if there is no evidence of the cycle of violence.[11]

The cycle theory provided legal system actors with an easy benchmark for measuring the existence of domestic violence. If the phases of Walker's cycle were present, you had domestic violence. The problem, of course, was the converse—if the cycle was not present, no domestic violence was occurring. Walker herself never made this argument, but the ubiquity of the cycle of violence suppressed other discourse within the legal system about how to identify abuse in intimate relationships and established the cycle of violence as the standard against which women's claims of violence would be tested.

Power and Control Wheel

While Walker's work on the cycle of violence was gaining currency across the country, women discussing their experiences with abuse were identifying a range of behaviors their partners used to keep them in check. Ellen Pence, one of the founders of the Domestic Abuse Intervention Project (DAIP) in Duluth, Minnesota, met repeatedly with women's groups in Duluth, asking, "What . . . is it like to live with a batterer?"[12] Women reported that, in addition to abusing them physically and sexually, their partners isolated, intimidated, and threatened them; abused them emotionally and economically; minimized, denied, or blamed their partners for their abuse; and used men's privileged status in society and their own children against them. In 1984, the DAIP collated this information into the Power and Control Wheel.

This graphic representation of the women's descriptions connects the hub of men's power and control over their partners, which the DAIP theorized was the ultimate goal of abuse, to the physical and sexual violence women experienced through spokes representing the various tactics men used to reinforce that power and control over their partners. The Wheel situated the abuse women experienced within a broader context of controlling behaviors and stressed the intentionality of that abuse.

The Power and Control Wheel has become one of the most frequently used tools to illustrate the experience of being abused. The Wheel has been adapted to describe abuse experienced by teenagers, immigrant and refugee women, and lesbians, among many others. Expert testimony about the Wheel has been admitted in both criminal and civil cases; the Wheel has been offered into evidence in litigation as well.[13] The Power and Control Wheel is regularly used in trainings to help legal system actors understand how the tactics of power and control reinforce the deployment of physical and sexual violence to ensnare women in violent relationships.

While the Power and Control Wheel provided a more complete picture of the structure of an abusive relationship, it did not fundamentally alter the legal system's understanding of domestic violence. Like the cycle of violence theory, albeit to a lesser extent, the Power and Control Wheel prioritizes physical abuse. Although the Wheel more fully articulates the range of behaviors that can be used to obtain power and control over a partner, the external circle of the wheel, the force that holds all of the other types of controlling behavior together, is physical and sexual violence. Without the presence of those forms of abuse, the spokes of the wheel would have no foundation.[14] As sociologist Michael Johnson writes, "[W]ith the addition of violence, there is more than entrapment. There is terror. . . . When violence is added to such a pattern of power and control, the abuse becomes much more than the sum of its parts."[15] Despite its more expansive definition of domestic violence, the Wheel, too, reinforced the legal system's understanding of abuse as primarily a physical phenomenon, with other tactics used to greater or lesser extents to augment control over a partner.

The Theory of Coercive Control

Advocates for women subjected to abuse began to focus on control as the motivation behind men's abuse early in the battered women's movement. In the early 1980s, social work professor Susan Schechter coined the term "coercive control" to describe the constellation of behaviors used to restrain women's liberty and monitor their behavior. Throughout the 1990s, sociologist Evan Stark refined the theory of coercive control, reconceptualizing the intention of abusive behavior and the role of abuse in control.

In his 2007 book, *Coercive Control: How Men Entrap Women in Personal Life*, Stark argued that previous explanations of the mechanics of domestic violence missed important aspects of women's experiences. The cycle theory of violence, Stark contended, was flawed in a number of respects. It looked at assaults as one-time events, rather than as part of a larger pattern of ongoing coercion and control. Stark explained that tension building could be chronic throughout the life of the relationship or happen not at all. Stark also disputed the ubiquity of the honeymoon period Walker described, contending that men were much more likely to minimize the abuse or blame their partners than to apologize.

Stark argued that instead of seeing it as a cycle, abuse was best understood as the combination of coercion, defined as "the use of force or threats to compel or dispel a particular response," and control, "structural forms of deprivation, exploitation, and command that compel obedience indirectly by monopolizing vital resources, dictating preferred choices, microregulating a partner's behavior, limiting her options, and depriving her of supports needed to exercise independent judgment."[16] Men deploy a number of tactics designed to establish dominance and privilege, prevent escape, repress conflict, and secure resources. Those tactics include intimidation, surveillance, degradation, shaming, and isolation.

Intimidation, Stark explains, is used to instill fear, secrecy, dependence, compliance, and loyalty in the woman; intimidation robs the woman of psychological strength. Threats, surveillance, and degradation inform the woman's understanding of her partner's capacity for control and reinforce her sense of vulnerability. Surveillance deprives the woman of privacy and isolates her from family, friends, and sources of support. Surveillance conveys the message "that the perpetrator is omnipotent and omnipresent," that the woman is being watched and her partner is gathering information that can be used against her.[17] Women's driving habits, their expenditures, and their daily routines are monitored. That monitoring is sometimes reinforced by oral or written recordkeeping of their activities. Donna Balis, one of Stark's patients, was required to keep a logbook that recorded every detail of her day, including any and all purchases, no matter how small, a list of the people she saw and talked to, and a monthly menu of meals. Each night, Donna's husband would question her about the entries in the log, assaulting her if she gave an answer he did not like.

Degradation denies women self-respect. Degradation can include marking a woman with tattoos, bites, or burns or forcing her to engage in behavior that is "intrinsically humiliating or is contrary to her nature, morality, or best judgment."[18] Degradation often involves rituals around sex or basic bodily functions, including eating, showering, dressing, sleeping, or using the bathroom. Men force women to eat without utensils, shower in cold water, forgo toilet paper, or sleep standing up. Isolation prevents women from disclosing their partner's behavior and from seeking help or support. Isolation also instills dependence in women and ensures that all of their skills and resources remain available only to their partners.

Coercively controlling men micromanage their partners' everyday lives, controlling access to necessities like food, money, sleep, housing, transportation, necessary medical care, and communication. These tactics, Stark explains, work by "exploiting a partner's capacities and resources for personal gain and gratification, depriving her of the means needed for autonomy or escape, and regulating her behavior to conform with stereotypic gender roles."[19] Ultimately, coercively controlling men seek to deprive women of their freedom and their potential for action, ensuring that they remain entrapped in the relationship.

Violence in and of itself does not constitute abuse in Stark's theory. Although men use violence in coercively controlling relationships, its role is less central and the violence less severe and more routinized. Violence becomes abuse only when the intent of the violence is control. Most victims of physical assault, Stark contends, remain autonomous in key areas of their lives despite those assaults; the intent of the assault is physical domination to secure compliance with an immediate demand. By contrast, coercive control's aim "is dominance rather than physical harm; it targets autonomy, liberty, and personhood; and the tactics deployed are far broader and more insidious."[20] Stark believes that coercive control is a reaction against the increase in formal equality and independence among women in the United States. In countries where women are still unable to assert their independence economically, politically, or socially and/or are obliged to be dependent in their relationships, Stark argues, women live under sufficient external domination that using violence alone enables men to exert control in their relationships. In countries like the United States, by contrast, such external control is either nonexistent or ineffective, driving men to seek control in personal life, where inequalities persist as a function of sex discrimination. Stark likens coercive control to hate crimes: conduct intended to further subordinate those who are already unequal in some way.

Coercive control's primary concern is with abuse as a form of liberty deprivation. Rather than viewing intimidation, isolation, and degradation as serving only to reinforce physical and sexual abuse, Stark contends that these tactics are essential components of the attempt to rob women of their autonomy and that physical violence, in fact, is secondary to these other forms of control. The concept of coercive control resonates with women's common assertions that emotional abuse is often the worst of what they suffer in their relationships.

Stark is not the only social science researcher working with the theory of coercive control. Arguing that coercive control has not been adequately conceptualized or measured in the social science literature, psychologists Mary Ann Dutton and Lisa Goodman draw on social bases of power theory to inform their model of coercive control. Dutton and Goodman define coercive control as "a dynamic process linking a demand with a credible threatened negative consequence for noncompliance."[21] They contend that men use a number of strategies to set the stage for coercion in a relationship. These strategies include communicating the intent and ability to control through past actions or explicit statements; creating or exploiting conditions that leave the woman vulnerable to control; undermining the woman's resistance by depleting her tangible, social, or personal resources; and establishing and exploiting emotional dependency. When the stage is set for coercion, an abuser can exercise control across any of nine domains: personal activities and/or appearance; support, social life, and/or family; household; work, economic, and/or resources; health; intimate relationships; legal; immigration; and children.

Coercion can only be maintained if the threat is credible. A woman must truly believe that her partner has the ability to effectively punish her or to withhold a meaningful reward. As in Stark's version, physical violence is not an essential element of coercive control, but violence does reinforce the credibility of the threat by reminding the woman of the likelihood that violence could recur. A negative consequence need not necessarily result from the threat, so long the woman believes that that consequence will occur if she fails to comply with her partner's demand. Like Stark, Dutton and Goodman also cite surveillance as a necessary component of coercion.

Coercive control has had a limited impact on legal definitions of domestic violence, although, as law professor Tamara Kuennen notes, legal reforms like mandatory arrest and no-drop prosecution grew in part from concerns that women experiencing abuse were not free to request arrest or participate in prosecution because of their partners' control.[22] Where coercive control has been incorporated into legal definitions of abuse, it has been drawn much more narrowly than either Stark or Dutton and Goodman's work would suggest captures women's experiences with abuse. Although some state civil protective order provisions identify coercion, false imprisonment, and/or restraint of liberty as abuse, those terms are usually defined by reference to actual or threatened physical force or violence. Only Illinois allows a petitioner to seek a protective order based on interference with personal liberty, defined as "committing or threatening physical abuse, harassment, intimidation or willful deprivation so as to compel another to engage in conduct from which she or he has a right to abstain or to refrain from conduct in which she or he has a right to engage."[23] On the criminal side, only Missouri recognizes purposeful isolation as a form of domestic assault.[24] Few reported cases reference coercive control; among those that do, ironically, are cases that use the concept to justify terminating the parental rights of mothers who have failed to protect their children from abuse or neglect as a result of coercive control.[25] No state defines abuse as the course of conduct depicted by Stark or the demand/threat described by Dutton and Goodman, although several scholars have proposed definitions of abuse based on coercive control. Those proposals will be discussed later in this chapter.

Johnson's Typology of Domestic Violence

Since the 1970s, scholars have argued about whether domestic violence is a gendered phenomenon. Some contend that domestic violence is a crime primarily perpetrated by men against women; others counter that men and women are equally violent. Both claim that research supports their respective positions. Sociologist Michael Johnson has proposed a fairly simple resolution to this raging debate: there is more than one type of domestic violence, and because scholars are measuring different phenomena, they are arriving at radically different results.

Johnson explains that there are, in fact, four distinct types of intimate partner violence. Intimate terrorism is Johnson's term for the kind of abuse generally described as domestic violence in the social science literature: coercively controlling tactics, including physical violence, threats and intimidation, monitoring, and undermining the will and ability to resist, used by men in intimate relationships to establish power and control over their female partners. Intimate terrorism is similar, but not identical, to Stark's conception of coercive control. Situational couple violence, by contrast, is not used to control a partner, but rather arises out of a specific conflict, "as the tensions or emotions of a particular encounter lead someone to react with violence."[26] Disputes over relationship status, money, children, division of labor within the home, and/or alcohol or drug use are all associated with situational couple violence. Situational couple violence might be used to get someone's attention, to express anger or frustration, or to obtain physical domination in the moment, but it does not involve the generalized control over all facets of a partner's life that characterizes intimate terrorism. Violent resistance is Johnson's term for women who fight back against their abusive partners; this, too, is violence without a control motive, violence used to defend against or delay an attack, to send a message about the woman's displeasure at being physically abused, to retaliate for past abuse, or to escape from a violent relationship. Finally, Johnson explains, there is a small subset of couples in which each partner is attempting to use violence to control the other and to control the relationship. Johnson labels this use of violence mutual violent control.

Johnson explains that one group of researchers, family violence scholars, has been much more likely to find situational couple violence than any of the other forms of abuse because those researchers surveyed data obtained from the general population. Their claims that women were as violent as men came from studies that equated a push, shove, or slap with more severe violence, like choking or punching, and did not measure other control tactics at all. Feminist researchers, by contrast, surveying shelters, hospitals, police, and courts, were more likely to find intimate terrorism's typical pattern of coercive control. Researchers were essentially comparing apples and oranges, Johnson argues, setting the stage for the gender symmetry debates that ensued.

The research on Johnson's typologies is still fairly new. Some studies support his distinctions among types of violence and establish both that women are much more likely to experience intimate terrorism or controlling violence than men and that the violence involved with intimate terrorism is more severe than in other forms of domestic violence. Others question whether what Johnson labels situational couple violence is really just nascent intimate terrorism, measured before the perpetrator becomes controlling enough to be counted in that category.[27]

Johnson's is not the only typology that distinguishes among forms of abuse. In their attempt to answer the question, "[W]ho is doing what to whom and with what impact,"[28] sociologists Ellen Pence and Shamita Das Dasgupta have suggested that there are five categories of domestic violence: battering, resistive/reactive violence, situational violence, pathological violence, and antisocial violence. Pence and Dasgupta define battering as the ongoing use of intimidation, coercion, violence, and other tactics to establish dominance over a part-ner—similar to Stark's coercive control and Johnson's intimate terrorism. They argue that social and historic conditions promote a sense of entitlement among men that normalizes their behavior and often accompanies the use of violence to establish control. Women engage in resistive/reactive violence to escape or stop abuse that they are experiencing or to establish some parity within the relationship that will enable them to protect themselves and/or their children from abuse. Situational violence is used to express anger or disapproval or to accomplish a particular goal, but does not involve control or a pervasive fear of the abusive partner. In fact, "the position of the victim and perpetrator may shift and change continuously" in relationships involving situational violence.[29] Alcohol or drugs, mental illness, physical disorders, or neurological damage can trigger pathological violence; ending the pathology can stop the violence where there is a causal link between the two. Antisocial violence is generally perpetrated by those who are abusive across social settings by individuals who feel no shame or remorse at their actions and fail to understand the conse-quences of their behavior. Pence and Dasgupta argue that understanding what kind of violence is being employed in a particular situation is essential in creat-ing effective interventions.

Defining Domestic Violence in the Law

Despite the development of the social science research, the law continues to define domestic violence largely around physical abuse: assaults, threats, sexual abuse, and forcible restraint. The vast majority of state criminal laws define domestic violence as physical injury, battery, or assault; a smaller number also include acts with intent to cause fear of bodily harm in their definitions. Only two states, Nevada and Rhode Island, define criminal domestic violence much more broadly. In addition to the types of physical violence that are actionable in most states, Nevada includes sexual assault, stalking, arson, trespass, larceny, destruction of property, injuring or killing an animal, false imprisonment, and forcible entry in its criminal domestic violence statute. Rhode Island's criminal domestic violence law covers van-dalism, disorderly conduct, trespass, kidnapping, child snatching, sexual assault, homicide, stalking, violation of a protective order, refusal to relin-quish/damage to a telephone, burglary, and arson. Even in these states, how-ever, the primary focus is on physical violence. State civil protective order laws are somewhat broader, but not comprehensive. Law professor Margaret E. Johnson's survey of state civil protective order law reveals that while all of the states remedy physical violence and most cover criminal acts, only one-third of the states provide any remedy for coercion (generally involving a threat of physical harm), restraint of liberty, or false imprisonment, and one-third address some forms of psychological or emotional abuse.[30]

These definitions are sufficient to provide redress for some women. But for Patricia Connors, the law's insistence on physical violence meant that the abuse she experienced was not actionable, not legally relevant. The law currently leaves unregulated a wide swath of behavior that many would consider abusive unless that behavior is accompanied by some form of physical violence. Absent that one slap or punch, years of emotional, economic, and other forms of abuse go unaddressed.

The profanity, insults, public humiliation, and degradation that Patricia Connors experienced all constitute emotional or psychological abuse (the terms are often used interchangeably). Sociologists' categorizations of emotional/psychological abuse vary. The Follingstad and DeHart Psychological Abuse survey asks about conduct including treatment of women as inferior and humiliation and/or degradation; isolation; emotional or sexual withdrawal or blackmail; verbal attacks; economic deprivation and threats of harm; destabilization of a woman's perception of reality; use of male privilege; control of personal behavior; jealousy and/or suspicion; intimidation; and the failure to live up to expectations. Sociologist Richard Tolman's Psychological Maltreatment of Women Inventory (PMWI) questions women about relationship experiences ranging from a partner calling her names, swearing, and yelling at her to a partner interfering with family relationships, monitoring her time, and making her feel insane. The PMWI captures two broad categories of emotional/psychological abuse: dominance/isolation abuse involves adherence to rigid gender roles, enforced subservience, and isolation from resources, while emotional and verbal abuse is characterized by withholding emotional resources, verbal attacks, and degradation.[31]

Current law provides a remedy for some aspects of emotional/psychological abuse. Missouri and Nevada, for example, have criminalized forms of emotional/psychological abuse; Missouri prohibits knowingly causing isolation, while Nevada includes harassment in its criminal domestic violence statute.[32] In their definitions of abuse, the civil protection order laws of some states, including Delaware, Hawaii, Illinois, and New Mexico, specifically cover conduct that causes the petitioner emotional distress or injury.[33] Harassment and stalking, often defined by reference to criminal law, are actionable under the civil protection order laws of a number of other states; these provisions are sometimes broad enough to cover emotional/psychological abuse.

But emotional/psychological abuse is far more than just the harassment or stalking covered by most domestic violence laws. The majority of the states fail to capture the relentless belittling, the degradation of being made to beg for money or having to ask for (and be denied) a new towel, and the torrent of verbal abuse that women like Patricia Connors endure, abuse that is as, if not more, painful than much of the physical violence to which women are subjected. An advertisement from Thailand makes the point graphically. Men are depicted with arms thrusting out of their mouths to punch, grab, and pull the hair of their partners, equating verbal abuse with the physical impact of being attacked. Some women never face physical violence at all, but their experiences with abuse are no less affecting. As one woman subjected to abuse explained, "He became relentless, and his verbal assaults escalated to the point where he didn't have to hit me. He actually never hit me, but that made it scarier. My best friend told me, 'If he does ever hit you, he won't stop until you're dead.'"[34]

Economic abuse, tactics that "control a woman's ability to acquire, use, and maintain economic resources, thus threatening her economic security and potential for self-sufficiency,"[35] has largely been ignored by the legal system, although scholars have long recognized the interplay between economics and abuse. A lack of economic security makes it difficult for women to leave abusive relationships; men control women's access to economic resources to prevent their partners from amassing the kind of power that could allow them to survive on their own. Psychologists from Michigan State University have suggested that economic abuse consists of two components: economic control and economic exploitation. Economic control includes tactics like preventing women from working, taking and withholding women's resources from them, dictating how money is spent, and requiring strict accountability when money is spent. Stealing money or property, building debt and destroying credit, refusing to work, and squandering money can all be considered economic exploitation.[36]

In her work with women on welfare, sociologist Jody Raphael documented a wide range of economic control tactics used by the women's partners. Men destroyed the books, training materials, and homework of partners enrolled in educational programs; kept women up all night before tests or interviews; inflicted facial injuries on their partners, preventing the women from attending school or work; failed to provide promised transportation or child care; and harassed women on the job, sometimes until they were terminated.[37] These tactics work with women across socioeconomic classes. Bruce Connors used both economic control (keeping Patricia from using the computer while she was in graduate school, taking her paycheck without giving her access to the joint checking account, requiring that she submit requests for money before it was spent and receipts afterward) and economic exploitation (building up tens of thousands of dollars in credit card debt in her name) to control Patricia. A 2008 study of women who experienced psychological and physical abuse found that 99 percent of the women surveyed—almost every woman researchers asked—had also been subjected to economic abuse.[38]

Economic abuse entraps women in violent relationships. Raphael explains the double bind experienced by economically vulnerable women: "Men use violence to keep women economically disempowered and dependent on them. Then, men manipulate these very conditions of poverty to further abuse women, who are thus trapped in poverty and abuse."[39] Yet only one state, Michigan, includes a narrow definition of economic abuse in its civil protective order law. Michigan permits a court to issue a protective order upon a finding of reasonable cause to believe that a person is interfering with the petitioner at the petitioner's place of employment or education or otherwise engaging in conduct that impairs the petitioner's employment or educational relationship or environment.[40] While such provisions provide relief for some women experiencing economic abuse, they reach only one aspect of a much larger source of control for abusive partners.

A newer area of inquiry for researchers is reproductive abuse. Men control their partners by interfering with, even terminating, their pregnancies. Studies have long established that homicide is a leading cause of maternal mortality.[41] The man's physical violence need not be the instrument of termination, however. As Evan Stark recounts, Donna Balis's medical records revealed that she had undergone an abortion "at her husband's insistence and against her wishes and religious scruples."[42]

Creating an unwanted pregnancy is another means of control. A recent study of young women seeking services from family planning clinics found that a significant number of women experience pregnancy coercion (the use of demands, threats, and violence to pressure a partner to become pregnant) and birth control sabotage (denying women birth control, destroying or sabotaging contraceptive devices). Those women are much more likely than other women to report physical and sexual violence as well.[43] The study's principal investigator, Dr. Elizabeth Miller, describes patients whose partners monitor their periods, for example, to ensure that they are not using Depo-Provera contraceptive shots. Miller explains, "Just like violence, it's a power thing. . . . The man is taking away a woman's power to decide she's not going to have a child," believing that the child will bind her to him.[44] Requests to use birth control can also trigger abuse. Worried that her HIV-positive husband could expose her to the virus, one woman asked her husband to use a condom. He responded by accusing her of infidelity and threatening, "Tell me who he is. Tell me. I hope this guy is worth dying for. I hope he's worth dying for." The woman opted to have unprotected sex with her husband because it was easier than insisting he use a condom.[45] No state directly regulates reproductive coercion, and Miller questions the propriety of doing so, given physician reporting requirements: "I'm not sure that a young woman telling me that her partner flushed her birth control down the toilet necessitates me reporting that to the authorities."[46]

Impairing a woman's spiritual life, self, or well-being can be a form of abuse as well. Social work researchers Nicole Dehan and Zipi Levi document three levels of spiritual abuse within the Haredi Jewish culture in Israel, a culture in which living in accordance with religious tradition and law is "an integral, intensive, and all-encompassing dimension of life, as Jewish law demands the incorporation of spirituality into every facet of living."[47] Spiritual abuse can consist of demeaning the woman's spiritual worth, beliefs, or deeds; preventing the woman from engaging in spiritual acts; and causing the woman to violate spiritual obligations, all of which, given the importance of religious performance in the lives of Haredi women, can damage their identity and self-worth. Dehan and Levi tell the stories of women who are precluded from carrying out rituals specifically assigned to women, like baking and separating challah (homemade bread) for the Sabbath, or who are forced to transgress by having sex while menstruating, which left one woman "full of shame and unable to accept herself. She had the sensation of being far from the Almighty and unworthy of His love." They conclude, "[B]y transgressing and forcing his wife to transgress such a central religious prohibition, the husband made her a participant in a very serious spiritual wrongdoing."[48] Although spiritual abuse has received little scholarly attention, other studies have documented spiritual abuse including preventing women from attending religious services or reading spiritual literature.[49]

Although some states cover a broader range of conduct in their domestic violence statutes, theoretically enabling women subjected to abuse to seek relief through those avenues, many forms of abuse remain beyond the purview of domestic violence laws. Legal redress could, however, prove valuable to some women. As a practical matter, civil protective order laws give women access to a range of remedies that other laws fail to provide, like temporary custody of children, economic support, and provisions requiring abusive spouses to vacate shared properties. Criminal prosecution can bring with it specialized counseling and access to services for both the perpetrator and the complainant. On the normative level, incorporating other forms of abuse into legal definitions of domestic violence would capture a vital aspect of women's experiences with domestic violence and serve the expressive function of recognizing and remedying emotional/psychological, economic, reproductive, and spiritual abuse.

Expanding Legal Definitions of Domestic Violence

Scholars and advocates agree that existing legal definitions fail to capture the scope and complexity of domestic violence. As philosopher Beth Kiyoko Jamieson writes about Jane:

> Jane's husband did not break her bones or blacken her eyes, but he did terrorize her. That counts as intimate violence. He did not beat her to a pulp but he did use sex to illustrate his capacity to control her. That counts as intimate violence. He did not pummel her kids or kick her dog, but he did take every opportunity to belittle her, to make her question her perceptions, to demean her. That counts as intimate violence. He did not destroy her belongings, but he did destroy her finances. That counts as intimate violence.[50]

The failure to look beyond physical violence leaves countless women without a legal remedy for the abuse that they suffer. As law professor Margaret E. Johnson has argued, the legal system's preoccupation with physical violence causes judges to prioritize claims that involve physical violence over other forms of equally damaging abuse and desensitizes judges to claims that do not involve physical violence, preventing women from securing relief through the civil protective order system.[51] Whether the law should include non-physical forms of abuse depends to a great extent on the law's goal in regulating abusive behavior. If, as a society, we are simply interested in ensuring that individuals do not physically harm one another, current definitions are sufficient. But domestic violence law could have more ambitious goals: to prevent or alleviate coercive control, to stop psychological intimidation and degradation, and to protect the liberty and autonomy of women. To achieve these broader goals, current definitions of domestic violence must be expanded. How to redefine domestic violence is a trickier question.

Any redefinition of domestic violence has to determine what kinds of abuse should be redressed through the law. Johnson's typologies provide a useful framework for considering this issue. The law already reaches situational couple violence: physical violence that emerges out of a particular set of circumstances, unlikely to be repeated. Both criminal and civil law provide ample redress for victims of physical violence. What current law often fails to reach, however, is what Johnson terms intimate terrorism and Stark calls coercive control. Although the law covers discrete acts of physical violence and some other forms of abuse, it does not provide a forum for redressing the course of conduct described by those theories, and, as a result, denies protection entirely to women subjected to emotional, economic, reproductive, or spiritual, rather than physical, abuse. The incident-based focus of current law often leads to inappropriate punishment for women engaged in violent resistance against their abusive partners.

Scholars have argued that the law could better reflect social science's understanding of intimate partner abuse as a function of coercive control. Sociologist Evan Stark suggests the criminalization of coercive control as a course-of-conduct crime, similar to harassment or stalking, with an emphasis on the deprivation of liberty and autonomy associated with coercive control. Based on the work of Stark and others, law professors Deborah Tuerkheimer and Alafair Burke have each proposed a new crime of domestic violence based on the concept of coercive control. Tuerkheimer's crime of battering would require a finding that a perpetrator had intentionally engaged in a course of conduct that he knew or reasonably should have known would result in establishing substantial power and control over another. The course of conduct must involve two acts that are illegal under the criminal code. Tuerkheimer argues that defining the crime of battering in this way would enable judges and juries to consider the context in which the instant offense has occurred, allowing prosecutors to offer evidence of other kinds of abuse—emotional/psychological, economic, reproductive, spiritual—that are not criminal in order to establish the existence of coercive control within the relationship. Placing the intent requirement in the course-of-conduct prong of the statute deflects the inquiry away from the status of the victim, Tuerkheimer argues, relieving prosecutors of the necessity of proving that the woman was, in fact, subordinated by the perpetrator's actions and avoiding victim stereotypes depicting women subjected to abuse as lacking agency.[52]

Burke's crime of coercive domestic violence is similarly intended to focus on the perpetrator's use of coercive control within a relationship. In Burke's conception, however, the intent requirement focuses directly on the attempt to gain power and control (defined as restriction of freedom of action) over another through the commission of two or more specified crimes of violence—assault, harassment, menacing, kidnapping, or sexual offenses. Burke argues that coupling the intent requirement to the power and control element captures the primary harm caused by abuse and utilizes the expressive function of the law to condemn the desire to limit the autonomy of another person. Criminalizing the attempt to establish power and control also renders the victim's response to that attempt irrelevant; culpability is based not on her reaction, but on his actions. As in Tuerkheimer's proposal, evidence of emotional and other forms of abuse would be relevant to show the intent to limit the autonomy of another, but would not be elements of the underlying crime.[53]

In the civil context, law professor Jeffrey Baker has suggested that states add coercion to the definitions of abuse in their civil protection order laws. Coercion, under Baker's definition, would consist of willful or knowing acts, demands, or credible threats intended to compel a petitioner "to engage in conduct from which the person has a right to abstain, or to abstain from conduct in which the person has a right to engage; . . . with intent to coerce or maintain coercive power" over another, and which would reasonably cause the person to engage in or refrain from the contemplated conduct.[54]

Tuerkheimer's, Burke's, and Baker's proposals would provide relief to women not eligible for redress under current law. It is not clear, however, that any of them would help a woman like Patricia Connors. Neither Tuerkheimer's nor Burke's proposal really expands existing law, criminalizing abusive acts that were not criminal before. Instead, the proposals provide a framework for bringing the entirety of the relationship before the court, enabling the court to consider the relevant criminal acts in the context of other exercises of control. Fundamentally, though, the definition of abuse remains the same, tethered to existing crimes and largely dependent on a showing of physical violence. Burke is quite clear that her intent is not, in fact, to reach other forms of abuse, but rather "[to question] the adequacy of the substantive criminal law's current response to the physical abuse that is unquestionably within the criminal law's reach."[55] Even under Tuerkheimer's proposal, with its more expansive list of predicate crimes, two violations of the criminal law are still necessary. Shoehorning what they are subjected to on a daily basis into the elements of existing crimes might not be possible for women experiencing economic or emotional/psychological abuse. Depending on state law definitions, for example, the behavior that so altered Patricia Connors might not constitute criminal behavior, precluding her from making a case for Tuerkheimer's crime of battering. Moreover, the requirement that other forms of abuse be tied to violations of the criminal law ascribes to them a second-class status, reinforcing the centrality of physical violence and denying the harm that stems from emotional/psychological, economic, reproductive, and other forms of abuse.

A larger issue for all three proposals involves the question of intent. Each proposal requires a finding that the perpetrator's goal in abusing his victim was to establish power and control: Burke and Baker by making an intent to coerce or control an element of the claim, and Tuerkheimer by requiring a showing that the perpetrator knew or reasonably should have known that his actions would result in the assertion of power and control over another. The motivation behind these proposals was to place responsibility for his actions squarely on the perpetrator, preventing his partner from being scrutinized for indicia of subordination. But sociologist Ellen Pence questions whether men who abuse really intend to establish power and control through their actions. Pence explains,

> [T]he women weren't telling us men did it in order to get power and control, what they said was that they ended up with all the power and all the control when they did this.
>
> . . . And I always interpreted it as that women were saying that men desired power and control, and when I did my men's groups I would say that I would always think that you were desiring, but I never heard the men say that.[56]

Psychologists Mary Ann Dutton, Lisa Goodman, and R. James Schmidt note that although the intent to control is widely ascribed to men who abuse, no study has measured the motives of these men, only their tactics. They ask, "Can a behavior be considered 'coercively controlling' without the intent?"[57] Looking back on her work with men who abuse their partners, Pence concluded, "By determining that the need or desire for power was the motivating force behind battering, we created a conceptual framework that, in fact, did not fit the lived experience of many of the men and women we were working with. . . . Eventually, we realized that we were finding what we had already predetermined to find."[58]

Defining domestic violence around coercive control poses a number of additional problems. As law professor Tamara Kuennen has noted, and as the work of psychologists Mary Ann Dutton and Lisa Goodman underscores, there is no single definition of coercive control. Without agreement as to what coercive control encompasses, defining around the concept is difficult. This problem is exacerbated by variation in type and degree of coercion: should domestic violence law reach only serious coercion, or should mild coercion be actionable as well? Moreover, coercion is highly contextual; what controls one woman or works within one relationship may have no impact on another. Coercion, Kuennen argues, is a subjective experience. Consent to coercive tactics may also make definition more difficult, argues law professor Cheryl Hanna.[59] Consent is a defense to criminal prosecution in most, although not all, instances, and consent is particularly problematic in those areas not currently considered actionable, like economic abuse. It may be difficult to argue that a woman consented to having her eye blackened; her signature on a credit application (regardless of how it was obtained) may be easier to produce.

One way to address many of these concerns is to define coercion around the experience of the targeted woman, rather than around the intent of the perpetrator. Defining coercion from the woman's perspective acknowledges just how contextual and subjective abuse can be and that the amount of coercion needed to exert control varies depending upon the woman involved. Establishing a standard that focuses on how a woman experiences abuse, rather than on what her partner does to her, makes the woman central in any legal proceeding and forces the legal system to consider the impact of coercion on this woman in this relationship, rather than some essentialized woman subjected to the same behavior. As law professor Catharine MacKinnon argued in the context of rape law, the question of whether an act constitutes abuse should be asked from the woman's point of view. The failure to use the woman's perspective as the touchstone for determining whether abuse is occurring allows police, prosecutors, and judges to substitute their judgments as to whether a woman is being coerced for hers. The experience of one Maryland woman seeking a protective order illustrates the importance of this perspective. After hearing her story, the judge denied her request for a protective order, explaining to the woman,

> "I don't believe anything that you're saying." He said, "The reason I don't believe it is because I don't believe that anything like this could happen to me. If I was you and someone had threatened me with a gun, there is no way that I would continue to stay with them. There is no way that I could take that kind of abuse from them. Therefore, since I would not let that happen to me, I can't believe that it happened to you."[60]

In MacKinnon's words, in the context of rape law, "it really is her perspective against his perspective, and the law has been written from *his* perspective. . . . Which is to say, only male sexual violations, that is, only male ideas of what sexually violates us as women, are illegal."[61]

Defining coercion as any intentional action or course of action that causes a petitioner to experience a loss of liberty, freedom, or autonomy would empower women to bring claims based on a broad range of abusive acts and would capture the types of behaviors that Stark and others have identified as so damaging to women subjected to abuse. It shifts the focus from the intent to control a woman's liberty (which the man may not possess) to the intent to commit whatever acts—emotional/psychological, physical, sexual, reproductive, spiritual, or other abuse—constrain her freedom. It avoids having to amend the law every time a new form of abuse comes to light—no mean feat in a climate where legislatures often resist any expansion of current law, fearing that women fabricate claims of abuse to gain advantage in divorce and custody matters. Maryland's legislature, for example, has repeatedly rejected attempts to include harassment, trespass, and destruction of property in the protective order statute's definition of abuse. The Chair of Maryland's House Judiciary Committee explained his reluctance to vote for the measure: "My wife says I harass her all the time. Should she be able to go to court for it?" Defining coercion around the woman's experiences also addresses Hanna's concern about the use of consent as a defense by empowering judges to consider whether consent can be meaningful in the context of coercion that women describe.

An individual-centered definition of coercion captures the experiences of women who are not physically abused but nonetheless find that their liberty and autonomy are restricted as a result of their partner's coercive tactics—women like Patricia Connors. Such a definition recognizes that different women may be controlled in different ways. That not every woman would have suffered the fundamental change in personality and behavior that Patricia Connors did as a result of her husband's degradation should not prevent her from securing relief from his abusive treatment.

Focusing the inquiry around the impact of coercion on the individual woman seeking the state's assistance need not be stigmatizing, as Tuerkheimer and Burke fear. In a legal system willing to listen to different women responding to abuse in different ways, a subordination narrative is far from the only story that could be told. If the legal system's understanding of domestic violence expanded beyond stereotypical images of victims and stock stories colored by outdated theories like battered woman syndrome, it could make room for a multiplicity of narratives of abuse, all of which would be equally actionable. Resisting coercion and describing a life circumscribed by abuse can both point to the exercise of control by an intimate partner if the woman is given space to explain just how the abuse has affected her. In her autobiography *Escape*, Carolyn Jessop describes the many small rebellions she engaged in before she was finally able to flee her emotionally abusive husband, Fundamentalist Latter Day Saints leader Merril Jessop. Merril's control of Carolyn and her sister wives was extreme; at various times in her marriage, Carolyn was not permitted to drive, go to college, hold a job, save or spend money, wear certain colors, use birth control, decide who would be in the delivery room when she gave birth, or take her children to see doctors. This control was achieved through a combination of repressive religious doctrine stressing obedience to the male "priesthood head" of the family and verbal abuse. That Carolyn was able, on occasion, to work, save money, avoid sex with her husband, and obtain medical care for a gravely ill child despite her husband's wishes does not negate her horrific story of abuse. The legal system could concurrently consider coercion and resistance; women's narratives of abuse can synthesize those experiences.

Centralizing the impact of abuse on individual women also provides a framework for better understanding women's use of force—what Johnson calls violent resistance. The rise in the rates of dual arrests and arrests of women, particularly women of color, as primary offenders in cases involving domestic violence and the prosecution of women who fight back against their abusers both highlight the legal system's tendency to focus only on specific incidents and punish women's use of force or discredit their claims of abuse without understanding the backdrop for their use of violence. As battered women's advocate Sue Osthoff has argued, despite the criminal system's unwillingness to consider context and its rigidity in definition, "[n]ot everyone who hits their partner is a batterer. A hit is not a hit is not a hit. Context matters. A lot. A whole lot."[62] Enabling women to describe their use of force as a resistance strategy designed to combat coercion could prevent inappropriate prosecution of women subjected to abuse and check the judicial tendency to dismiss claims of abuse made by women who fight back against their abusers.

The goal of domestic violence law and policy could be to hear and validate women's stories of abuse and to provide legal remedies to help them escape that abuse. This goal could be achieved by defining abuse broadly and providing a forum for women subjected to abusive tactics to put their actions and the actions of their partners in perspective. Defining abuse around the woman's experience could be a cornerstone of a woman-directed legal system, a system that values her testimony about the impact of her partner's actions on her life and relies on her participation with prosecution, giving her the option to tell her story if doing so best meets her goals. While a broader definition of abuse would expand the reach of the criminal law into women's lives, the need for women to affirmatively engage the system by testifying to the impact of that abuse would serve as a check on unwanted intrusions by that system.

Defining coercion around the subjective experiences of individual women could raise due process concerns, particularly in the criminal context. For a criminal statute to meet the requirements of due process, it must provide potential offenders with fair notice of the action deemed criminal, using language that is sufficiently specific to avoid invalidation for vagueness. Defining the harm around the victim's subjective experience of the perpetrator's conduct is not unfamiliar in criminal law—criminal harassment and stalking statutes, for example, penalize intentional conduct directed at a specific person that alarms, annoys, or harasses that person. The crime turns to some extent on whether the targeted person was, in fact, alarmed, annoyed, or harassed. Courts have repeatedly upheld such statutes so long as the language used in those statutes was unambiguous. Criminal and civil statutes in some states use a person's subjective experience of harm as the touchstone for determining whether harassment or abuse of some kind has occurred. Both Washington's criminal harassment statute and Maryland's civil protective order statute apply an individualized objective standard, requiring that the person actually feel fear and that the fear be reasonable in evaluating the believability of threats of harm. Careful statutory drafting would be needed, but crafting a definition of abuse centered on an individual's experience of coercion is not impossible.

Revising the definition of abuse has consequences not just for criminal and civil protective order law, but also in a variety of legal settings in which abuse is relevant: divorce, custody, employment, and housing law, for example. Abuse is a ground for divorce and a factor in alimony and property distribution determinations in many states that still consider fault.[63] In some states, evidence of domestic violence is considered in determining whether a father should have joint or sole custody of or unsupervised visitation with his children.[64] Employers in some states are precluded from failing to hire or terminating workers they believe have experienced domestic violence,[65] and some states require employers to provide leave or to make other reasonable accommodations to assist employees subjected to abuse.[66] Landlords in some states are forbidden to refuse to rent to or terminate the leases of tenants because they have been abused.[67] Domestic violence provides tenants in other states with a defense to eviction or a right of early lease termination to establish safety.[68]

The definition of abuse need not necessarily be as broad for all of these purposes. The use of reproductive coercion to restrain a woman's liberty may have a different relevance in a custody or visitation case than it does in the housing or employment setting. If the overarching goal of domestic violence law and policy is to capture the true harms experienced by women subjected to abuse, the broader definition should be universal across different areas of the law. But, as Dutton and Goodman recognize, it may be appropriate to have different definitions of abuse for different purposes. An anti-essentialist definition of domestic violence would allow for variability dependent upon the legal context in which the woman is seeking relief.

Law exists to guide behavior and redress violations of socially mandated standards of conduct. Some may not be ready to accept that women are subjected to abuse in myriad ways well beyond the physical. But law can push social change, helping society to see that behavior once deemed inoffensive or, if not laudable, certainly acceptable within relationships is, in actuality, serving to restrict the liberty of the women in those relationships. If the law is to combat domestic violence, it must address all of the ways in which women experience abuse. Until such changes are made, the legal system will never meet the needs of Patricia Connors and women like her.

Deconstructing the Victim

Valoree Day was not a victim of domestic violence. Day's boyfriend, Steve Brown, repeatedly assaulted her, causing bruises, black eyes, swelling, bite marks, and welts. Brown punched Day in the face, causing a voluminous nosebleed and cut lip, spattering her clothing with blood. Brown attempted to strangle Day early in their relationship. He tried to run Day over with his car. Brown threw a boulder at Day's car as she drove to work. Brown repeatedly threatened to harm Day over the course of their relationship and heaped humiliating verbal abuse upon Day in public. During the night of June 10, 1988, Brown threatened to kill Day twice, using a knife to force his way into the home that they shared after Day locked him out to protect herself. Brown pushed his way into the bedroom where Day had barricaded herself and came at her with a knife. Nurse Maureen Wertz catalogued Day's bruises, redness, swelling, cuts, and abrasions after Day was arrested for stabbing and killing Brown. Those injuries were still visible five days later, when Dr. William Jefford Stiers examined Day. Nevertheless, the State of California argued, Day was not a victim of domestic violence because she was not "docile, submissive, humble, ingratiating, non-assertive, dependent, quiet, conforming and selfless"[1]—the way that a woman subjected to abuse is expected to behave.

Over the past 30 years, the public, the media, and the legal system have coalesced around a stereotypical image of women subjected to abuse. Before the battered women's movement, the assumption was that domestic violence happened to "them"—poor women of color who lived in slums. Advocacy by the battered women's movement around the idea that domestic violence is endemic to all races, ethnicities, religions, and socioeconomic classes, coupled with the advent of battered woman syndrome and its reliance on the theory of learned helplessness to explain why women subjected to abuse stay in abusive relationships, changed that understanding. The image of the victim of domestic violence morphed from a low-income woman of color to a passive, middle-class, white woman cowering in the corner as her enraged husband prepared to beat her again—a vision consistent with the dominance feminist conception of subordinated women in fear of all-powerful men. That victim, though, is not representative of the vast majority of women subjected to abuse. Nonetheless, because that stereotype is what legal system actors expect to see, women who defy the stereotype are at a distinct disadvantage in the legal system.

Pre-Movement Images of Victims

Early research on women subjected to abuse theorized that masochism was at the root of domestic violence. Drawing on psychiatrists Sigmund Freud and Helene Deutsch's contentions that all women are, at core, masochists, "their suffering . . . inherently bound up with erotic pleasure,"[2] researchers argued that domestic violence fulfilled the masochistic needs of women married to men who abused them. In a 1955 study, psychiatrists Albert A. Kurland, Jacob Morgenstern, and Carolyn Sheets argued that wives who had survived brutal, life-threatening attacks by their husbands were involved in a "sado-masochistic" interaction, sadistically causing the men to accumulate guilt and masochistically accepting the abuse resulting from the outburst of violence caused by that accumulated guilt.[3] In their much-cited 1964 study, *The Wifebeater's Wife: A Study of Family Interaction*, psychiatrists John E. Snell, Richard J. Rosenwald, and Ames Robey described men who committed abuse as passive, indecisive, and sexually inadequate and their wives as aggressive, masculine, frigid, and masochistic—ironic, given the drastically different picture the battered women's movement would later paint both of women subjected to abuse and their partners. The husband's violence "served to release him momentarily from his anxiety about his ineffectiveness as a man, while, at the same time, giving his wife apparent masochistic gratification and helping probably to deal with the guilt arising from the intense hostility expressed in her controlling, castrating behavior."[4] In 1979, psychiatrist Natalie Shainess wrote that while not all victims of abuse and rape "are masochists . . . a goodly number are, in subtle ways."[5] At a time when very little was being written about women subjected to abuse, much of that literature centered on the role of abuse in filling women's innate masochistic needs.

This research colored the attitudes of professionals working with women subjected to abuse. Social work professor and activist Susan Schechter describes how, during presentations by the Chicago Abused Women's Coalition in the late 1970s, professionals grappling with the information given about women subjected to abuse situated the causes of abuse in women's personalities.[6] Despite the emergence of research refuting the theory of women's masochism in the late 1970s and early 1980s, in 1985, the American Psychiatric Association proposed the addition of Masochistic Personality Disorder to the Diagnostic and Statistical Manual of Mental Disorders (DSM), a widely used resource in diagnosing mental illness. The new category would have labeled women who remained in abusive relationships masochistic. Only strong dissent from the American Psychiatric Association and American Psychological Association's Committees on Women prevented the category from being permanently added; instead, it was listed as requiring further study in the revised third edition of the DSM and excluded from the fourth edition altogether.[7]

Research suggested that a substantial segment of the public shared the belief that women subjected to abuse were essentially masochistic. In a 1987 study, psychologists Charles Patrick Ewing and Moss Aubrey asked whether the public accepted what the battered women's movement was by then describing as one of the "myths" of domestic violence: that women subjected to abuse are masochistic. Ewing and Aubrey surveyed 216 members of the public, giving them a hypothetical situation involving a woman experiencing violence at the hands of her husband and asking a number of questions about that hypothetical. Ewing and Aubrey found that 38 percent of those surveyed believed that the woman was at least partially responsible for her husband's violence; 41 percent felt that if she remained in the relationship and continued to be assaulted, the woman was "at least somewhat masochistic."[8] Judges echoed these sentiments. One advocate for women subjected to abuse described how, after watching a judge dismiss criminal charges in "first time assault" cases all morning, her client admitted that it was not the first time that she had been beaten by her husband. The judge responded, "Well, it sounds like you must enjoy getting beaten up if it has happened before. There's nothing I can do."[9]

By the late 1970s, however, new research was emerging that challenged the conception of women subjected to abuse as masochistic. In her 1980 article, "Overview: The 'Wife-Beater's Wife' Reconsidered," psychiatrist Elaine Hilberman argued that contemporary researchers were abandoning the conception of women subjected to abuse as masochists in the face of "little enthusiasm or supporting data for the theories of masochism that have been traditionally invoked to explain why women remain in violent relationships."[10] Although the myth of masochism would linger for some time, researchers had moved on to a new theory to explain the behavior of women subjected to abuse: learned helplessness.

Learned Helplessness

By the late 1970s, psychiatrists and psychologists were searching for a new paradigm to treat women subjected to abuse, one that replaced a belief in women's innate masochism with an understanding of how the context of the abuse colored women's behavior. Building on her own earlier research, in 1979 psychologist Lenore Walker changed the way that society, and particularly the legal system, looked at women subjected to abuse by proposing a response to the question perennially asked of those women: Why doesn't she leave? In her seminal work, *The Battered Woman*, Walker drew on the theory of learned helplessness to suggest an answer.

Psychologist Martin Seligman developed the theory of learned helplessness through laboratory experiments in the late 1960s and early 1970s. In his experiments, Seligman placed dogs in cages and administered electrical shocks to the dogs at unpredictable intervals. At first, the dogs attempted to escape from the shocks. Later, however, when the dogs seemed to realize that their actions could not prevent them from being shocked, the dogs stopped attempting to avoid punishment and became "compliant, passive, and submissive. . . . In fact, even when the door was left open and the dogs were shown the way out, they remained passive, refused to leave, and did not avoid the shock."[11] Only after being dragged repeatedly to the door of the cage were the dogs able to learn how to avoid being shocked again. Seligman also applied the theory of learned helplessness to the behavior of both rats and humans. Learned helplessness was later used to explain depression; the behavior of prisoners of war, concentration camp detainees, and institutionalized patients; the lack of motivation among welfare recipients; fatalism among peasants in the developing world; and the economic failure of industrial towns.[12]

Walker analogized the behavior of women subjected to abuse to that of the dogs in Seligman's experiments. She theorized that over time, women subjected to abuse, finding that they cannot anticipate, control, or stop the violence against them, begin to suffer from learned helplessness. This inability to exercise control, according to Walker, leads women subjected to abuse to assume that they are powerless to affect the violence. Instead of actively seeking to escape violent relationships, women sink into passivity, self-blame, and fatalism born of the randomness of the violence. As Walker explained,

> Repeated batterings, like electrical shocks, diminish the woman's motivation to respond. She becomes passive. Secondly, her cognitive ability to perceive success is changed. She does not believe her response will result

in a favorable outcome, whether or not it might. Next, having generalized her helplessness, the battered woman does not believe anything she does will alter any outcome, not just the specific situation that has occurred. She says, "No matter what I do, I have no influence." She cannot think of alternatives. She says, "I am incapable and too stupid to learn how to change things." Finally, her sense of emotional well-being becomes precarious. She is more prone to depression and anxiety.[13]

In *The Battered Woman*, Walker argued that the only way to alleviate learned helplessness in women subjected to abuse, as with the dogs in Seligman's early experiments, would be to drag them out of their relationships or somehow separate them from their partners. Later, in her 1984 book, *The Battered Woman Syndrome*, Walker developed a series of "learned helplessness survival techniques" designed to help women escape abusive relationships: "becoming angry rather than depressed and self-blaming; active rather than passive; and more realistic about the likelihood of the relationship continuing on its aversive course rather than improving."[14]

Walker's appropriation of learned helplessness to explain the behavior of women subjected to abuse shifted the focus from women's intrinsic characteristics that invited violence (masochism or some other pathology) to the constraints on women created by the violence itself. Women were not inherently unable or unwilling to respond to violence; domestic violence rendered women unable to respond. Women subjected to abuse were not innately victims—domestic violence transformed them into victims. This conception of the victim dovetailed with the dominance feminist view of women as victimized by virtue of their physical and sexual subordination at the hands of men. Walker's work grew from this feminist orientation. As Walker wrote in *The Battered Woman*, "I am aware that this book is written from a feminist vision. . . . I view women as victims in order to understand what the toll of such domestic violence is like for them."[15]

Shortly after the publication of *The Battered Woman*, the concept of learned helplessness as a justification for why women subjected to abuse did not leave their partners made its way into the legal literature. The theory of learned helplessness was used to explain how women subjected to abuse were so conditioned to live with violence that they could not take affirmative steps to leave their relationships. Law review articles and state court cases cited the concept, particularly in the context of women who killed their abusive partners. Courts allowed expert witnesses to use learned helplessness to explain why a woman would recant a previous statement regarding abuse during the trial of her partner.[16] Courts have also used learned helplessness to establish that a woman had not, in fact, been abused. In a 2007 child abuse and neglect case, a Georgia court found that a mother was not abused because her work outside of the home and her attempt to confront her husband about his inappropriate discipline of their children established that she was not suffering from learned helplessness.[17]

Learned helplessness was not without its critics. Scholars challenged Walker's research, pointing out flaws in the research design. Learned helplessness as applied to women subjected to abuse, argued sociologist Edward Gondolf, "is a notion . . . that appears to be rooted in assumptions and observations rather than hard fact."[18] Others contended that learned helplessness promoted problematic stereotypes of women subjected to abuse. The name itself, Walker notes, was deemed "politically incorrect." Walker explains, "Learned helplessness was confused with being helpless, and not its original intended meaning of *having lost the ability to predict that what you do will make a particular outcome occur.*"[19] For just that reason, notwithstanding Walker's original intent, the theory of learned helplessness was the first step toward defining women subjected to abuse as passive and ineffectual, too fearful to act to stop the violence.

Battered Woman Syndrome

In 1984, Walker propounded a comprehensive theory designed to explain the behavior of women who killed their abusive partners. That theory, known as battered woman syndrome, would have profound implications not just for the criminal law, but also for the way in which women who had been abused were viewed throughout the legal system.

Defining battered woman syndrome is more difficult than it might seem. In the first iterations of the theory, Walker paired learned helplessness with the cycle theory of violence to describe how abusive relationships operated and how the inability to control the cycle of violence affected the women in those relationships. In the early legal literature on battered woman syndrome, as well as case law from the 1980s, battered woman syndrome is framed around these two elements. Later, Walker tied battered woman syndrome to the Post-Traumatic Stress Disorder (PTSD) category in the DSM, arguing that battered woman syndrome has six groups of criteria that have been tested scientifically and can be said to identify the syndrome. The first three groups of symptoms are the same as for PTSD [intrusive recollections of the trauma; hyperarousal and high levels of anxiety; and avoidance behavior and emotional numbing— depression, dissociation, minimization, repression, denial] while the additional three criteria groups are present in intimate partner victims [disrupted interpersonal relationships as a result of the partner's power and control; body image distortion and/or physical complaints; sexual intimacy issues].[20]

Advocates, expert witnesses, and courts did not always confine themselves to either of these versions of battered woman syndrome, however. As law professor Elizabeth Schneider notes, battered woman syndrome has become "a catch-all phrase . . . to describe a great range of issues: a woman's prior responses to violence and the context in which those responses occurred; the dynamics of the abusive relationship; a subcategory of post-traumatic stress disorder; or woman abuse as a larger social problem."[21]

Early proponents of the theory believed that battered woman syndrome would help to dispel the myths that prevented women subjected to abuse from securing assistance through the courts, counteracting prevailing beliefs that women were masochistic and were free to leave abusive relationships whenever they chose. Walker's theory of women subjected to abuse as passive non-actors trapped within a cycle of violence quickly spread throughout the legal world, primarily (and counterintuitively) to justify the actions of women who killed their abusers rather than leaving their relationships—to explain, for example, why Valoree Day did not leave Steve Brown before their fatal altercation on the night of June 10, 1988. In case after case, courts allowed experts (including Walker) to use battered woman syndrome to debunk the received wisdom and common myths about domestic violence and to explain why women subjected to abuse stayed with their abusers and how those women perceived the potential for violence against them. Ultimately, the majority of the states allowed expert testimony on the impact of domestic violence on women, in some states defining in statute and case law what it means to be a "battered woman." Legal system actors were also schooled in battered woman syndrome; as former prosecutor and law professor Alafair Burke notes, "[C]ounselors, police officers, prosecutors, parole board officials, and social-service providers" study battered woman syndrome, in theory "to improve the quality of their responses to domestic violence."[22]

Again, though, battered woman syndrome met with a fair amount of criticism. Walker's own research did not support some of the theory's core concepts: that women subjected to abuse suffered from low self-esteem, were more depressed, and perceived others as controlling their lives. Moreover, the theory was internally contradictory: how could learned helplessness, which stresses women's sense of their inability to control their environments, explain why women took the extremely active step of killing their abusers? Walker explains away the contradiction in her book *Terrifying Love: Why Battered Women Kill and How Society Responds*, claiming that in the moment before she kills, a woman subjected to abuse experiences a flash of insight into the relationship. That insight convinces her that she must kill to save her own life, suggesting that at that moment, the woman who has been abused understands exactly what she must do to escape—a far cry from a whipped dog unable to leave her cage. Critics noted that Walker's conception of battered woman syndrome was at odds not only with her own work, but also with research suggesting that some women fought back against their abusers throughout the course of the relationship, suggesting that women were neither as passive nor as unable to formulate effective responses to abuse as Walker theorized.[23] Walker answered these critics in the third edition of *The Battered Woman Syndrome*, arguing that what domestic violence takes from women is the ability to predict the outcome of their struggles or to believe that they will ever escape the violence, not the ability to minimize injury or to fight back from within the relationship. Leaving her partner, then, is the ultimate line of demarcation, the step that a woman subjected to abuse must take (but cannot take) to break the cycle of violence.

Most problematic, though, was the way in which battered woman syndrome portrayed women subjected to abuse. Battered woman syndrome reinforced preexisting sexist stereotypes about women's fragility and passivity, suggesting that, in the cases of women subjected to abuse, that fragility and passivity were somehow pathology. As law professor Melanie Randall argues,

> [T]he "battered woman syndrome" is arguably little more than a more compassionate and gender sensitive version of the traditional psychiatric view of women as "irrational" or even "insane," except that this version incorporates a recognition that the women's alleged "irrationality" or psychological incapacity results from the infliction of abuse upon her by a male intimate.[24]

The Political Redefinition of the Victim: Survivor Theory

Not everyone saw women subjected to abuse as the passive non-actors of Walker's theory, however. Nine years after the publication of *The Battered Woman*, sociologists Edward Gondolf and Ellen Fisher developed an alternative theory intended to explain the behavior of women subjected to abuse. Survivor theory created a different narrative for women subjected to abuse, one that purported to explain why they remained in violent relationships without labeling them as passive or weak. In an effort to shift the conversation about why women subjected to abuse remained in abusive relationships, Gondolf and Fisher recast them as survivors who actively took measures to protect themselves and their children from within the relationship, rather than passive victims immobilized by the failure of past efforts to forestall violence. Having determined that help is not available, Gondolf and Fisher argued, women subjected to abuse may come to the rational conclusion that they are more likely to survive if they endure physical violence within the relationship than if they attempt to leave. In their research, Gondolf and Fisher found that women increased their attempts to find help as they perceived their situations becoming more dangerous. The failure, Gondolf and Fisher argued, was not with the women, but with the sources of help that purported to be available to them. Gondolf and Fisher sought to shift the focus of interventions from Walker's "psychotherapeutic focus on 'solving' battering" to improving and increasing the availability of social supports and resources that would enable women subjected to abuse to "become more independent and leave the batterer."[25]

Women subjected to abuse embraced this theory and its language of survival, which emphasized their strength, resilience, and ultimate triumph. As bell hooks noted, such language was essential for women fighting to preserve their sense of self:

> Women who are exploited and oppressed daily cannot afford to relinquish the belief that they exercise some measure of control, however relative, over their lives. They cannot afford to see themselves solely as "victims" because their survival depends on continued exercise of whatever personal powers they possess. It would be psychologically demoralizing for these women to bond with other women on the basis of shared victimization.[26]

Support for Gondolf and Fisher's hypothesis came from an unlikely source: Lenore Walker, whose research corroborated the idea that women subjected to abuse developed what she called "survival or coping skills that keep them alive with minimal injuries."[27]

But while survivor theory provided an alternative narrative to Walker's helpless victim, it similarly failed to capture the experiences of many women subjected to abuse. Like the battered woman syndrome, survivor theory focuses on why women do not leave their relationships, as if leaving is every woman's ultimate goal. Survivor theory recasts a victim's passivity as a conscious choice to stay in a violent relationship, but does not account for affirmative actions that a woman might take—like fighting back against her partner. The problem with reframing victims as survivors, psychologist Sharon Lamb notes, is that, like Walker's theory, it oversimplifies the experience of being abused. She writes, "If the culture overemphasizes the helpless victim, and if victims overemphasize the survivor victim, we are caught between two stereotypes that preclude a range of experiences and the unifying awareness that victimization is too frequently a part of every woman's life."[28] The stories of women subjected to abuse are too complex to be shunted into the overarching categories of "victim" and "survivor." Creating such categories had the unintended but nonetheless harmful consequence of penalizing those women who did not fit neatly within them.

Survivor theory has never had the impact within the legal system that it has had among others who work with women subjected to abuse—and among women themselves. In the legal system, the paradigmatic victim is still very much the model for how women subjected to abuse are expected to present. For women who violate these norms, the costs can be steep.

The Paradigmatic Victim and Her Non-Conforming Sisters

As the image of "the battered woman" shaped by Walker's theories took hold, stereotypes about women subjected to abuse began to dominate discourse within the legal system. Defining the victim became a function of integrating Walker's theories with the historical and political images of victims and battered women. The resulting construct of a passive, white, straight woman became the paradigmatic victim of violence.

Defining the Victim by Passivity

In the literature on domestic violence, women subjected to abuse have been described as scared, helpless, meek, blameless, weak, and powerless. Women subjected to abuse have also been depicted as deferential, submissive to authority, compliant, vulnerable, ashamed, dependent, unassertive, depressed, and defenseless. The paradigmatic victim, sociologist Evan Stark writes, is a descendant of the Victorian "respectable woman" who deserves protection, juxtaposed against the "rough woman," who does not.[29] Although the paradigmatic victim wants to leave the relationship, she is powerless to do so. She is expected to cooperate with the legal system—with police who want to arrest and prosecutors who want to convict her abuser. By all accounts, the paradigmatic victim comports with societal notions of the "victim." She does not use violence against her partner unless she is convinced that she must do so or face imminent death herself. Other than retaliating when she sees no other viable option, the victim does not fight back.

The passivity stereotype creates particular problems for women who fight back against their partners. Studies of women who use force against their partners indicate that overwhelmingly large numbers of those women have been subjected to abuse. In her study of women arrested for domestic assaults, sociologist Susan Miller found that 95 percent of the women had used violence in reaction to a partner's violence. The vast majority of women who use violence do so to defend themselves or their children or to prevent an impending attack. But women cite other reasons as well: to stand up for themselves in an attempt to salvage their self-worth, get their partners' attention, earn their partners' respect, and retaliate for threats against their families or their partners' abusive behavior. Sociologist Evan Stark argues that women use violence in order to express their identities as beings independent of their controlling partners. Describing Nathaline Parkman, a 35-year-old African American woman who stabbed her abusive partner the day after he threatened to cut her, Stark writes,

> The main damage Nate suffered had less to do with physical or psychological trauma—though both were present—than with her feeling that Larry had so circumscribed her capacity to freely act that she was dying as a distinct person. . . . What drove her into the street that night was the existential threat to her standing as a free woman, the fact that Larry intended to subordinate her purposes to his as well as hurt her physically, to make her his thing. This, she could not allow.[30]

Susan Miller has organized women's use of violence into two categories: defensive behavior (the attempt to escape or avoid a violent incident against the woman or her children, typically after the man has already used violence against her) and frustration responses (expressive acts conveying the woman's frustration over her inability to escape abuse or control the situation).

Men obtain control over their partners through abuse. By contrast, very few women who fight back are seeking to exercise control over or induce fear in their partners, and even fewer are successful in doing so. In her study of women who had been violent toward their partners, sociologist Shamita Das Dasgupta found that neither the women nor their partners believed that the women's violence had made their partners fearful for their safety. In fact, one study found that men were frequently amused and laughed when their partners initiated violence, suggesting that they did not take their partners' violence seriously. Ironically, women's use of force may lead to escalation of the violence and make women who fight back more vulnerable to serious injury. Ultimately, Dasgupta concludes, "[G]enerally women are quite unsuccessful in achieving their objectives through violence. That is, in most cases, women are able to neither control violence against themselves nor modify their abusive partners' behaviors according to their own will by using violence against them."[31]

Women who fight back are more likely than men to admit to using violence and to take responsibility for their violent behavior. These women tend to include a great deal of detail in their stories, including exactly where they struck their abusers and how hard they hit. This willingness to admit to and minutely recount their violence may be tied to how society perceives violence by women. Because women are socialized to refrain from using violence, they may perceive their own violence as violating societally dictated gender norms, making these episodes more memorable. Society may share these perceptions. As Dasgupta argues, "[S]ocieties that believe in the stereotype of feminine passivity and tolerance . . . may perceive a woman who uses violence against her intimate partner as 'unnatural,' 'freakish,' and 'criminal by nature' and deal with her accordingly."[32] Once a woman subjected to abuse uses violence, her status as "victim" is imperiled.

Women who fight back may be fearful but are not passive—they actively resist their abusive partners. When seeking help, these women must overcome the stereotype that they defy: the weak, passive, and helpless battered woman. Consider, for example, the following exchange between a prosecutor trying the case of a woman subjected to abuse who killed her partner and a witness who had known both parties. Asked by the prosecutor how Dianne reacted when abused by her husband, the witness stated, "You know, Dianne was really calm. You know, Dianne would be really calm until he smacked her and then she'd smack him back. I never seen her do anything to him, you know, it was always him doing it to her, and then she would fight back." The prosecutor remarked, "She could probably hold her own, though," to which the witness replied, "Well, she tried. No, not, well, I don't think she could hold her own, but she was pretty tough, she's a pretty tough girl, you know."[33] The prosecutor used this exchange to bolster his contention that because Dianne could defend herself, she could not have been abused. Women who fight back not only have their experiences minimized or denied—they also have the weight of the legal system that frequently fails to protect them brought to bear against them by prosecutors who (literally and figuratively) indict them for their actions.

The dissonance between the passive victim and the stories of women who fight back is fairly easy to see. The relationship between the passive victim and mothers subjected to abuse is somewhat more complex. Mothers subjected to abuse face a classic Catch-22: if they act in conformity with victim stereotypes, they lack the agency to be trustworthy, protective, "good" mothers. If they defy the stereotypes, they can't really be experiencing domestic violence. Either way, mothers subjected to abuse lose in the legal system.

The story of Hedda Nussbaum illustrates the front half of the equation: victim of domestic violence equals unprotective mother. Nussbaum became infamous after her paramour, Joel Steinberg, beat their six-year-old adoptive daughter Lisa to death in 1987. Lisa wasn't Steinberg's only victim. Hedda Nussbaum's startlingly disfigured face appeared in newspapers, magazines, and on television during the trial as she explained how Joel Steinberg had systematically rendered her incapable of caring not only for her children, but also for herself. Nussbaum is covered with scars resulting from Steinberg's abuse. In a 2002 *New York Times* article, Nussbaum documented her injuries: numerous surgeries on her nose and face to reconstruct damage done by Steinberg; a left eye so disfigured from being gouged that it continuously tears; a ruptured spleen that required surgery after Steinberg punched her. At trial, psychiatrists testified that Nussbaum had been isolated, brainwashed, and tortured by Steinberg, explaining that she was so incapable of independent thought or action that she acquiesced when Steinberg told her to smoke crack with him instead of seeking medical help for Lisa while she lay dying on the ground. On the basis of these expert opinions, prosecutors dropped charges against Nussbaum, who would later testify against Steinberg. While feminists split over Nussbaum's culpability—Gloria Steinem supported Nussbaum, while Susan Brownmiller sharply criticized the decision not to prosecute her—Nussbaum's "decision" to side with her abusive partner to the detriment of her child defied societal expectations of what a "good mother" should do. Because Nussbaum could not act as a good mother as a result of her victimization, it was not difficult for many to link the stereotype of "bad mother" with that of "victim of violence"—particularly given how closely Nussbaum adhered to the profile of the paradigmatic victim.

Nussbaum is far from alone in that category. When judges believe that mothers subjected to abuse lack the capacity to act on behalf of their children, they are not hesitant about intervening to "protect" those children. In the District of Columbia's dedicated domestic violence court, it was not unusual for one judge to call child protective services whenever an allegation was made that the children had been present during an act of domestic violence, notwithstanding the fact that the mother was taking what most would perceive as protective action by seeking a protective order in his court. Similarly, other legal system actors perceive mothers subjected to abuse as unable to care for their children. In its report, *Battered Mothers Speak Out*, the Wellesley Centers for Women documented the experiences of mothers subjected to abuse with the Massachusetts court system. One mother, Lorie, explained how state actors' failure to understand the effects of abuse colored their assessments of the parties' credibility or stability:

> [The guardian ad litem] was saying [that I] was psychologically unstable and, you know, irrational, emotional, and angry. It's like, yeah, if you've been through 10 years of what I've been through. . . . You go through hell and try to get out of hell and they punish you, saying, "Oh, you cry too much and you're upset, so you know, the kids are more stable with the father, there's no emotion."[34]

Stereotypes about the passivity of women subjected to abuse may, in fact, be more powerful than reality. Take the case of Sharwline Nicholson. In 1999, Nicholson was 32, a full-time college student, working full-time, and the mother of two children, an eight-year-old son and a three-year-old daughter. Nicholson lived in New York. Her son's father was not involved with her or the children, and her daughter's father, Mr. Barnett, lived in South Carolina, but visited occasionally. On January 27, 1999, during one of his visits to New York, Nicholson informed Barnett that she wanted to end their relationship because they lived so far apart. Although he had never been violent or threatening toward Nicholson in the past, Barnett became enraged, punching, kicking, and throwing things at Nicholson while her daughter slept in her crib in another room. Her son was still in school. Bleeding profusely, Nicholson called 911 and asked a neighbor to babysit for her children while she was at the hospital. The neighbor agreed to meet her son at his bus stop and watch both children until she returned.

At the hospital, doctors found that Barnett had broken Nicholson's arm, fractured her ribs, and injured her head. Nicholson was visited by police officers in the hospital, who suggested that her children might be better off with a family member than a babysitter. Nicholson provided the officers with the telephone numbers of two cousins and her daughter's godmother. Notwithstanding the arrangements she had made for her children's care, New York's Administration for Children's Services ordered the children removed from Nicholson's custody. Police came to the babysitter's home that evening with guns drawn to remove the children. The social worker assigned to the case testified that he believed the children were in "imminent risk if they remained in the care of Ms. Nicholson because she was not, at that time, able to protect herself nor her children because Mr. Barnett had viciously beaten her."[35] The agency refused to tell Nicholson where her children had been placed, instructing her to appear in court the next week if she wanted to see her children. Nicholson asked that her children be placed with relatives; the agency refused, instead placing the children in foster care. The social worker assumed that Barnett lived with Nicholson. In reality, Barnett lived in another state and did not have a key to Nicholson's apartment. As the agency requested, Nicholson attempted to obtain an order of protection against Barnett after leaving the hospital but was denied because Barnett lived out of state and Nicholson did not know his address.

Sharwline Nicholson was charged with neglect for "engaging in domestic violence" in the presence of her daughter and for failing to cooperate with services to ensure her children's safety. On February 4, 1999, the family court ordered her children returned to her. The agency did not return the children until February 18, 1999, 21 days after their initial removal.

Sharwline Nicholson clearly was not a stereotypical victim of violence. Barnett had never abused her before January 27, 1999. She made provisions to care for her children before being taken to the hospital with serious injuries. She sought a protective order against Barnett. She worked with police to prosecute Barnett. She was not passive in the face of violence, but rather worked actively to safeguard her children as she healed from an incomprehensible attack. Sharwline Nicholson could not have differed more from the stereotypical passive victim, but she was treated as one nonetheless.

New York law was in part responsible for this injustice. At the time that Nicholson's children were removed from her care, New York law allowed the child welfare agency to remove children from parents who had "engaged in" domestic violence. A parent could engage in domestic violence simply by being the victim of a violent attack, without reference to context: the length of the relationship, the extent of the abuse, the presence of the children during the abuse, any actions taken by the parent to protect herself. New York law, in essence, defined mothers who had been abused as passive victims and therefore not protective. The law assumed, as some system actors assume, that a mother subjected to abuse was not fit to care for her children—she had "engaged in" domestic violence and was neglectful. As a result of these assumptions, Sharwline Nicholson's children were placed in foster care, she was charged with neglect, and long after those allegations had been dismissed, Nicholson remained listed in New York's child abuse and neglect registry as a neglectful parent.

Sharwline Nicholson had undeniably been abused, and therefore, must have been passive (despite all evidence to the contrary). But when mothers are not passive—when they act to protect themselves and their children—the legal system frequently assumes that they are not experiencing abuse. The legal system is profoundly skeptical about mothers' claims that they have been abused, a skepticism that is clear in the areas of child custody and international parental abduction.

Because judges often perceive allegations of domestic violence in the context of divorce and child custody as trivial, nothing more than the anger and hurt feelings arising from personality conflicts or failed relationships, they discount the credibility of women who claim to have been subjected to abuse. Professionals who lack experience with domestic violence may rely instead on courthouse assumptions about the dubious legitimacy of domestic violence claims and the pretextual reasons women have for filing them. Judges question the ulterior motives of women bringing domestic violence cases—"they are often considered manipulators and liars intent on using the court to achieve some wrongful purpose, such as revenge or advantage in a divorce case."[36] Judge Susan Scott of the Superior Court of New Jersey was uncommonly candid in discussing this problem. She admitted that it was difficult to discern which claims of domestic violence were true because the "word around the underground" was that domestic violence claims were fabricated to evict men from their homes using protective order statutes. The judge recounted a case in which a judge denied a protective order after finding that the woman's allegations were likely fabricated, only to have the respondent kill himself and his partner shortly thereafter.[37]

Skepticism surrounding claims of domestic violence creates a dilemma for a mother subjected to abuse who is involved in litigation: if she doesn't raise the issue of abuse, the court has no context for considering her actions or any reluctance she expresses about sharing custody or permitting unsupervised visitation with her former partner. The court cannot attempt to protect the mother or her children if the mother does not provide the court with a justification for doing so. If she discloses the abuse, however, it is unlikely that she will be believed. "Rather," law professor Joan Meier argues, "her very status as a litigant, a mother, and battered, seems to ensure that she will be viewed as, at best, merely self-interested, and at worst, not credible."[38]

Similar problems plague mothers who flee across international borders with their children. The Hague Convention on the Civil Aspects of International Child Abduction, a private international treaty currently ratified by 81 countries, governs the return of children wrongfully removed from their states of habitual residence. The Hague Convention was drafted with the assumption that the majority of abductors would be fathers depriving primary caretaker mothers of custody. In such a factual scenario, the Hague Convention's remedy of returning the child to the place of the child's habitual residence, and to the care of the primary caregiver, for adjudication of custody makes perfect sense. In reality, however, the vast majority of child abductors are mothers and primary caretakers. Many of these mothers claim to have fled with their children to escape domestic violence. At a recent meeting of signatories to the Hague Convention, country after country affirmed the frequency with which domestic violence is raised and expressed concern about the Convention's operation in these cases.

Mothers who are subjected to abuse and who flee with their children face the same type of dilemma as mothers who take action to protect their children in custody cases. By acting, they undermine judicial notions about how women subjected to abuse should behave, rendering their claims of abuse suspect. Moreover, by fleeing with their children, they run headlong into societal norms about the harm caused by child abduction; as law professor Merle Weiner explains, "[T]hey are presumptively bad mothers because exit inherently is believed to cause harm."[39] Stay and expose your child to abuse and risk the intervention of the child welfare system because you are a paradigmatic victim and a bad mother who fails to protect her child; fight for custody or flee, and your experience of abuse is doubted or ignored and your motives for taking action sharply questioned. Either way, the passivity associated with victimization constrains the choices of mothers subjected to abuse.

Defining the Victim by Identity

The paradigmatic victim is white. Victimhood is intimately tied to traditional notions of womanhood, notions that have been largely defined by a white norm. As law professor Shelby Moore argues:

Victim status . . . is readily accessible to white women because both the Anglo American tradition and the social development of women have established "true women" as pious, pure, submissive, and domestic. Generally speaking, white women in America are, and have been, best able to enjoy the benefit of victim status because they are expected to be "true women." Comparatively, African American women, whose stereotype was created by slavery, have been and continue to be denied "true woman" status as defined by American culture.[40]

The word victim implies whiteness, a connotation that deprives women of color of victim status and its associated protections.

The language used at the start of the movement to stop violence against women also cast victims as heterosexual. The early battered women's movement talked about "wife abuse" rather than "domestic violence" or "intimate partner violence," underscoring the assumption that abuse between partners happened within marriages. By definition, lesbians could not be battered women, because they could not be wives. Violence in lesbian relationships was also at odds with early feminist theories about domestic violence. Battered women's advocates rooted the causes of domestic violence in the patriarchy, viewing violence as yet another manifestation of men's privilege and the oppression of women. This analysis does not apply well to lesbian abuse, although some theorists have reconfigured their patriarchal analyses to account for abuse within lesbian relationships.[41]

The laws of many states similarly fail to account for lesbian abuse. Same-sex abuse is not recognized under the civil protection order laws of six states. Other states' laws do not explicitly authorize same-sex partners to petition for relief; those women are dependent on individual judges to interpret the law in ways that afford them protection. Prior to the U.S. Supreme Court's holding in *Lawrence v. Texas* that private sexual activity between adults cannot be criminalized, lesbians in some states would have had to admit to illegal sexual conduct to qualify for protective orders. If the face of the paradigmatic victim of violence is that of a white woman, the face of her abuser is certainly that of a man.

White, straight victim stereotypes fail to account for the diversity among women subjected to abuse. Reliance on these stereotypes and on the experiences of white, straight women to shape law and policy pushed the experiences of other women to the margins. But women experience abuse differently based on differences in identity. Race, sexual orientation, immigration status, class, disability status, and location all shape women's experiences with abuse, reinforcing their disempowerment and dictating their needs.

Simply by virtue of their race, women of color face an uphill battle in having their abuse recognized and rectified, even when they attempt to mimic the stereotypical victim. April, an African American woman subjected to abuse, described her experience:

> I was told to act like a little white girl . . . to look sad, to try to cry, to never look the jury in the eye. It didn't really work for me because the judge took one look at me and said, "You look pretty mean; I bet you could really hurt a man."[42]

When confronting abuse, women of color may perceive that outside assistance is unavailable to them, because service providers are not easily reached or culturally competent (and may even seem hostile). Women of color may also be reluctant to engage state systems for assistance, given the history of racism ingrained in those systems and the stigma attached to those who air a community's "dirty laundry." Cultural norms may pressure African American women to maintain a strong front and handle their problems without interference.[43] For Latinas, language, religion, and family ties are often barriers to seeking outside assistance.[44] Mistrust of the white institutions historically responsible for genocide and family destruction, fear of ostracism from their families, and language and cultural differences may prevent Native American women from leaving their partners.[45] The importance of patriarchy, gender role norms, and family primacy can shape Asian American women's responses to abuse.[46]

The experiences of immigrant women are constructed by many of the same factors—economic instability, isolation (both within their own cultural communities and within the larger community), family, cultural, and religious pressure to make their relationships work or to keep their private lives private, a dearth of support services particular to their culture, lack of trust in law enforcement and other government systems—but the obstacles created by those factors are often exacerbated for immigrant women. Law enforcement is particularly unresponsive to the needs of immigrant women who do not speak English. In a study of immigrant Latinas subjected to abuse in Washington, DC, researchers found that police spoke to the women in Spanish (through interpreters or directly) in only 34 percent of cases.[47] That number is certainly lower in cases involving women who speak less common languages.

For undocumented immigrant women, there are additional stressors related to the insecurity of their immigration status. Fear of engaging public systems with the power to deport them prevents undocumented immigrant women from accessing legal assistance. "No tengo papeles" ("I don't have papers"), responded Vicky, an undocumented immigrant woman, when asked whether she had ever called police about or sought a protective order against her abusive husband.[48] Maria Bolanos did call the police after an altercation with her partner on Christmas Eve in 2009. Charges against her partner were later dropped, but Bolanos, an undocumented immigrant, was arrested by the responding officer for allegedly selling a $10 phone card to a neighbor, a charge that Bolanos denied and that was later dismissed. Bolanos was fingerprinted and her fingerprints were shared with Immigration and Customs Enforcement through the Secure Communities program. As a result of her call to the police for help, Bolanos will likely be deported. Addressing concerns that such actions would discourage undocumented immigrant women from calling police for assistance, Bolanos says, "You would have to be crazy to call the police. . . . I would never call the police again."[49]

Abusive partners threaten to expose undocumented women to authorities, have them deported, withdraw or interfere with legal actions designed to provide immigrant women with legal status, and take their children if they report abuse. The likelihood that immigrant women have children born in the United States can increase that anxiety; deportation of the undocumented immigrant woman can mean separation from her children, particularly if a U.S. court order grants her partner custody rights.[50] Undocumented immigrant women may lose their ability to find employment if their immigration status is disclosed, making them more reliant on their abusive partners for economic support.

Low-income women are particularly vulnerable to abuse. Social science research demonstrates that the lower the household income, the higher the rates of violence within a relationship. Women on welfare are especially at risk, experiencing abuse at ten times the rate of the general population. Economic resources—stable housing, work, affordable and safe child care, transportation, income for food and utilities—are often necessary for women to leave violent relationships. Even if they are not economically dependent on their partners, low-income women may be so geographically or socially isolated that they are unaware of or unable to access services. The partners of low-income women sabotage their efforts to achieve self-sufficiency. The stigma of collecting welfare benefits may prevent some low-income women from seeking assistance. Wanda, a rural Kentucky woman, described her exchange with a county attorney handling her domestic violence case: "The County Attorney's like, 'Well women like you, I work for women like you to raise your kids on welfare. I don't appreciate you being on welfare.' And I told him, quit his damn job, that's what I told him."[51]

Lesbians may fear airing their problems before a homophobic community, particularly if they have not come out to family, friends, and/or co-workers. When they do disclose the abuse in their relationships, lesbians often find their stories of abuse minimized as "cat fights" or dismissed because a "femme" partner could not brutalize a "butch" woman. Service providers are sometimes uncomfortable living and working with lesbians in shelter settings. Lesbians may also perceive shelters and mainstream services as the province of straight women. Even when the law provides protection for women in same-sex relationships, the outright homophobia or discomfort of some system actors with same-sex relationships makes the prospect of interacting with the legal system fraught for lesbians subjected to abuse.

Fear of disclosure may be a concern for women with disabilities as well. For a woman with HIV, for example, the threat of having a partner publicize her HIV status to unknowing family and friends can be sufficient to keep her in an abusive relationship, as can threats to abandon her when she is too ill to care for herself. Unwillingness to publicly discuss HIV-related abuse may cause women to avoid seeking police intervention or judicial assistance. Disabled women are vulnerable to disability-specific abuse, including destruction of medical devices and manipulation of medication.[52] The fear of losing a primary caretaker may outweigh a disabled woman's desire to leave an abusive relationship. Betty, a deaf and physically disabled woman in her sixties, recently came to a prosecutor's office after police arrested her partner of 35 years. Upon investigation, prosecutors learned that police had been called to Betty's home 25 times over the past three months (never by Betty, only by her neighbors, whom she did not know). Betty admitted that her partner had been physically abusing her for the past 30 years. But Betty refused to assist prosecutors in building a case against her partner, because successful criminal prosecution of her partner could mean losing her sole source of companionship and communication with the world, as well as physical and economic support. Betty relied on her partner for transportation to doctors' appointments, food, shelter—survival. Because prosecutors could not provide her with the level of support that her husband provided, Betty opted not to cooperate with prosecution.

Isolation is a problem for many women subjected to abuse; for rural women, it can be overwhelming. Men intentionally isolate their partners geographically, both as a form of abuse and because isolated rural settings are conducive to abuse. Men who abuse in rural areas remove phone receivers and disable or destroy motor vehicles to prevent their partners from seeking assistance. Two-thirds of rural households lack telephone service, rendering calls for help impossible.[53] Given the paucity of economic opportunity in many rural areas, the economic stability needed to escape abuse may be impossible to achieve. State-run systems are often staffed by people who are related to or know the abusive partner personally—a "good ol' boys" network that narrows women's options. Bertha, who lived in rural Kentucky, described her interaction with police: "One of them . . . he looked at Kenny and he says, 'Kenny, give me one good reason to put that bitch in jail and I will.' And he's never liked me. And he's always been softy, softy to Kenny."[54] When your husband's brother is the constable in your rural area, it is unlikely that your husband will be arrested and prosecuted for abusing you. Rural police may be unable to respond quickly to calls for assistance even when they are inclined to do so, given limited resources and large service areas. Those constraints combine to create stories like this one:

> I'm kind of disappointed. I know this is not a good thing to say, but I'm disappointed in the sheriff's department because this [being raped and beaten by her former partner] happened to me on the tenth and Gary wasn't arrested for thirteen, you know, until thirteen days later. . . . They just kept dragging it out. They had a warrant and what not and I'm, like, four broken ribs.[55]

Limited resources affect service providers as well. Rural shelters are often in poor physical condition and offer a narrow range of assistance; as one shelter worker asked, "Would you like to stay in a place like this, even for a short time?"[56] Rural women are forced to make choices between bad and worse options. After Cynthia Hage's boyfriend slammed her hand on to a table hard enough to draw blood, she had three choices: stay in their trailer, hide in an outhouse, or run to her car and lock the doors. Hage chose the last option, and was sitting in her car, which was not running (although the keys were in the ignition), when the police arrived and arrested her for drunk driving. The trial court denied her request for a jury instruction on self-defense/retreat, finding that she had other options for refuge in her isolated rural area. She was convicted.[57]

Some of these concerns may also be reasons that white, straight, middle-class women choose not to seek assistance. But white, straight, middle-class women are relatively advantaged in their experiences with abuse, as compared with women of color, immigrant women, disabled women, rural women, poor women, and lesbians. By fostering law and policy that is unresponsive to their needs, defining the victim around white, straight stereotypes both highlights and exacerbates the economic and social marginalization experienced by women with other identities.

The Consequences of Non-Conformity

Police, prosecutors, and judges rely on victim stereotypes to analyze the cases they encounter. They, too, have seen victims represented as white women, with all of the historical baggage that designation carries. The legal system is still predominantly white, male, and middle class, more likely to envision and sympathize with the women they know—their daughters, their sisters. Domestic violence trainings that emphasize battered woman syndrome and victims who are passive, dependent, weak, and afraid reinforce these beliefs. System actors who internalize these messages are looking for a particular kind of victim telling a particular kind of story: a white woman telling a story of passivity, dependency, fear, and inability to address the abuse without the assistance of the legal system. For the "perfectly constructed plaintiff . . . a white, married, church-going, tee-totaling, homemaker, with no criminal record—not even a parking ticket,"[58] these stereotypes present no problem. But women who tell a different story might be unable to secure the kinds of assistance that could help them avoid further abuse. One example: a woman who is unwilling to admit her fear, or who does not fear her abuser but nonetheless believes that he is likely to harm her, might find herself ineligible for civil protection in some states. The civil protection order statutes of Indiana, Kansas, Kentucky, Maine, Maryland, and a number of other states cover threats that place another in fear of imminent serious bodily harm. Women who are threatened but will not admit to or do not feel that fear are denied the protection of the courts because they fail to conform to a standard that assumes that a threat would cause a woman to feel fear, an assumption enshrined in law to the detriment of non-conforming women. When a woman who has been threatened asserts, "I'm not afraid of him" to a judge who is looking for that fear to substantiate her claim, she renders herself ineligible for assistance.

Victim stereotypes validate the claims of a narrow subset of women subjected to abuse. Simultaneously, those stereotypes create barriers to accessing support for women who fail to conform—like angry women. Anger is a common response to trauma. Women may be angry that they have been abused, angry with their partners for subjecting them to abuse and for destroying their families, and angry that having fled the abuse, their lives are far from perfect. Seeking assistance may make women subjected to abuse feel safe enough to express that anger. That anger, though, may cause police, prosecutors, and judges to turn against them. Anger expressed when police arrive at the scene may mean that the woman is arrested. Anger in the courtroom can lead to admonishments like this one, given by a judge in Baltimore, Maryland: "If you find you need to come back to court, you need to learn how to conduct yourself first."[59] One woman subjected to abuse, Jane, described her observations of the court system:

> I think the vast majority of the women that go into court do so upset and the minute they show that they are out of control in any way, no matter how legitimate it might be, the court takes offense to that. They either deal with you in a very negative way, or they decide not to deal with you. And it takes you months, sometimes years, to get that credibility back with the judge.[60]

An angry woman is simply not a good victim.

Non-conforming women, as Jane recognized, lose credibility with the legal system. The credibility of women subjected to abuse is tenuous in any event. Studies document the skepticism with which police officers, judges, and jurors meet claims of abuse.[61] Stories that challenge preexisting understandings of victim behavior are even more likely to raise doubts about women's credibility. Women subjected to abuse who fail to conform to victim stereotypes face a cruel choice: tell your authentic story and face the consequences of failing to conform, or tailor your story to the prevailing narrative and deny the reality of your experience. Linguist Shonna Trinch has documented the impact of this type of narrative reconstruction on Latinas subjected to abuse applying for civil protective orders. Trinch describes how state representatives, in interviewing and compiling court papers for women subjected to abuse, construct women's stories in ways that track state definitions of and expectations about abuse. Trinch describes these interviews as a "linguistic battle of wills" between women committed to telling their stories and institutional actors determined to conform to established norms of victim behavior.[62] Trinch notes that institutional service providers tend to emphasize aspects of women's identities that underscore their victimization and downplay women's descriptions of fighting back against their partners. Ironically, this narrative reconstruction may ultimately harm the women whose stories are edited, as only they will be called to account for any inconsistencies between their pleadings and their courtroom testimony. Trinch concludes that narrative reconstruction can be interpreted as "giving voice" to victims of domestic violence to ensure that they are heard. On the other hand, it can be seen as mutating or erasing the victims' voices, leaving a historical record in the form of a court document that does more to reflect what the law considers to be important in these cases than it does to represent what the women's experiences are and what they consider to be of relevance.[63]

Defining the victim is a normative act. In creating categories like battered woman syndrome, "the legal language of recognition can become the language of constraint," confining women subjected to abuse to narrow victim stereotypes.[64] Basing law and policy on those stereotypes ignores the ways in which women's intersecting identities construct the experience of abuse.

Intersectionality challenges us to consider how different identities, particularly marginalizing identities, contribute to women's experiences with and responses to abuse. As law professor Kimberlé Crenshaw explains,

> Many women of color . . . are burdened by poverty, child care responsibilities, and the lack of job skills. These burdens, largely the consequence of gender and class oppression, are then compounded by the racially discriminatory employment and housing practices women of color often face, as well as by the disproportionately high unemployment among people of color that makes battered women of color less able to depend on the support of friends and relatives for temporary shelter.[65]

In a policy world that embraces the essentialized victim of violence, there is no room for this type of analysis, further marginalizing non-conforming women subjected to abuse by failing to incorporate their experiences into law and policymaking.

Definition can also be a transformative act. In the context of self-defense law, for example, law professor Jeannie Suk has argued that reformulations of the castle doctrine—the right to use deadly force to defend oneself within the home—intended to address concerns about the use of the defense by women who kill their abusers have created two categories of individuals: the person and the victim. The ordinary person who uses force within the home, Suk argues, is the true man. The victim, by contrast, is

> the subordinated woman unable to retreat. . . . She was not asserting her rights in a place where she had a right to be. She was, rather, the recipient of the state's protection, a supplicant who had to prove she was disempowered and coerced in order not to be punished for defending her life.[66]

This conception of the victim will undoubtedly benefit some women on trial for killing their partners. But the cost to all women subjected to abuse is significant—the loss of personhood required by taking on, and by enshrining in law, the identity of victim.

There is a clear theoretical progression from dominance feminism to the creation of the paradigmatic victim. A philosophy centered on the subordination of women as the defining feature of women's social existence leads directly to the kind of victim stereotyping that characterized the early battered women's movement. That victim stereotyping, in turn, excludes women from protection, forces women to rewrite their lives in order to get assistance, and limits creative thinking about how domestic violence law and policy can benefit all women subjected to abuse.

Separation

Dixie Shanahan did not have to kill her husband, according to Susan Christensen. Shanahan shot her husband Scott after enduring 19 years of abuse, including black eyes, bruises, threats, being dragged by her hair, held at gunpoint, tied up and left in a basement for days, and regular verbal abuse and degradation in front of family and friends. Shanahan shot her husband after a morning of being beaten, after being threatened at gunpoint, after her husband promised, "This day is not over yet. I will kill you." At her murder trial, Shanahan testified that she shot her husband because she believed that she and her unborn child would not survive to see the next day unless she acted. Nonetheless, Susan Christensen believed, Dixie Shanahan had options, options that would have prevented that final confrontation on August 30, 2002. As Christensen testified during Shanahan's trial, "I don't believe this case had to end this way. I think that there were choices that we gave Dixie, in particular, that she chose not to take and those choices have been proven over and over to be effective if allowed to take their course."[1]

Susan Christensen, the Assistant County Attorney for Shelby County, Iowa, had, in the years leading up to Scott's death, offered Dixie Shanahan two choices: to seek a protective order against her husband and to cooperate with his criminal prosecution. Shanahan did, at various times, avail herself of those options. She filed for, and received, a protective order in 1997. She cooperated with the state during its first criminal prosecution of Scott that same year; Scott pled guilty to punching Dixie and spent two days in jail. Three months later, Scott was again prosecuted for assaulting his wife. On that occasion, Dixie refused to assist prosecutors, asking instead that the charges be dismissed. Scott was convicted and served four days in jail. Upon his release, Scott redoubled his abuse. Three years later, when the state of Iowa prosecuted Scott for felony domestic violence, Dixie refused to return from Texas (where she had fled to escape Scott's abuse) to testify against him. While Christensen originally took "some comfort knowing that there was some distance between"[2] Dixie and Scott, she later condemned Dixie's decision not to return for the trial, which forced prosecutors to drop the charges. Christensen testified that although neither of the earlier prosecutions had stopped Scott's violence against Dixie (and in fact, the violence had increased after each prosecution), she believed that if Dixie had cooperated that third time, the violence would have ended.

That Christensen would equate separation with successful termination of the violence is hardly surprising; indeed, the inclination to conflate the two has oriented domestic violence law and policy since the early days of the battered women's movement. Like many aspects of domestic violence law and policy, the focus on separation owes its preeminent position to psychologist Lenore Walker and the theory of learned helplessness. Walker argued that to eradicate learned helplessness, women must be removed from the context of the violent relationships that engender the condition. The only remedy for learned helplessness was separation. Law and policy development within the legal system accordingly prioritized separating women subjected to abuse from their abusive partners and made separation the litmus test for determining whether a victim was worthy of assistance. As law professor Christine Littleton writes, "[The legal system] does not blame *all* battered women for their plight, only those who do not immediately sever their relationships and leave their batterers."[3]

The demand that women subjected to abuse separate from their abusive partners rewrites cultural norms about women's roles in relationships. Historically, women were urged to stay in violent relationships, to preserve their families and support their spouses. The law made it difficult for women to leave, setting impossibly high standards for divorce on the grounds of cruelty and denying them custody, child support, and marital property if they insisted on divorcing. The new norm, though, requires women subjected to abuse to leave their partners and use the legal system to enforce that separation through protective orders and criminal proceedings. The failure to immediately and willingly separate from a man who abuses has implications for a woman's credibility. Judges, police, and prosecutors, vested in their roles as those who rescue women from abuse, are skeptical of the claims of women who are reluctant or unwilling to separate or who do not separate quickly enough.

Christensen's testimony highlighted her certainty that remedies like protective orders and criminal prosecutions, which are designed to separate the parties, would stop Scott Shanahan's violence (although on cross-examination, she conceded that about half of the women who she assisted with protective orders reported further problems with their partners). That position is founded on two troubling assumptions. First, it assumes that separation is effective in stopping abuse. Second, and more important, it assumes that separation is the only appropriate response to domestic violence—and that, as a result, all women should want to separate (or be separated from their partners, whether they want to or not).

But separation-based remedies didn't work for Dixie Shanahan. In part, separation failed because her husband was not deterred by the intervention of the courts. But separation also failed because contextually, it was not the option that best met her needs. Early on, when her husband sought counseling for his anger, and she believed that he could change and be a good husband and father to their children, separation was antithetical to Dixie's ultimate goals: to have a strong marriage, to honor a pledge that she had made to Scott's mother to take care of him, to give her children a father. Later, when it became clear that all that separation, via the intervention of the legal system, brought her was intensified abuse, separation-based remedies made her less, rather than more, safe.

Despite the experiences of Dixie Shanahan and countless women like her, who have found that separation was not the panacea that it was made out to be, domestic violence law and policy continues to rely almost exclusively on separation-based remedies. The focus on separation springs from a core belief that women in violent relationships should not remain in those relationships. Since the inception of the battered women's movement, the question "why doesn't she leave?" has dogged advocates and women subjected to abuse. The question highlights both the assumptions people make about domestic violence (that everyone in a violent relationship can actually just get up and leave, and that everyone in a violent relationship should want to get up and leave) and the public's ignorance about the complexity of abusive relationships.

"Why doesn't she leave?" is not a surprising question—looking at an abusive relationship from the outside, it can be difficult to understand why a woman subjected to abuse does not simply open the door and walk out. Even the most seasoned advocates (reluctantly) admit to having occasionally questioned why their clients don't leave their partners. The early battered women's movement struggled to overcome the perception that women remained in abusive relationships because they were masochists, gratified by their victimization. Advocates developed a laundry list of reasons that explained why women stayed in abusive relationships: children, economics, religion, immigration status, extended family ties, community sanction, housing, employment, culture, disability, fear, and love. The literature that purports to explain why women subjected to abuse don't leave is troubling, though. By and large, discussions about why she doesn't leave assume the validity of the desire to separate women from their abusive partners. These explanations accept that there must be some justification for a woman's failure to separate, and that all women would leave violent relationships if they had appropriate support and intervention. Women don't leave, the argument generally goes, because leaving is unsafe, unduly burdensome, or otherwise harmful in some way, not because they do not want to leave. To be seen as a real victim of abuse, a woman must want to leave and either be unable or be struggling actively to do so. Domestic violence law and policy similarly reflects the idea that women would leave if they could, if only sufficient support was provided. Leaving is thought to be every woman's goal.

Separation and Separation-Based Remedies

Separation—the act of leaving an abusive partner—must be distinguished from separation-based remedies. Although separation is the ultimate goal of domestic violence law and policy, few still believe that physical separation alone—simply closing the door of a shared home and walking out into the night—will be sufficient to safeguard women subjected to abuse. The statistics on and stories about the prevalence of post-separation assault are simply too persuasive to ignore. Research shows that a large percentage of intimate partner violence occurs after the termination of the relationship—post-separation.[4] The risk of homicide to women subjected to abuse dramatically increases after separation as well.[5] As a practical matter, total separation from an abusive partner may be impossible; as researchers Ruth E. Fleury, Cris M. Sullivan, and Deborah I. Bybee note,

> The complexities of women's lives . . . make avoiding the batterer, even after the relationship is over, that much more difficult, particularly if children are involved. Women may need to continue contact with their batterers due to custody and visitation issues. Even when children are not involved, survivors and batterers may still live in the same area or have other social connections to each other. Expecting survivors to move away or to cut important social ties as a means of protecting themselves is unrealistic and unfair.[6]

Separation, in and of itself, does not end domestic violence—an insight that was no revelation to women who continued to be abused after leaving their partners. Researchers theorized that violence increased after separation as abusive partners sought to regain the control they ceded when their partners left the relationship. Law professor Martha Mahoney called this phenomenon "separation assault" and argued that, given its prevalence, the legal landscape facing women subjected to abuse needed to be reconstructed to acknowledge and account for it.[7]

Separation-based remedies are an attempt to reconstruct that landscape. Because an abusive man may equate separation with an assertion of independence by his partner, and may respond violently in seeking to regain control, domestic violence law and policy developed interventions around separation that are intended to make separation safe. Arrest, prosecution, criminal stay-away orders, and protective orders use the authority and enforcement power of the legal system to reinforce the physical separation the woman achieves by leaving. The obvious question, then, is how successful these remedies are in keeping women safe while separated.

Arrest

Arresting men who abused their partners seemed an easy answer to enforcing separations. Prior to the activism of the battered women's movement, the most common police response to a "domestic call" was to advise the husband to take a walk around the block and cool down. Arrests were incredibly rare, even in cases involving visible injury. For poor people and people of color, law professor Donna Coker argues, police reluctance to arrest is tied to a perception that violence is the norm in those communities. Police intervention was (and is) perceived as unlikely to make a difference in an abusive relationship.

The immediate benefits of arrest in the context of separation are obvious: while an abusive partner is being arrested, transported, booked, arraigned, and (likely) released, a woman has the opportunity to leave. Arrest is a state-enforced period of separation, albeit often a short one. Whatever value arrest may or may not have in deterring future abuse, arrest absolutely stops the immediate incident and provides a window of opportunity for the woman subjected to abuse to flee.

This cessation of violence in the moment makes arrest incredibly appealing as a separation strategy. But the promise of arrest is illusory. Sometimes arrests don't happen immediately; as described in chapter 3, one woman in rural Ohio waited for her former partner to be arrested for thirteen days after he raped and beat her, during which time, as she lay on the couch with four broken ribs, he stole her car and destroyed her clothing.[8] In some communities, the time between arrest and release is ridiculously short, providing little window for a woman subjected to abuse to collect herself, her important information, her resources, her belongings, and possibly her children and find somewhere for all of those things to reside in the short term. In *Saving Bernice: Battered Women, Welfare and Poverty*, sociologist Jody Raphael tells the story of Bernice Hampton, a woman subjected to serious abuse at the hands of her long-time partner, Billy. Bernice called police repeatedly to report Billy's stalking. Raphael writes,

> "After he was arrested," says Bernice, "he would come out of the police station and say, 'You don't get the message. There is nothing that anyone can do to me. I will always get out. And when I get out, what do you think you are going to get?'" Then he would choke Bernice on the street across from the police station.[9]

The impracticality of holding all of the men arrested for abusing their partners means that most will be released, usually after posting minimal bail. Between Saturday, May 29, 2010, and Monday, May 31, 2010, Jeffrey Pavano was arrested three times for abusing his wife. First arrested on Saturday night and released on $5,000 bail, Pavano returned to his home in West Hartford, Connecticut, on Monday at noon, was again arrested, posted bail of $10,000—and was back home by 5:36 Monday evening. Bail for the third arrest was set at $500,000.[10] Only after the third arrest was Pavano prevented from returning to his home, because he was unable post bail.

Even if her partner is arrested, a woman subjected to abuse may not have the time or the resources to find safety. The number of shelters in the United States is still insufficient to house the thousands of women who seek their services. In rural areas, the nearest shelter space may be counties away, inaccessible without transportation and other resources. Women may be unable to seek refuge with friends or family, either because those supports don't exist or are unwilling to get involved or because women fear endangering friends who offer to help. Such fears are well-founded. On June 6, 2010, Geraldo Regalado went to the restaurant in Hialeah, Florida, where his estranged wife, Liazan Molina, worked, and shot not only Molina, but also her cousin, Yasmin Dominguez, who took her in after the couple separated. Yasmin had come to the restaurant that day to protect Liazan. Molina and three of her co-workers were killed; Dominguez was sent to the hospital in critical condition.[11] Arrest may enrage the abusive man, spurring him to seek revenge against his partner—thus creating separation, but not safety. In short, while arrest can create immediate separation, its prospects for enabling women to separate permanently and safely are limited at best.

Prosecution

But arrest is only one component of the criminal justice system's separation-based policy. In some cases, arrest leads to prosecution, yet another tool that advocates of the criminal law response to domestic violence believe is essential in keeping women safe. Prosecution was, if anything, rarer than arrest in cases involving domestic violence prior to the reforms of the late 1980s. Prosecution rates were ridiculously low. In 1989, prosecutors in the District of Columbia brought fewer than 40 cases of misdemeanor domestic violence; by 1996, that number was approximately 4,500.[12]

Prosecution could, in theory, facilitate separation in a variety of ways. Prosecution can lead to incarceration, a period of state-enforced separation, or to the imposition of a state-ordered separation via the issuance of a criminal stay-away order as a condition of probation or parole. Prosecution can also serve as the wake-up call that an abusive man needs to understand that his best strategy for avoiding future involvement with the criminal system is to remain apart from his partner.

The reality of prosecution's ability to enable women to separate safely is more complicated. Remarkably few domestic violence cases are prosecuted—even when arrests are made or charges brought. In a study published in 2000, researchers Patricia Tjaden and Nancy Thoennes found that only 7.3 percent of physical assaults, 7.5 percent of rapes, and 14.6 percent of stalking cases involving intimate partners were prosecuted.[13] The vast majority of cases involving domestic violence are prosecuted as misdemeanors rather than felonies. Misdemeanors typically carry very short jail sentences—90 days or less. Even in cases of egregious violence, sentences of a day or two are not uncommon. Dixie Shanahan's husband Scott was sentenced to 30 days' incarceration with all but two days suspended, for punching Dixie in the face and slamming her head into a car window—a misdemeanor. He was again sentenced to 30 days but served only four days for his second misdemeanor conviction, after beating Dixie's head and legs with a metal object, causing her to bleed from her ear. She was pregnant at the time.

But Scott Shanahan spent time in jail; many misdemeanor convictions result in no jail time at all. To process the enormous number of misdemeanor cases coming through state court systems, prosecutors routinely offer plea bargains that dispense with jail time in lieu of batterer intervention programs, probation, and criminal stay-away orders. Even a felony conviction may not bring significant jail time. Kenneth Woodruff of Lacombe, Louisiana was first arrested for domestic violence in 2005, convicted of a misdemeanor, and sentenced to probation and community service. In 2006, a second misdemeanor conviction carried a sentence of probation. In 2008, Woodruff was given a plea deal that allowed him to plead guilty to a "second, second domestic violence offense" in order to avoid a felony conviction. Later in October 2008, Woodruff was again arrested and convicted of felony domestic violence, but sentenced to time served. In February 2009, he was convicted of another felony, sentenced to a year in jail, and given credit for time served. Later in October 2009, Woodruff was arrested and convicted for a sixth act of abuse—all against the same woman—and finally received a significant sentence: 15 years' imprisonment. Eight years of the sentence were suspended, however.[14]

Prosecution carries many of the same risks associated with arrest—particularly the risk of renewed abuse. Because jail time for domestic violence is rare and often minimal, abusive men are likely to be back in the same communities as their partners in a short period of time—and are likely to be angry about their exposure to criminal liability. Men who are convicted and placed on probation face scant restrictions on their freedom; as a practical matter, probation officers are not shadowing men who abuse to ensure that they stay away from their partners. Judges issue criminal stay-away orders, requiring that men who abuse maintain their distance from their partners, but those orders are only as effective as the willingness of men to comply with them and the police to enforce them. Again, while prosecution might provide some time during which a woman subjected to abuse can separate from her partner, it is unlikely to give her much time, or to ensure her safety during the separation.

Even incarceration is no guarantee of separation or safety. Tiffany Gates began working with prosecutors after her ex-boyfriend, Robert Ridley, threatened to set her on fire in front of her nine-year-old child, kicked her, punched her, and hit her with a knife. On August 13, 2008, Gates went with police to retrieve her belongings from the Washington, DC, apartment they had shared; Ridley set the couch in the apartment on fire. Ridley was arrested, charged, pled guilty to arson, and was released to a halfway house on October 9, 2008, with sentencing set for December 2008. Ridley escaped from the halfway house on October 29. Around midnight on November 21, 2008, Gates called 911 to report seeing Ridley. At 12:19 a.m., she begged a marshal specially assigned to apprehend Ridley for help. At 1:25 a.m., the marshal arrived but waited outside for assistance. The marshal was on the phone with Gates as Ridley kicked in the door to her apartment. When the police finally entered Gates's building, they found

Gates bleeding from multiple stab wounds outside the door of a neighbor's apartment. Ridley was quickly apprehended in another apartment in the building. Tiffany Gates was pronounced dead at 2:20 a.m.[15]

Civil Protection Orders

On the civil side, protective orders are widely hailed as facilitating separation by equipping women with a range of remedies designed to provide the essentials for a safe separation. Available in every state, such orders might include, depending on state law, provisions requiring that the respondent not assault, threaten, or harass his partner; that he not contact his partner; and that he stay away from his partner's home, school, place of employment, and children's school or day care facilities. Such orders also have the power to establish custody, child support, and spousal support, grant use and possession of family homes and vehicles, and require reimbursement for expenses incurred as a result of abuse. Some social science research indicates that protective orders are associated with decreased subsequent violence,[16] and women report that they believe the decision to seek a protective order is often a good one.[17] Protective orders, then, could keep abusive men physically away from their partners and give women subjected to abuse the tools that they need to maintain the separation—safety at home, work, and school, stability for their children, a place to live, and financial resources to support their families.

Protective orders could do all these things, but it's worth asking how often they actually do. There are studies that find protective orders reduce future violence, but there are also studies associating protective orders with increased violence and homicide.[18] Protective orders were intended to be easy to pursue without counsel by women needing immediate assistance. Hearings were to be held quickly in response to emergency situations. Remedies were meant to be expansive and flexible, enabling women to request the particular tools they needed to address their individual situations. Enforcement would be swift and carry real penalties, so that men who abused their partners understood that a civil protection order demanded the same respect as the criminal law.

But simply filing for a protective order can prove deadly. On September 15, 2009, a West Virginia domestic violence program held a vigil to honor a woman whose abuser set her on fire after she filed for a protective order, killing her. Filing can send a signal that a woman is no longer willing to be controlled by her partner and is seeking assistance to change the balance of power. Danielle described her unwillingness to seek a protective order to sociologist Kathleen Ferraro:

[A] man like Tony, I woulda served him with a piece of paper saying he couldn't be around me, I wouldn't be around today for that paper to mean anything because that would've been an insult to him, that would've been disrespectful to him, that would've been a slap in his face because I took something that was private and let it be known public.[19]

In November 2010, Robert Gold-Smith beat his wife outside of a Joliet, Illinois courtroom after a hearing during which a judge refused to rescind the protective order his wife, Victoria Smith, had taken out against him after he threatened to kill her. Gold-Smith's attack left his wife with 15 stitches around her eye and chipped teeth.[20] Attacks associated with filing protective orders are a powerful example of the danger of separation violence.

Securing protective orders without the assistance of counsel has proven more challenging than advocates had hoped. The vast majority of protective order petitioners are not represented in these court proceedings. Although petitioners can craft their own pleadings and represent themselves in protective order cases, women are far more successful in obtaining protective orders when they are represented. In a study of women seeking protective orders in Baltimore, Maryland, researchers found that 83 percent of the women with attorneys were granted protective orders, as opposed to 32 percent without attorneys.[21] Other studies show similar, if less stark, results. Social scientists suggest that these discrepancies reflect the inability of many women subjected to abuse to create on their own the kinds of narratives that will persuade judges of their need for protection. Persuasive narratives include detailed information about the events that led women to seek protection and omit information that finders of fact deem superfluous (even when that information provides context or fleshes out the characters more fully). In some cases—those where either the abuse is severe and clear or the respondent does not appear—assistance with crafting the narrative may be unnecessary. But, sociologist Alesha Durfee argues,

In contested cases . . . where respondents retained a lawyer and/or filed affidavits disputing the petitioner's claims of abuse, there was no external documentation of the abuse, or it was unclear whether the incidents described met the legal criteria for an entry of protection order, variations in the form, content, and structure of the narrative had important implications for case outcomes. . . . In these cases, legal representation is critical for victims.[22]

In some jurisdictions, protective order hearings are not held nearly as swiftly as advocates had intended. Service of process has become a major hurdle to having cases heard in some areas. In Baltimore, Maryland, for example, protective order hearings are routinely postponed because the police are unable to serve the respondent with notice of the action. Women seeking protection are forced to return to court week after week, often with children in tow, having asked their employers to be patient just one more time, only to find that their cases are still stalled for lack of service of process. One survey found that half of the women seeking protective orders were unable to proceed because service efforts had failed.[23] Other surveys have found service-related denials of orders in 12 percent to 91 percent of cases, depending on the jurisdiction.[24] In some jurisdictions, protective order proceedings are put on hold while criminal charges are pending, denying relief for the women seeking assistance until after the criminal matter has been resolved.

The scope of the court's remedial power varies from jurisdiction to jurisdiction. In the District of Columbia, the protective order statute includes a catch-all provision, enabling the judge to order a respondent "to perform or refrain from other actions as may be appropriate to the effective resolution of the matter."[25] In neighboring Maryland, however, judges are restrained by statute from ordering any relief beyond what the law explicitly provides. Even in those places where judges have broad authority to grant remedies, they remain reluctant to provide women with the tools that they need to ensure safe separation. Most problematic are economic resources and safe custody and visitation provisions.

Judges are sometimes unwilling to provide women with the economic resources they need to safely separate, preferring to defer adjudication of spousal and child support claims until divorces or custody actions are filed. Although many state statutes empower judges to order respondents to vacate the family home, judges sometimes hesitate to evict a man who claims he has nowhere else to go or whose name is the only one on the lease. A judge in the District of Columbia refused to evict a man from the home he shared with his wife and six children, despite entering a protective order against him. Instead, the judge permitted the man to reside in the basement of the home, which had a separate entrance. His wife was forced to return to court the next day; her husband had spent the previous evening banging on the basement ceiling, causing her to fear for her safety and for the safety of her children. Similarly, in a 2008 Maryland case, Judge Bruce Lamdin refused to order a man out of the family home despite finding by clear and convincing evidence that the man, with a knife in hand, had threatened to kill his wife, the latest of numerous incidents of abuse the woman alleged. The woman and her three children lived with her attorney until the matter was heard on appeal and her husband voluntarily left the home a month later.[26] The case likely became public only because Lamdin had previously been suspended for his mistreatment of litigants in his courtroom. It is impossible to know how often such decisions fly under the radar, part of the everyday operation of the protective order system.

Unsafe custody and visitation provisions undermine the effectiveness of protective orders for women with children. Judges routinely order women to "work out" visitation provisions with their partners only minutes after entering protective orders finding that the partner has been abusive. When women are hesitant about unsupervised visitation, judges sometimes punish them by awarding custody or unsupervised visitation to their partners or name paternal relatives, who may turn a blind eye to the threat posed by their family member, to serve as visitation supervisors. Even paternal relatives with the best of intentions may underestimate the threat that the father poses. Jessica Jacobsen's father-in-law certainly did. Jacobsen's protective order required her father-in-law, Reginald Jacobsen, to supervise visitations between her estranged husband, Jeffrey, and her children. As they arrived to pick up the children, Jeffrey asked his father to get Jessica, so that he could ask her a question (a violation of the protective order). When, at Reginald's request, Jessica came out of the house, Jeffrey shot her in the chest and later shot himself. Reginald Jacobsen must have been horrified; he could not possibly have known what his son planned to do. But he never should have been in the position of facilitating his son's request for access to Jessica Jacobsen in the first place.

Enforcing protective orders has also been a challenge. Most states provide for enforcement of protective orders either through criminal contempt (proceedings held in the civil system and brought by the woman) or by criminalizing violations of protective orders (usually as misdemeanors, prosecuted by the state). Stories of violated protective orders are common, both in the media and among lawyers, advocates, and women subjected to abuse. Those anecdotes are supported by social science research suggesting that between 23 percent and 70 percent of women report violations of protective orders; a meta-analysis of 32 studies found that about 40 percent of orders were violated.[27] The media is replete with the stories of women who do "everything right": who turn to the legal system, who get protective orders, and whose partners violate those orders, often with tragic results. Alison Kirby is one of those women. In March 2006, Kirby sought a protective order in Mary-land after her boyfriend, Christopher McCann, threatened her with violence. Kirby showed a judge cell phone pictures of McCann's knife collection and testified to her fear. Judge Michael Finifter of the Circuit Court for Baltimore County, Maryland issued a protective order prohibiting McCann from assaulting, threatening, harassing, or approaching Kirby. It didn't matter. On May 1, 2006, McCann followed Kirby to a Wal-Mart and attacked her in the parking lot, stabbing her 12 times in the head, face, and arms. McCann was later convicted of first-degree murder.

Strict enforcement could increase the effectiveness of protective orders, but enforcement has been uneven at best. As law professor Sally Goldfarb notes, "Even where laws requiring strict enforcement have been enacted, they are too often ignored. In fact, poor enforcement may be largely responsible for the results of studies showing high rates of non-compliance with protective orders."[28]

Despite state laws that seem to require police to stringently enforce protective orders, police are under no constitutional obligation to protect the individual women who receive them. So said the U.S. Supreme Court in 2005 in *Town of Castle Rock v. Jessica Gonzales*. Jessica Gonzales's protective order set firm restrictions on her ex-husband Simon Gonzales's visitation with their three children, Leslie, Katheryn, and Rebecca. When Mr. Gonzales snatched the children from the front lawn of Ms. Gonzales's home on June 22, 1999, he violated the provisions of that order.

Ms. Gonzales's order included a "Notice to Law Enforcement Officials" that read:

> YOU SHALL USE EVERY REASONABLE MEANS TO ENFORCE THIS RESTRAINING ORDER. YOU SHALL ARREST, OR, IF AN ARREST WOULD BE IMPRACTICAL UNDER THE CIR-CUMSTANCES, SEEK A WARRANT FOR THE ARREST OF THE RESTRAINED PERSON WHEN YOU HAVE INFOR-MATION AMOUNTING TO PROBABLE CAUSE THAT THE RESTRAINED PERSON HAS VIOLATED OR ATTEMPTED TO VIOLATE ANY PROVISION OF THIS ORDER.[29]

Believing that the order meant what it said—that law enforcement was responsible for enforcing the terms of the order—Gonzales called the police around 7:30 p.m., shortly after her daughters disappeared. Simon Gonzales should have been familiar to the Castle Rock police. He had had seven contacts with them, many domestic violence related, over the previous three months. But Jessica Gonzales was told to call back at 10:00 p.m. She called again at 8:30 p.m., after hearing from her husband that he and the children were at a nearby amusement park, and was again told to wait to see if he returned with the children. She called at 10:10 p.m., and was told to wait to see if the children were still missing at midnight. At midnight, she called to say the children were still missing, and went to her husband's apartment to look for the children. She called the police at 12:10 a.m. from the apartment and was told to wait for an officer. No officer arrived. At 12:50 a.m., she went to the police station and made an incident report; the officer who took the report responded to her urgent pleas by going to dinner. At 3:20 a.m., Simon Gonzales arrived at the police station and opened fire. Police returned fire, killing Gonzales. When the shooting ceased, police found the bodies of the Gonzales girls in the cab of Simon Gonzales's pickup truck, riddled with bullet holes of varying sizes.

Jessica Gonzales sued Castle Rock for its failure to enforce her restraining order, notwithstanding the mandate to police to arrest or seek a warrant for the arrest of the restrained person when there was probable cause to believe that the restrained person had violated the order. The Supreme Court denied Gonzales's claim, holding that the mandatory language in the statute quoted on Jessica Gonzales's restraining order wasn't mandatory at all. Justice Antonin Scalia wrote for the Court, "We do not believe that these provisions of Colorado law truly made enforcement of restraining orders *mandatory*,"[30] because police discretion continued to exist despite the language of the statute. Because the law was not truly mandatory, Ms. Gonzales was not entitled to have it enforced. Because Ms. Gonzales was not entitled to enforcement of the law, there could be no property right, and no violation of due process, when the police failed to enforce the protective order that was intended to provide a safe separation for her and her children.

Castle Rock undermines the effectiveness of protective orders as a tool for separation. While *Castle Rock* involved a violation of the visitation provision of a protective order, the Court's opinion applies to all provisions of protective orders—including provisions that forbid further assaults, threats, or contact. Protective orders can only deter men who abuse from further abuse if there is a credible reason to fear the ramifications that will result from their violation. Creating that fear requires that men who abuse believe that police will enforce the orders. If police have no duty to enforce, the likelihood of enforcement decreases. Orders become less credible, and the potential for creating safe separation for women who want that separation more remote.

Divorce and Custody

Divorce provides women with legal separation from abusive partners; physical separation is more difficult to effectuate (although divorce courts in many states can issue protective orders as part of a final decree). Divorce courts could provide women with the economic resources to remain separate and safe, but often fail to do so. Awards of alimony are becoming increasingly rare in America. A recent study of family law judgments in Maryland found that alimony is requested in only 16 percent of filed cases, and awarded in only 6 percent.[31] Alimony is frequently awarded on a short-term basis, which may not be sufficient for a woman subjected to abuse to establish a new life away from her spouse. For women from low-income families, economic support may be even more elusive. Courts consider the ability of the partner to pay alimony in making determinations; the court can't award what the person does not have. Similarly, the parties may not have sufficient property for the court to make an award that would enable a woman subjected to abuse to start over on her own.

For women who share children with their partners, the prospect of permanent separation is exceedingly unlikely. Judges are extremely reluctant to deprive even men who abuse of contact with their children, and frequently enter custody and visitation orders that give them access to their former partners. The Wellesley Centers for Women's Battered Mothers' Testimony Project documented numerous instances where judges refused to protect women during visitation exchanges and required that women subjected to abuse share custody with their partners, despite the danger created by doing so in those cases.[32] Child support orders provided men who abused with excuses for badgering their ex-wives about how their money was being spent. Debra described her experience:

> While the children were growing up, I learned the hard way—the ways abusers continue to abuse after the separation or divorce. After 17 years of marriage, the father of my four children used the child support money as a means to verbally and emotionally harass me on an ongoing basis. He thought paying child support gave him the right to demand an "accounting" for the way in which I spent the money, never stopping to think it rarely covered the monthly rent payment![33]

Custody and child support orders could be crafted in ways that reinforce safety and separation, but often are not.

The stories of women subjected to abuse highlight the difficulties of using the legal system to create and maintain separation. Regan Martin's husband, John Samolis, began abusing her while they were dating. The physical, sexual, and emotional abuse continued for six years, culminating in an assault in May 2006 that left her hospitalized, covered with bruises, with a split and swollen lip and bloody wounds. Martin agreed to press charges against her husband, signing the complaint from her hospital bed, but later took Samolis back, dropped her protective order, and refused to testify. Samolis continued to harass her, and in October 2006, Martin sought a new protective order and agreed to testify against her husband. Samolis pled guilty to aggravated domestic battery and entered prison in February 2007; he was eligible for release in 19 months. For 19 months, Martin should have had separation and some measure of safety, thanks to the legal system.

Instead, Martin continued to receive threatening letters and phone calls from Samolis despite the order of protection. Prosecutors charged Samolis with violating the order of protection, but delays meant that Samolis's bail hearing was held on the day he was to be released from prison. A judge set bail at $3,500; Samolis was out of jail in four hours. Although by this time Martin had divorced Samolis, her request for permission to move her children out of state was still pending. After Samolis's release, a judge granted her request—but gave Samolis phone contact and supervised visitation. Martin was forced to provide Samolis with her new address and phone number. Predictably, Samolis began to harass Martin by phone, calling 30 times and sending 15 text messages in five days. He threatened to follow her to her new state. Samolis was again arrested for violating the protective order, pled guilty, and was again incarcerated.[34]

Like Regan Martin, Denise tried to separate from her ex-husband:

After 5 years, and more moves than I can remember, I was able to obtain a divorce. This did not stop the stalking, the breaking and entering, the calls, or the abuse. Even after he remarried he would still call, threaten, and break into my home, where he could find us.

For almost 7 years I lived in fear. We would move and hide. Change cities, states, names.

He would find us, break into the house in the middle of the night. I would be hurt. The police were no help. By the time the police would arrive, it was over. Orders of protection were worthless. His parents couldn't keep him away. My friends and family were long gone. They had been hurt and couldn't risk it anymore.

The abuse didn't stop until her ex-husband was convicted of killing his girl-friend and imprisoned.[35]

In both of these cases, the legal system's preferred tools for enforcing separation failed. Men violated protective orders. They were arrested and released. They were convicted, served time, and even while incarcerated continued to abuse, threaten, and harass their partners. Regan Martin and Denise both wanted separation—but the legal system couldn't deliver on its promises.

For women who want to separate, then, the tools that the legal system offers aren't always effective. That those tools fail to live up to their promise is a critical problem for women who want to use them. That those remedies are, by and large, the only things that women subjected to abuse are offered in a society that disproportionately relies on the legal system to address domestic violence, is tragic.

The Women Who Stay

For women who don't want to separate, the legal system has even less to offer. By enacting and funding separation-based remedies to the exclusion of other responses, the state has made a normative choice about the value of relationships that involve abuse. As sociologist Phyllis Baker writes, "The overall goal of the cultural script for battered women is to leave and to stay away from their abusers."[36] The script for the legal system is the same. The law's reliance upon separation-based remedies reflects a judgment that all women subjected to abuse should want separation from their partners because their relationships are not worth supporting and cannot be made viable.

That judgment reflects an unwillingness to accept women's calculations about the relative merits of remaining in or leaving their relationships, calculations based on factors like assessments of safety, economics, immigration status, community support, and children. At a deeper level, though, that judgment reflects a profound ambivalence about, and even a dismissal of, the value of the continued existence of those relationships. But as law professor Donna Coker reminds us, "[S]ome marriages are worth saving. Sometimes women are successful at getting their partner to stop the violence."[37] Similarly, psychology professor Esther Jenkins has argued, "Black women don't want men removed from their families. . . . They want their relationships fixed."[38] Studies have repeatedly shown that love and the desire to maintain relationships with their partners lead women subjected to abuse to remain with their partners and to opt out of legal remedies—to refuse to cooperate with prosecutors, to dismiss petitions for protective orders or ignore their terms.[39] Women continue to see good in their partners—to view them as dependable or affectionate—even while those men are being abusive.[40]

Love has been described as a basic human need, "one of the foremost preoccupations of humankind."[41] Some psychologists believe that love stems from a deeply rooted human need to foster emotional interdependence—that we are programmed to love. Love can provide happiness, security, confidence, and safety. When the attachment to an object of love is severed, we may experience restlessness, difficulty concentrating, interrupted sleep habits, anxiety, tension, and anger. The yearning for the lost object of love can last for years. For many of us, love is the most important thing in our lives, the thing without which our lives are not complete. Women subjected to abuse are no different than the rest of society in their desire for love. As one woman explained, "I just wanted him to stop punching me whenever he damn well pleases . . . but I still care for him, miss him when he's not around. . . . We do have a lot of good times together. . . . I even love him after everything he's done to me."[42]

To say that women subjected to abuse should separate from their partners is, as a theoretical matter, easy—it is not difficult to make the case that no one should remain in a relationship where she is being abused in some way. But the lived experiences of women subjected to abuse suggest layers of complexity that make that assertion more complicated. Sociologist Beth Richie discovered that in her sample of Black women subjected to abuse, the abuse began, on average, two years into the relationship.[43] In his interviews with women subjected to abuse who chose to remain with their partners, sociology professor Lee Bowker found that women used a variety of informal strategies, with varying levels of success, to attempt to stop the abuse themselves, from within their relationships.[44] In a longitudinal study, nursing and public health professor Jacquelyn Campbell and her colleagues found that more than a year had elapsed since the last incident of violence for approximately a quarter of the women in the study who had previously been subjected to abuse.[45] One woman had experienced violence only once at the beginning of her marriage—approximately 23 years earlier.[46]

These studies begin to provide that complexity. From Richie's work, we can imagine a relationship involving two years of love and affection, two years of building a life together, two years of emotional investment and the belief that the relationship would provide stability and partnership well into the future. After that two-year period, once abuse has occurred, Bowker teaches us that women can devise successful strategies from within their relationships to stop that abuse. From Campbell, we know that it is possible that long periods of time may elapse between violent incidents, and that some relationships may, in fact, remain non-violent. In the face of these studies, it is harder to justify policy responses that demand that women leave their partners when they are not otherwise inclined to do so.

The battered women's movement is deeply ambivalent about the role of love in relationships involving abuse. Law professor Christine Littleton describes the dilemma for advocates: "How could we possibly take seriously women's accounts of love and hope without undermining the little protection from male violence women have been able to wrest from the legal system, without indeed increasing our already overwhelming vulnerability?"[47] This ambivalence stems not only from the fear of losing those gains that have already been made, but also from the need to prevent a return to discredited theories about why women subjected to abuse stayed with their abusers. Researchers once theorized that masochism kept women from leaving abusive relationships. Walker's theory of learned helplessness was meant to refute that contention, although some have claimed that learned helplessness is simply masochism devoid of its erotic component.[48] Walker argued that women remained bound to their abusive partners out of a misguided love for them; as law professor Anne Coughlin argues, "Walker's observation that women subordinate themselves to and endure abuse from the men they love is reminiscent of the works of nineteenth-century scientists, who found that love has a powerful coercive effect on a woman."[49] The love that women subjected to abuse express for their partners is tainted by questions about its authenticity and its implications.

The domestic violence literature tiptoes carefully around the concept of love. The literature accepts the idea that some women subjected to abuse do, in fact, continue to say that they love their partners despite the abuse. But the literature explains this love away, almost apologizing for the desire of women to continue their relationships. Love becomes pathology in Walker's cycle of violence, the bridging phase between an acute battering incident and the resumption of tension building. Love prevents women from seeing through the claims that he'll never do it again, that he didn't mean to hurt her, and that he loves her, too. Love becomes a problem to solve so that the woman subjected to abuse can be cast in a sympathetic light (the poor, misguided woman) and so that her problems can be addressed in the legal system's preferred manner, through separation. Because, of course, if a woman stays with her partner out of love, the domestic violence service system has very little to offer her. As one woman subjected to abuse observed,

[T]hese people think that if I call them, they'll come and get me and I'll stay with them, but that's not the help, that's what I felt like in the meetings I come to, everyone says, the guy's a jerk and you're all right, don't let him make you think it's you and they give you all these ways of getting a place to stay or food to eat, but they don't tell you how to go back and deal with the person and I bet you nine out of ten of them go back, end up seeing the person again because you're not learning how to deal with it at the time, you're learning how to run away, you know what I mean?[50]

Love as pathology reaches its apex with the concept of traumatic bonding. Introduced by sociologists Donald Dutton and Susan Painter in 1981, traumatic bonding theory posits that the power imbalance between a woman subjected to abuse and her partner and the intermittency of abuse combine to enhance the emotional bonds between the woman and her partner, making it more difficult for the woman subjected to abuse to leave the relationship. The exercise of power by the man who abuses reinforces the woman's negative self-image, convincing the woman that she cannot function without her abuser and preventing her from separating from her partner. The woman is further cemented to the relationship by the alternating of violence and affection and warmth, a phenomenon known as intermittent reinforcement, which makes it difficult to break free from the relationship. What the woman subjected to abuse identifies as love Dutton and Painter recast as an unhealthy attachment created by a power imbalance and reinforced by the prospect of occasionally affectionate behavior.

Traumatic bonding has been used in social science research to explain why women who profess to love their abusers and want to continue their relationships decide not to seek separation-based remedies, like protective orders. One study found that women who reported loving their partners were less likely to complete the process of applying for and obtaining a protective order. The researchers argue that their result is consistent with traumatic bonding theory, and suggest that

> those in a position to help should prepare women for the possibility that when fear subsides, positive memories and emotions about the partner may emerge. They should help the women remember the negative aspects of the relationship and the possible negative outcomes associated with continuing the relationship. . . . Ultimately, these practical strategies may help increase the number of women who not only file for a temporary restraining order, but also follow through with the difficult process of ending an abusive relationship.[51]

Similarly, finding that emotional attachment spurred a majority of women subjected to abuse to return to their partners, another study recommended that counselors discuss these findings with their patients because the failure to address the role that attachment plays in decisions to return "may inadvertently undermine our own efforts to help battered women in the process of terminating abusive relationships."[52]

The battered women's movement has stressed the importance of listening to women subjected to abuse, particularly in the context of the threat of harm that they face from their abusers. Women subjected to abuse have been called the experts on their own lives, attuned to the likelihood of future abuse. Their perceptions are to be deferred to and trusted when determining the danger an abusive partner poses. Why are those perceptions denied the same deference when a woman subjected to abuse says that she loves her partner or that she believes her relationship can be saved? As sociologist Phyllis Baker reminds us, women who decide to stay with partners who are abusive "were not dupes, they made choices."[53] Rather than listening to women who want to stay in their relationships, though, those women are said to have traumatically bonded or are told that they are rationalizing away the abuse in order to protect their emotional commitments. We must focus on love, the literature argues, in order to show women that they don't really love their partners, but rather are bonded with them in an unhealthy manner, and that separation, not saving their relationships, should be their goal. Because, as one "healthy relationships curriculum" developed by a women's advocacy organization tells teens, "When Push Comes to Shove . . . It's No Longer Love."

Martha Mahoney named a phenomenon experienced by innumerable women subjected to abuse. Mahoney's work on separation assault is insightful and nuanced, recognizing the complexity of the decisions women subjected to abuse face around ending their relationships and prioritizing their goals. Separation-based law and policy responses to domestic violence largely lack such nuance, however. Instead, such policies reflect a normative choice by the state that relationships between women subjected to abuse and men who are abusive are better destroyed than preserved. Hesitation or unwillingness to end a relationship means that the woman is being coerced, threatened, or controlled; from the feminist perspective, such women might be accused of "false consciousness." A woman's desire to work from within her relationship to end the abuse is evidence of learned helplessness, and the remedy for learned helplessness is clear—separate the woman from her abusive partner so that she can see what is best for her. Although learned helplessness has lost much of its currency among the battered women's movement, the underlying emphasis on separation as the key to safeguarding women subjected to abuse remains.

Expanding Separation-Based Remedies: The U Visa

Separation-based remedies are not a historical artifact of the early battered women's movement. In 2000, legislators chose to rely on a separation-based remedy to provide assistance to undocumented immigrant women subjected to abuse. The U Visa program provides a current example of a problematic separation-based policy choice.

Congress authorized the creation of the U Visa program in the Victims of Trafficking and Violence Protection Act, a section of the Violence Against Women Act of 2000. The Act makes 10,000 visas available each year to immigrants who have suffered substantial physical or mental abuse from being subjected to rape, torture, trafficking, incest, domestic violence, sexual assault, prostitution, kidnapping, murder, and other crimes in the United States, but only if the immigrant has information concerning the criminal activity that the immigrant is willing to use to help law enforcement investigate or prosecute. To prove that the immigrant has, in fact, assisted law enforcement, the immigrant must produce certification from police or prosecutors vouching for the immigrant's willingness to work with law enforcement authorities. The U Visa gives the immigrant temporary legal status in the United States, the ability to work, and, after three years, the opportunity to apply for permanent residency in the United States. To qualify for permanent residency, an immigrant must show that she has not unreasonably refused to provide assistance to law enforcement authorities investigating or prosecuting the crime against her, that she has been continuously present in the United States for three years, and that there are strong reasons for her to remain in the United States.

The U Visa program has had a troubled beginning. In the seven years after its inception, not a single U Visa was granted. The Department of Homeland Security failed to enact regulations implementing the program until September 5, 2007, depriving immigrant women subjected to abuse of the opportunity to use the program for the first seven years of its life. Those regulations were not promulgated, in fact, until after advocates filed a class action lawsuit asking that the Department of Homeland Security be required to issue the long overdue regulations.

The U Visa was intended to enable immigrant women to report and fully participate in the investigation and prosecution of crimes against them. Congress's purpose in enacting the legislation was to "strengthen the ability of law enforcement agencies to detect, investigate, and prosecute cases of domestic violence" and other crimes "while offering protection to victims of such offenses."[54] Congress found that providing legal status to undocumented immigrant women subjected to abuse was in keeping with the humanitarian interests of the United States, but only if those women were willing to cooperate with criminal justice interventions against their partners. The U Visa provides legal status in exchange for invoking the power of the criminal justice system against a partner, a partner who, if also undocumented, would be subject to deportation upon criminal conviction for a domestic violence offense.

Advocates for immigrant women subjected to abuse questioned the requirement that women cooperate with law enforcement in order to qualify for U Visa relief, arguing that participation with the criminal justice system can make women less safe. Leslye Orloff, Director of the Immigrant Women Program at Legal Momentum, testified before Congress, "[L]ots of times you have women who may want to cooperate but are legitimately terrified that if in fact they cooperate with law enforcement they will get killed."[55] But the U Visa program provides little relief for another group of women as well— those women with no desire to cooperate with law enforcement because they do not want to invite the criminal justice system into their relationships.

The U Visa program, like other separation-based remedies, is problematic from both the practical and normative perspectives. It restricts assistance to undocumented women subjected to abuse who are willing to help law enforcement officials, notwithstanding the myriad reasons that a woman might have for not wanting to go that route. The system offers nothing to the woman who decides to drop the charges against her partner or who refuses to testify. No help is available for the woman who weighs the costs of criminal justice intervention against the benefits of having a father for her children, an economic provider, a translator in the wider world, the support of her extended family and larger community, or the love of her partner, and decides against cooperating with law enforcement. The U Visa is, purely and simply, a tool of the criminal justice system, the original separation-based remedy for domestic violence. The U Visa is just more honest about its goals than other programs, admitting from the start that its intention is to facilitate prosecution, not necessarily to meet the needs of women subjected to abuse.

The U Visa requires undocumented immigrant women to employ the separation-based remedies of arrest and prosecution, with no particular reason to believe that they will work (as discussed earlier in this chapter), in a context in which criminal justice intervention may, in fact, be less effective. Language barriers may deprive police of an accurate description of events; the undocumented woman subjected to abuse could be denied a U Visa because her attacker's narrative (particularly if told in English) may be more persuasive than her own, leading to no arrest, or worse, her arrest. Few police officers and prosecutors speak a language other than English, and translators can be scarce. For the undocumented immigrant woman, making herself heard and understood may be impossible. Undocumented immigrant women may distrust the legal system, both because of the system's ineffectual response to abuse in their own countries and because of their fears of being deported, and may be wary of working with police and prosecutors. That caution is particularly warranted, given that the undocumented woman must rely on law enforcement to certify that she has worked willingly with them, without any guarantee of receiving such certification in the beginning of her relationship with them—and without any guarantee that immigration officials will credit the certification provided by law enforcement. If her partner is her sole source of economic support, invoking the criminal system against her partner may mean depriving the family of its income, not just in the immediate aftermath of an incident, but, if her partner is convicted, incarcerated, and/ or deported, for the future as well. The woman may also fear the loss of the support of her own family, her partner's family, and the larger community if she collaborates with the criminal system to have her partner arrested and prosecuted. Bringing the scrutiny of immigration enforcement officers into her community should she work with police is yet another concern. Some of these contextual factors make arrest and prosecution less likely, others make the woman's cooperation less likely—but all point to the difficulty of offering only a separation-based remedy to undocumented immigrant women.

As a practical matter, the U Visa may not be the most effective tool for enabling women to assist the criminal justice system. As a normative matter, the U Visa clearly sends the message to undocumented immigrant women subjected to abuse that, from the state's perspective, their relationships are not worth salvaging. The U Visa "treats battered women like children, granting legal benefits and remedies only if the women admit to making bad choices and comply with the schema that others have set out for their redemption."[56] That message is reinforced by the dire consequences of arrest and prosecution for undocumented immigrant men who abuse their partners. Conviction of a crime of domestic violence—even a misdemeanor—is grounds for deportation from the United States. The pressure to follow the cultural script, to be a "good victim" who not only accedes to the wishes of police and prosecutors but also provides active assistance to law enforcement, will mean the destruction of some immigrant families. For undocumented immigrant women who want separation from their partners, this may prove a fair trade. But for those undocumented women who are interested in keeping their families together, for whatever reason, the state offers nothing. In some sense, the U Visa is a tacit acknowledgment that the state does not know or care how to keep a woman subjected to abuse safe within her relationship. Calling the police without the intention of working with law enforcement to hold her partner accountable not only deprives an undocumented woman of a chance to gain legal residency, but also makes her vulnerable to adverse immigration actions. Given those options, the undocumented immigrant woman who wants to protect her relationship with her partner may conclude that her best option is to remain hidden from public view.

The U Visa is only one example of the way that domestic violence law and policy continues to require women to separate in order to receive assistance. In Wisconsin, a woman subjected to abuse is only eligible for unemployment benefits resulting from a domestic violence-related job loss if she can show that she was forced to leave her job because her protective order either had been or would be violated—a requirement that presupposes that every working woman subjected to abuse has the inclination, time, and ability to secure a protective order. Similarly, to take advantage of state laws allowing women subjected to abuse to terminate their leases early, in most states those women must show that they have sought the assistance of the legal system to separate from their partners, either by involving law enforcement or securing a protective order. The state is willing to provide women subjected to abuse with assistance, but only on the state's terms.

The law's focus on separation dovetails nicely with a dominance feminist view of the state, vesting the state with responsibility for taking the steps necessary to enforce separation and, in so doing, saving women subjected to abuse. The problem, of course, is twofold: the state has not done a particularly good job of creating safe separation between women and their partners, and some women don't want to be saved. Some may argue that the contextual factors that prevent women from wanting to separate—economics, family and community support, and immigration concerns, for example—are simply additional problems for the state to solve, but not reasons to justify decreasing our reliance upon separation-based policies. Until such time as the state is able to remove all of those constraints, however, we must accept that these are the contexts within which women make decisions about separation, and that separation serves many of them poorly, if it serves them at all. Even if the state did address all of these concerns, some women would still want to maintain their relationships, a goal that separation-based remedies reject as a valid choice for a woman subjected to abuse. Some women might want separation, with some of the benefits conferred by separation-based remedies like protective orders, but might not want to use the legal system to effectuate that separation. The task, then, is to create a diversity of options, legal and non-legal, for women subjected to abuse—some that offer (but do not require) separation, and others that are available to women who choose not to separate. In so doing, we must change the philosophical orientation of our system from one that makes separation a cultural imperative to one that sees separation as one option among many.

Twenty years ago, law professor Christine Littleton asked, "What would legal doctrine and practice look like if it took seriously a mandate to make women safer *in* relationships, instead of offering separation as the *only* remedy for violence against women?"[57] Looking at the current system of domestic violence law and policy, we still can't answer that question.

Mandatory Interventions

June 10, 1983. Charles Thurman dropped the knife that dripped with his wife's blood. Then, as police officers looked on, he kicked her in the head—and he still wasn't arrested. After months of phone calls and reports to police warning of Charles Thurman's violence and repeated threats against his wife, after a criminal conviction and a civil order both required Thurman to stay away from his wife, Charles Thurman was still able to stab his wife multiple times in the chest, neck, and throat, drop their son on top of her while she bled, and kick her repeatedly in the head. Thurman's vicious attack on his wife was facilitated by the Torrington, Connecticut police department's unwillingness to respond to numerous requests for assistance by and on behalf of Tracy Thurman and her son, Charles Jr.—inaction that continued after the stabbing. Charles Thurman wasn't arrested, in fact, until he again approached his wife while she was lying on a stretcher, waiting to be taken for medical treatment.

Tracy Thurman and her son sued the City of Torrington for its failure to intervene on their behalf and received $2.3 million in damages. The landmark suit not only provided Tracy and Charles Jr. with some small measure of compensation for what they had suffered (Tracy Thurman remains partially paralyzed and permanently scarred from that attack) but also—in conjunction with the settlement of lawsuits filed in Oakland, California, and New York City protesting the lack of police response to domestic violence calls—began a policy revolution designed to ensure that police could no longer ignore the pleas of women seeking assistance simply because their assailants were their husbands.

Throughout the country, legislatures imposed or police departments implemented policies requiring that police make arrests in domestic violence cases whenever they had probable cause to do so, ending the era of unfettered police discretion in determining whether individual incidents of domestic violence should be classified as crimes. Although Oregon passed the first such law in 1977, few jurisdictions had followed suit prior to 1983. After *Thurman v. City of Torrington*, however, seeing the potential for crippling judgments based on police inaction, other jurisdictions quickly enacted such policies. No longer would police officers be permitted to tell abusive men to take a walk around the block, allowing them to return to torment their victims whenever they pleased; instead, their attacks on their wives would be treated as seriously as if they had assaulted strangers. Battered women's advocates hailed the adoption of these policies, known as mandatory arrest laws, as a victory for women who had begged for police protection from their abusers to no avail.

Mandatory arrest policies were attractive to women subjected to abuse and their advocates because they deprived individual officers of the discretion to decide whether or not to treat a man's abuse of his partner as a crime. But police officers weren't the only ones to lose some measure of control with the inception of mandatory arrest. In a mandatory arrest regime, no party to the incident—abuser, officer, or victim—has the ability to preempt the involvement of the criminal system once the officer decides that he has probable cause to make an arrest. No longer could women subjected to abuse ask that their abusers not be taken into custody, no matter the reason for the request; a call to the police would now trigger a series of events leading directly to arrest, regardless of whether the woman subjected to abuse saw that as a desirable outcome. Mandatory arrest brought greater protection for many women, but at a sizable cost—the freedom of individual women to decide whether they wanted to be involved in the criminal system at all.

Mandatory arrest is not the only domestic violence policy that gave protection to women subjected to abuse with one hand, but took away their freedom to choose with the other. Both the criminal and civil systems enforce policies that purport to protect women by removing not only the system's ability to choose to protect, but also the woman's ability to decline the state's protection or intervention. The autonomy of women subjected to abuse is the price of these policies. The question is whether that has been too high a price to pay.

Mandatory Arrest and No-Drop Prosecution

In the criminal system, the best examples of policy initiatives that deprive women subjected to abuse of meaningful choice are mandatory arrest laws and "no-drop" prosecution policies—policies that enable, and in some cases, require, prosecutors to go forward with cases over the woman's objection.

Mandatory arrest laws, as described above, were thought to solve the "Charles Thurman problem"—the perpetrator who gets warning after warning from police but is never arrested, and who, as a result, feels secure in his ability to continue to harass, threaten, and abuse his partner free from state sanction. Frustrated with years of police inaction in the face of severe abuse, advocates for women subjected to abuse saw police discretion as a crucial weakness in the criminal justice system, particularly because police were trained to use that discretion to avoid arrest whenever possible. Remove police discretion not to arrest, advocates believed, and domestic violence would be treated just as seriously as any other crime. Moreover, mandatory arrest laws would prevent police from citing discretion when choosing to credit the stories of abusers who said that their wives were simply overwrought, when ordering women subjected to abuse to leave their own homes, or when blaming women for provoking attacks. Mandatory arrest laws were thought to serve as a deterrent to individual abusers, sending the message that domestic violence was criminal activity warranting the intervention of the justice system. No longer would men be able to abuse their wives with impunity; they would now have to consider whether that abuse was worth the consequences they could face. These laws would give women subjected to abuse a respite without requiring them to affirm that they wanted to pursue charges, eliminating the potential for pressure and coercion by abusers around the decision to arrest.

On a societal level, proponents believed mandatory arrest laws would remove domestic violence from the privacy of the home and subject it to the harsh light of community scrutiny. Before the battered women's movement began to publicly characterize attacks on married women as criminal assaults in the late 1960s and early 1970s, abuse of one's wife was widely viewed as a husband's prerogative. State authorities were inclined to ignore such acts as being beyond the province of the state, regardless of the injury inflicted on the woman or her pleas for assistance. As law professor Elizabeth Schneider writes of that time, "Privacy says that violence against women is immune from sanction, that it is permitted, acceptable and part of the basic fabric of American family life. Privacy says that what goes on in the violent relationship should not be the subject of state or community intervention."[1] Advocates for women subjected to abuse fought to expose the abuse that occurred in private and to ensure that it was treated and penalized just as violence between strangers would have been. The shift from private to public reflected the belief that women subjected to abuse wanted domestic violence to be brought into the public sphere and that they would welcome state intervention. Mandatory arrest laws were an important step in that direction. Confronted with the costly results of unfettered police discretion—the successful lawsuits in Connecticut, California, and New York—convincing state legislatures to pass such laws was far easier than earlier legislative advocacy on behalf of women subjected to abuse had been.

Historically, police officers were unable to make arrests without warrants in misdemeanor cases unless they witnessed the assaults themselves. The first statutory changes won by the battered women's movement eased these restrictions, allowing officers to arrest whenever they had probable cause to believe that an act of domestic violence had occurred. But even after legislative revisions freed police to make warrantless arrests in misdemeanor cases, arrest rates remained low, and arrests for domestic violence continued to be rare. In 1984, however, attitudes among law enforcement began to change after the U.S. Department of Justice released the report of the Attorney General's Task Force on Family Violence, which recommended a strong criminal justice response to domestic violence and touted preferred arrest policies as a key element of that response.

Early efforts to enact mandatory arrest laws were also bolstered by research indicating that arrest was linked to lowered rates of recidivism among perpetrators of domestic violence. In 1981 and 1982, studies in Minneapolis suggested that the arrest of men who abused their partners deterred them from future abuse. Lawrence Sherman, one of the authors of that study, later wrote, "Although the authors cautioned against passage of mandatory arrest laws for domestic violence until further research could be conducted, by 1991 the results contributed to the passage of such laws in 15 states."[2] Subsequent research in six additional cities would validate his words of caution; while arrest proved a deterrent to future violence in some locations, in others there was no deterrent effect, and worse, some evidence that arrest contributed to increases in future violence. Sherman and his colleagues hypothesized that arrest was a more effective deterrent for some offenders than others, particularly those who had a greater "stake in conformity," or believed that they had a great deal to lose by acting in a manner considered deviant or out of the norm. Sherman's studies found that those who were married and employed had a greater stake in conformity, and therefore, were more likely to be deterred by arrest. Race also factored into the deterrent effect of arrest. In cities with large African American populations, arrest was positively correlated with future violence, suggesting that arrest policies endangered African American women. Nonetheless, Sherman's early work was cited as justification for continuing to implement mandatory arrest policies regardless of the demographics of the jurisdiction.

Mandatory arrest laws got a further boost from the Violence Against Women Act. As previously noted, the Violence Against Women Act of

1994 required states to certify that they had adopted either pro – or mandatory arrest policies to be eligible for federal funding under the Grants To Encourage Arrests program—a program that provided millions of dollars to state and local police departments. Eager to ensure that they would be able to access this funding, those states that had not already adopted such laws quickly did so. Today, every state has some form of pro-arrest policy in cases involving domestic violence.[3]

Once advocates had convinced states to enact mandatory arrest laws, they turned to the next obstacle in ensuring accountability using the criminal system: prosecutors. Just as police officers historically had used their discretion not to arrest perpetrators of domestic violence, prosecutors, too, had routinely chosen not to pursue cases against the few perpetrators of abuse who police had actually arrested. Ironically, prosecutors' failure to pursue cases involving domestic violence has been cited as yet another reason police declined to arrest.

Scholars have posited a number of reasons for the low rate of prosecution in domestic violence cases: the lack of evidence, the patriarchal views of prosecutors, skepticism about the seriousness of the crimes involved, prosecutors' perceptions that judges were not interested in entertaining such cases. The justification most frequently offered by prosecutors for their reluctance to pursue domestic violence cases was their inability to rely on their star witnesses—the wives and girlfriends of the men they were prosecuting. Women's unwillingness to testify to the abuse they had suffered deprived prosecutors of their best, and often their only, witnesses and hamstrung prosecutions in which the testimony of the involved parties was the only available evidence. The failure of women subjected to abuse to participate in prosecutions was widely attributed to victims' fear of repercussions at the hands of their abusers, a credible fear given that even after successful prosecution, sentences for domestic violence offenses were ridiculously light and jail time was rarely imposed in misdemeanor cases. Prosecutors began to look for ways to ensure that cases could be brought successfully even if women chose not to participate—a method that has come to be known as victimless prosecution.

The success of victimless prosecution hinges on the willingness of police officers to respond to cases involving domestic violence differently and more thoroughly than they would ordinary assault cases. Police officers were trained to carefully investigate crime scenes, make detailed reports, and collect evidence that would allow prosecutors to pursue cases even when women were unwilling to testify. Prosecutors relied on physical evidence, photographs of both the woman and her partner (to show his demeanor at the time of arrest and any injuries, defensive or otherwise), recordings of 911 tapes, statements made to police, medical records, and other witness statements to secure convictions in cases that previously, without such careful attention to evidence gathering, would have been impossible to successfully prosecute without the woman's participation. Victimless prosecution allowed prosecutors to circumvent the woman's wishes by replacing her testimony, which previously had been viewed as essential, with other evidence sufficient to persuade a finder of fact beyond a reasonable doubt that the charged crime had actually been committed. Victimless prosecution also enabled prosecutors to undermine the testimony of women who appeared on behalf of their partners, impeaching them with prior inconsistent statements to police, or confronting them with photographs of injuries and their own words on 911 tapes.[4]

Despite the implementation of these increasingly sophisticated methods of preparing domestic violence cases, prosecutorial reluctance to bring domestic violence cases and women's unwillingness to testify continued to hamper successful prosecutions of domestic violence cases. The adoption of no-drop prosecution was meant to address both of these issues. No-drop means exactly what it says—prosecutors would not dismiss criminal charges in otherwise viable cases simply because women were not interested in, or were even adamantly opposed to, pursuing them. Advocates of no-drop prosecution strategies offer three justifications for the policies. First, they argue, no-drop prosecution in domestic violence cases is good for society, in that the purpose of the criminal system is not to bend to the wishes of individual crime victims, but rather to punish offenders and to deter others from committing similar crimes. The role of the prosecutor in the American criminal system is to reinforce the state's conception of the boundaries of acceptable behavior by ensuring compliance with the laws that define and regulate what individuals are and are not permitted to do. The failure to prosecute domestic violence cases, whether attributable to prosecutorial recalcitrance or victim unwillingness, sends the message that abuse of one's intimate partner is acceptable, in direct contravention of the criminal laws against such abuse. Consistent enforcement of the law is essential in ensuring respect for that law; allowing intimate partners to continue to flout those laws without fear of repercussion enables perpetrators of domestic violence to believe that the laws against abuse can be taken as seriously as most individuals take speed laws on major highways—which is to say, not seriously at all.

The second justification proffered for no-drop prosecution is women's safety. Prosecuting those who commit domestic violence increases safety both for the individual woman, by removing the immediate threat to her, and for future partners of the same perpetrator. The woman's inability to thwart the process is a particularly important guarantor of her safety. Because the woman no longer has the ability to stop the prosecutor from bringing the case to court, her partner has no motivation to pressure her to do so. Shifting the burden of deciding whether the prosecution will proceed from women to prosecutors was thought to significantly safeguard women from further coercion and violence.

The final justification for no-drop prosecution policies was, ironically, empowerment. Women subjected to abuse, the argument went, would derive strength and validation from the experience of participating in prosecution. This argument assumed successful prosecution of the case and positive treatment of the woman throughout the process.

One important distinction in the realm of prosecution policy is between "hard" and "soft" no-drop policies. In "soft" no-drop jurisdictions, women's testimony is not compelled; instead, prosecutors work with women subjected to abuse to help them feel comfortable with the system and offer them resources and supports (such as, for example, rides to hearings or a special advocate to explain the system) that make compliance with the prosecutor's request to assist in the prosecution possible. If the woman subjected to abuse is ultimately unwilling, unable, or uninterested in assisting prosecutors, she will not be forced to do so (although the services and supports upon which the woman may be relying may no longer be available if she chooses not to cooperate). "Hard" no-drop policies, by contrast, are the purest form of these policies—prosecutors pursue their cases regardless of the woman's wishes so long as sufficient evidence to prosecute exists. In a hard no-drop jurisdiction, then, when a woman is unwilling to appear voluntarily, prosecutors might subpoena her to compel her testimony, or, in the most extreme cases, issue a warrant for her arrest and/or have her incarcerated to ensure her appearance at trial. Law professor Cheryl Hanna, a former prosecutor, explains the necessity for such actions: "No-drop policies that do not compel victim cooperation lack credibility."[5] If both the abusive man and his partner are aware that the prosecutor will not follow through on the threat to force the woman's compliance, there is little incentive for him to refrain from pressuring his partner to withdraw her support for prosecution and even less for the reluctant woman to comply voluntarily. At core, these policies reflect a struggle over who will control the woman subjected to abuse; if the state does not exercise its control over her by compelling her testimony, her partner will, by preventing her from testifying. Hard no-drop policies express the state's belief that it has a superior right to the assistance of the woman subjected to abuse, in service of both the woman's needs and the state's objectives. Returning to Barbara Hart's hierarchy of the goals of legal interventions in domestic violence cases, hard no-drop policies clearly prioritize safety over all other aims, including fostering the agency of women subjected to abuse, and assume that safety can be achieved through prosecution.

(Not) Mediating Family Law Matters

As alternative dispute resolution grows more popular in the legal system, ever-increasing numbers of civil family law matters have been deemed appropriate for mediation. In some jurisdictions, a litigant cannot have a claim for divorce or custody heard without first engaging in mediation. Often described as cheaper, easier, and less formal than litigation, mediation is thought to give litigants greater control over the terms of the agreements they reach, encourage cooperation between the parties, and increase litigants' satisfaction with the legal process. From the outset of the mediation explosion, however, advocates for women subjected to abuse have been almost universally opposed to employing mediation to resolve cases involving domestic violence. Attorney Tara Lea Muhlhauser's position is representative: "Mediation is unequivocally wrong when the dynamics of violence exist in a relationship."[6] Or, as advocates Allen M. Bailey and Carmen Kay Denny ask, "[H]ow is a client, whose spouse shoved the barrel of a .44 magnum revolver into her or his ear and threatened to kill, supposed to benefit from a 'heart to heart' . . . talk with the battering partner and negotiate custody of their children or anything else?"[7] Theoretical and practical concerns about the appropriateness of mediating such cases drive this opposition.

Some opponents of mediation fear that mediating cases involving domestic violence trivializes these matters. Because safety is the overriding concern for many advocates, the inability of mediation to stop abuse and ensure safety is sufficient reason to avoid the process. Women should not have to negotiate for their safety; agreements that make the cessation of abuse contingent on some concession by the woman subjected to abuse (for example, an agreement that she will stop working or defer to her partner whenever they disagree) are completely unacceptable for that reason. But even when the abuse itself is not what is being mediated, using alternative dispute resolution to address cases involving domestic violence undermines the seriousness with which such cases are treated, critics contend. Relegating these issues to mediators rather than using the time and resources of the court system to resolve them sends the message that these cases are not as important as others; opponents of mediation have charged gender bias in the consignment of "women's issues" like domestic violence to alternative dispute resolution. Critics further contend that the development of the law in cases involving domestic violence is stunted when cases are resolved through mediated agreements rather than adversarial proceedings that can create binding precedent.

Privacy is again a concern in the debate over mediating domestic violence cases. Given the efforts of advocates to move domestic violence from the private sphere of the home into the public arena of the legal system, it is hardly surprising that the effort to shift resolution of cases involving domestic violence into a private dispute resolution system is unpopular. Allowing mediation of these cases "causes the re-privatization of family law resulting in a setback to the political and legislative progress of the battered women's movement."[8] Mediating cases involving domestic violence shields abuse from public scrutiny and makes it easier for the legal system and the public to underestimate the prevalence of abuse in family relationships and the toll that such abuse takes on women and their children. Moreover, mediating cases involving domestic violence allows men who abuse to avoid public sanction for their actions, undermining the goal of accountability. This is particularly true, opponents have argued, because mediation is future focused. Many mediators discourage discussions of past abuse and fail to consider how that abuse should affect the arrangements negotiated between the parties for interactions going forward. This future focus precludes women subjected to abuse from using mediation to confront their partners about their actions and the consequences of their abuse. This orientation can also prevent women from discussing how their fears of further abuse color their reactions to proposed custody and visitation plans or their concerns that their partners will use economic tools, like withholding alimony and child support, to continue to exercise control post-separation.

Another theoretical problem with mediating such cases is the inability to reconcile the ideology and practices of mediation with the realities of domestic violence. Mediation is frequently described as a method of resolving conflicts; by contrast, advocates for women subjected to abuse are quick to explain that domestic violence is not about conflict, but rather control, and the use of abuse to maintain that control. Mediation provides a man who abuses with yet another opportunity to attempt to exert control over his partner, an opportunity that may be particularly welcome to the abuser after the parties have separated and his access to his partner decreases. Even if it appears that individual areas of conflict between the parties over child custody and marital property are being resolved, the larger issue of control lurks in the shadows and may constrain the ability of the woman subjected to abuse to confidently assert her positions. As a result, the woman may not negotiate forcefully and may concede too much to avoid angering her partner. Her partner, in contrast, may contest points that are unimportant to him simply because he can, and because he knows that it will unnerve his former partner. Mediation is said to require cooperation between the parties; cooperation with someone who changes his demands only to demoralize the other participant is a practical impossibility. The scant possibility of reaching agreement makes mediation a costly addition to the legal process. Because settlement is unlikely, mediation (which may require payments to a mediator and counsel) becomes yet another hurdle that the woman subjected to abuse must clear before gaining access to the courtroom, where her concerns will finally be heard and her claims adjudicated.

Perhaps the most frequently cited justification for avoiding mediation in cases involving domestic violence is the power imbalance between the parties. One of the core principles of mediation is that the parties come to the table with equal power, equally able to assert their positions and to discuss and negotiate the terms of an agreement. Some critics contend that all women are at a disadvantage in mediation by virtue of their unequal economic and social power; most agree that women subjected to abuse are at a distinct disadvantage in mediation as a result of the coercion and violence that have characterized the relationship. The assumption is that a woman subjected to abuse is simply incapable of equaling her partner's power. As law professors Karla Fischer, Neil Vidmar, and Rene Ellis write, "[B]y its very nature the culture of . . . battering makes the couple unequal in subtle and pervasive ways,"[9] thus preventing productive mediation from ever being possible in cases involving domestic violence.

This theoretical concern about the innate power imbalance between a woman subjected to abuse and her partner is tied to a pragmatic concern about the mediator's inability to redress those power imbalances. The mediation literature is replete with references to the mediator's ability to "balance the power" between the parties, but descriptions of just how a mediator is able to balance power or how a party can be sure that the power is, in fact, balanced before a mediation proceeds, are rare. Power differentials in cases involving domestic violence are qualitatively unlike those in other kinds of relationships; the mediator may be attempting to balance power between parties who have been in unequal positions for years or who have never been equals within the relationship. Professors Fischer, Vidmar, and Ellis note, "[T]he notion that power which has been grossly imbalanced over the course of an entire multi-year relationship can be shifted within a two hour mediation session minimizes the seriousness of the impact of the abuse on battered women."[10] A mediator's assurances that he can balance the power sufficiently to ensure that her interests are protected in mediation may prove cold comfort to the woman subjected to abuse. Advocate Joan Zorza has argued that women subjected to abuse are so fearful and submissive that even mediators with a sophisticated understanding of domestic violence cannot bridge the power differential.[11]

Few mediators, opponents argue, have the kind of specialized training in and experience with domestic violence that would enable them to identify abuse in the first instance. Mediators are not always required by law to have training in domestic violence, although model standards developed for mediators in family law cases require such training. One survey of more than 200 mediation programs throughout the United States indicated that 30 percent of the programs do not train their staff to identify domestic violence.[12] Without such training, some fear that mediators will not recognize the kind of subtle manipulation that a man who abuses might use to prevent his partner from fully participating in the mediation. The man might even be able to turn the mediator against the woman subjected to abuse, contributing to a climate in which the woman feels that she cannot assert herself or have her concerns heard, or causing the mediator to pressure her to accept an unfair agreement.

Although many states require that mediators screen for domestic violence before beginning work with the parties, that screening may not be occurring, and if it is, it may not be effective in identifying abuse in the relationship. Two recent studies examining mediation of family law matters in Maryland, a state that prohibits mediation in cases involving domestic violence, found that mediations occurred in significant numbers of custody cases although abuse was clearly present.[13] Even when mediators screen for and identify domestic violence, they may not change their regular practices to account for the abuse. In their review of policies and practices for mediating custody cases involving domestic violence, researchers Nancy Thoennes, Peter Salem, and Jessica Pearson found that 75 percent of mediators sometimes conducted mediations in cases involving domestic violence without changing their regular practice; 3 percent of mediators with domestic violence training and 17 percent of mediators without training reported that they never changed their techniques in cases involving domestic violence.[14] These mediators, then, are unlikely to be taking special measures either to ensure the safety of the woman subjected to abuse or to balance the power between the parties.

Another problematic aspect of mediating domestic violence cases is the need for the woman subjected to abuse to articulate her own goals and needs during the mediation, a task that she simply may be unable to accomplish when confronted with her abusive partner. In her study of 129 divorced women with children, sociologist Demie Kurz found that 30 percent of women were fearful during their child support negotiations, 38 percent were fearful during custody negotiations, and 35 percent were fearful during marital property negotiations. These fears, Kurz discovered, were linked to the women's experiences of abuse during their marriages and separations, and were stronger for women subjected to more frequent or serious abuse. As a result of these fears, both past and future, Kurz found, these women reduced the amount of their requests for child support, and in some cases, abandoned their cases altogether. Kurz concludes, "[T]hese data suggest that a substantial group of women negotiate for resources in a 'climate of fear' in which their fear of violence can lead them to forfeit their rights."[15] Imagine how much more difficult it would be for a woman to forcefully assert her position while sitting in close proximity with her abusive partner in a process that expects her to be able to come to some agreement. While having counsel present during the mediation might alleviate some of these concerns, in many mediations counsel is not permitted to attend, let alone participate; even if counsel is present, these same concerns might prevent a woman from giving counsel either the information or the authority to negotiate freely on her behalf.

Safety concerns are another reason for discouraging mediation in cases involving domestic violence. Mediation may require that the parties share the same physical space, giving the man who abuses access to his partner that he may have been denied by separation or by court order. Court ordered mediation could, in fact, enable the abusive partner to circumvent the terms of a court order requiring him to stay away from his partner. Once granted that access, opponents argue, the potential for violence during the mediation itself exists, with few of the kinds of safeguards in place—court security personnel, metal detectors—that protect women subjected to abuse when they enter courtrooms to confront their partners. Mediation could trigger violence not just during the session itself, but afterward; having expressed her desires and, by so doing, undermined her partner's control, the woman subjected to abuse might fear that her partner will retaliate against her as a way of reestablishing his domination.

Recall the benefits of mediation listed earlier: cheaper, easier, less formal, gives litigants greater control, encourages cooperation, increased satisfaction. Few of these justifications for promoting mediation seem to operate in cases involving domestic violence, but potential dangers abound. For that reason, many advocates have fought to ensure that women subjected to abuse can avoid mediation. They have been remarkably successful. Most states require that mediators screen for domestic violence before beginning mediation. Many states allow women subjected to abuse to opt out of mediation if they can persuade the court or the mediator that there is a history of abuse in the relationship or if there is currently a protective order in effect. Delaware's law is typical:

> Notwithstanding any other provision of law to the contrary, Family Court mediation conferences shall be prohibited in any child custody or visitation proceeding in which 1 of the parties has been found by a court, whether in that proceeding or in some other proceeding, to have committed an act of domestic violence against the other party or if either party has been ordered to stay away or have no contact with the other party, unless a victim of domestic violence who is represented by counsel requests such mediation.[16]

Because they cannot feel confident that mediation will be a safe and productive process for women subjected to abuse, advocates routinely caution women against participating in mediation, encouraging them to use these provisions to opt out of the process whenever possible.

In a few states, women subjected to abuse have no choice to make regarding mediation. Cases involving domestic violence cannot be mediated, regardless of the wishes of the parties. Maryland law, for example, prohibits the court from ordering mediation in cases in which a party or child (or a mediation program that has screened the case) represents to the court that there is a genuine issue of physical or sexual abuse of a party or child.[17] Illinois, Minnesota, Montana, North Dakota, and Pennsylvania also prohibit courts from sending cases involving domestic violence to mediation. Such laws and policies ensure that women subjected to abuse cannot be further harmed by the process and must instead pursue their claims through the adversarial system—the ultimate protection that advocates can provide.

Autonomy and Agency

These policies all seem like perfectly reasonable responses to deficiencies in the legal system's ability to respond adequately to domestic violence. Before deciding that trading women's ability to control their participation in the legal system for the mandated protection of that system has been a good bargain for women subjected to abuse, however, we should first consider the values of autonomy and agency.

What does autonomy mean? For philosophers, this is a much more complicated question than it might appear. Autonomy has alternately been described as a basic state of being and as a competence that one must develop.[18] Contrast basic autonomy, which references individuals who are responsible, independent, and able to speak for themselves, with ideal autonomy, which requires that individuals operate in a state of maximal authenticity of choice, free of any self-distorting influences. Philosophers have defined autonomy as the theoretical capacity for self-governance, the actual condition of self-governance, the ideal of self-governance in a state of absolute freedom, and a set of rights that undergird the ability to establish sovereignty over the self.[19] Fundamentally, however, autonomy is constituted of the independence to deliberate and make choices free of manipulation by others and the capacity to make reasoned decisions about how to live one's life; as philosopher John Christman writes, "[T]he unifying idea behind the various uses of the notion of autonomy is that of 'self-government'—being or doing only what one freely, independently, and authentically chooses to be or do."[20] Law professor Margaret E. Johnson argues that autonomy is an essential component of women's liberty-based rights to human dignity.[21]

Autonomy is at the heart of liberal political philosophy. The idea that individuals should be able to choose how to govern their lives, without the state, through courts and legislatures, dictating those choices either to achieve its preferred goals or to protect individuals from choices it believes to be antithetical to their well-being, is central to the theories, for example, of Emmanuel Kant, John Stuart Mill, and John Rawls, whose work forms the basis of much American political thought. Not surprisingly, then, autonomy is also one of the cornerstones of the American legal system.

Feminists have long been conflicted about the role of autonomy in shaping the law. Many have rejected the individualistic bent of autonomy. Although autonomy would seem congruent with the feminist goal of liberation, some feminists have instead characterized autonomy as selfish and egotistical.[22] They argue that valuing the individualism of autonomy rejects the reality of women's lives, which are often deeply intertwined with the lives of others; in response, feminist philosophers have developed "relational" theories of autonomy, which stress the ability to achieve autonomy within a world in which individuals are socially constructed and shaped by their relationships to others.[23]

Feminist theorists have also argued that the emphasis on autonomy within liberal political philosophy and the law disadvantages women who, by virtue of their subordinated status as victims of a patriarchal system, are rarely able to exercise the sort of autonomy contemplated by philosophers. Philosopher Susan Wendell articulates this position:

> Much of what women appear to do freely is chosen in very limiting circumstances, where there are few choices left to us. Even where the circumstances present many choices, it is often the case that our knowledge, our ability to judge, and our desires have been so distorted and manipulated by social influences as to make a mockery of the idea that we choose freely.[24]

Because women can only contemplate options and make choices within a patriarchal frame, which constrains and distorts the options that are available, their choices can never truly be free. To value autonomy within a political system, then, is to ensure that women can never be equal actors within that system. As philosopher Morwenna Griffiths writes, "[A]utonomy is often thought to present a problem for women because (1) it is a desirable quality; and (2) women don't have it."[25]

Some feminist thinkers have attempted to incorporate the ideas underlying the concept of autonomy while rejecting the philosophical baggage that the term "autonomy" carries for feminists. The term autonomy has become so fraught, law professor Kathryn Abrams suggests, that it should be rejected in favor of the term "agency," which captures the key features of autonomy—self-definition and self-direction—but recognizes how social construction delimits the choices available to women. For Abrams, self-definition involves "determining how one conceives of oneself in terms of the goals one wants to achieve and the kind of person, with particular values and attributes, one considers oneself to be."[26] Abrams describes self-direction as the ability to formulate goals and plans free of the undue influence of others. Similarly, in her book *Real Choices: Feminism, Freedom and the Limits of Law*, philosopher Beth Kiyoko Jamieson suggests that feminists adopt the Agency Principle: "that individuals have the right to make their own decisions about how to live their lives, that individuals must be assumed to be capable of making ethical decisions, and that social reprobation (well-intentioned or not) must not inhibit the decision-making process."[27] A feminist conception of autonomy should include not only the ability to make choices within one's personal life, but also the ability to exercise choice within the larger society; Morwenna Griffiths defines autonomy as having "three interconnected strands: freedom to make oneself, freedom to live that self without fear of the consequences, and freedom to participate in public decisions that affect oneself."[28]

The question of whether women can act autonomously or with agency within a patriarchal system is complicated significantly by the presence of domestic violence. Some philosophers have questioned whether women subjected to abuse are ever capable of acting autonomously. They argue that abuse is inherently coercive, creating a context that precludes women subjected to abuse from being able to exercise free will. Others believe that while women subjected to abuse are still capable of exercising some form of autonomy or agency, their ability to do so is at best compromised and the choices that they make must be understood as being shaped by the context of the abusive relationship. In a coercively controlling relationship, they assume, the woman is not free to make her own choices or act independently because she is being subjected to the will of another. They believe that the autonomy of women subjected to abuse is undermined because their attention is too focused on safety to be able to fully contemplate their choices. Law professor Ruth Jones has gone so far as to suggest that courts should appoint guardians for women who have been coercively controlled, because their judgment has been so impaired and their autonomy so extinguished as to render them incapable of protecting themselves or separating from their partners. Jones writes,

> Coercively controlled battered women, immobilized by violence, need a more aggressive state intervention than those provided by empowerment-based remedies. Unable to act on their own, these women require an intervention that permits someone else to act on their behalf to protect them from their abusers until they can protect themselves.[29]

Concluding that the agency or autonomy of women subjected to abuse is constrained, a number of scholars have supported the use of mandatory legal interventions to protect these women. They justify these interventions by arguing that women subjected to abuse are incapable of making authentic choices to protect themselves—the choices they would certainly make, these scholars suggest, if their autonomy had not been impaired by abuse. As philosopher Marilyn Friedman writes, "Domestic violence . . . itself profoundly undermines a woman's autonomy. Anything that succeeds in deterring an abuser's future abusiveness promotes his victim's long-run autonomy."[30] In the short term, Friedman is willing to trade the decision-making authority of women subjected to abuse for the potential ability to exercise agency in the long term; as a result, she argues, "The law should therefore do what it can to prevent men from abusing their intimate female partners, even if it must do so against the wishes of the victims and by mandating the victims' cooperation."[31]

These arguments are based on a number of problematic assumptions. These thinkers tend to equate all abusive relationships with the exercise of coercive control and, moreover, to assume that all women within coercively controlling relationships are so subject to the will of their partners that they are unable to exercise the ability to choose. Jones's definition of coercive control highlights this assumption. Women who have been coercively controlled, according to Jones, lack access to resources and the ability to use them. What Jones ignores is that a woman's resources are not necessarily external. As survivor theory highlights, women subjected to abuse rely on their own knowledge of their partners and their innate abilities to survive; external resources might not be what a woman subjected to abuse needs. The choice not to access resources, then, is a poor measure of whether a woman is able to exercise her autonomy. More importantly, Jones's definition, which hinges on accessing external resources, seems to link the inability to choose to the inability to leave the relationship, which ignores the legitimate autonomous choices that some women make to remain with abusive partners.

These supporters of mandatory interventions focus primarily on the potential for severe physical violence; as Friedman asserts, "Helping to preserve someone's very life takes obvious precedence over respecting her autonomy."[32] What arguments like this miss, however, is that the lives of many women subjected to abuse are never at risk; lethality occurs too often in intimate relationships, but it does not occur in all of them, or even in the majority. Further, they assume that legal intervention prevents future abuse and that autonomy will not be of use to the woman subjected to abuse in the course of the legal intervention—that somehow the exercise of autonomy can wait until a later date. Although abuse can certainly involve coercion, these thinkers assume that the choice not to engage the legal system is necessarily a coerced choice. Given that mandatory policies frequently operate to deprive a woman of choice, it is worth questioning whether a woman subjected to abuse is free of coercion regardless of the measures she uses to address the abuse.

Other scholars believe that women can exercise autonomy and/or agency even when they are being abused. The exercise of autonomy does not require unfettered or entirely consistent choice. In fact, philosopher John Christman explains, "many external life situations display such contradictory and confusing characteristics that one's very survival may demand at least a partially conflicting set of desires and values."[33] Women subjected to abuse must be free to make choices that others disagree with or fail to understand, even if they choose to remain in situations that some would characterize as depriving them of autonomy. Law professor Kathryn Abrams argues that self-direction may exist even when others fail to see it, when women resist the institutional forces that conspire to limit their ability to choose. Abrams describes this phenomenon as "resistant self-direction," explaining that "women who resist in these ways may not be seeking to transform society in any systematic sense, but simply to pursue their own choices and plans in contexts where doing so evokes serious gender-based challenge."[34] One such situation, argues Abrams, is in the context of an abusive relationship. Building on the work of legal scholar Martha Mahoney and the ideas underlying survivor theory, Abrams argues that the efforts women make to safeguard themselves and their children within their relationships constitute exercises of self-direction, of agency, despite the existence of outside constraints on these women's ability to freely choose.

The arguments made by those who support mandatory interventions beg the conclusion that women subjected to abuse rarely, if ever, act autonomously, a problematic assertion given the primacy of autonomy in the American political and legal systems. Accepting the idea that women subjected to abuse are incapable of engaging in independent deliberation devalues these women as members of the political society and invites and justifies what some might characterize as paternalism on their behalf. Paternalism reflects a lack of respect for autonomy and for the individual as a person. A number of the policies adopted to address domestic violence—policies championed by many advocates for women subjected to abuse—are guided by what seem to be patently paternalistic views of these women as powerless, limited individuals incapable of acting on their own behalf.

A better way to characterize the spirit motivating these policy choices, at least on the part of advocates for women subjected to abuse, however, is that they exemplify maternalism. These policies come from a well-meaning place—the desire to protect women subjected to abuse from further intimidation and abuse, from their own inability to invoke the legal system given their fear of retaliation from their abusers, from losing their children or economic benefits in unfair mediations. This maternalism is born of advocates' experiences with a legal system that has too often failed to safeguard the rights and needs of women subjected to abuse and their belief that mandatory interventions are instrumental in ensuring that the system treats cases of domestic violence seriously. But maternalism is no better than paternalism, in that it, too, assumes that women subjected to abuse are incapable of considering the full range of possibilities and deprives them of the ability to make choices for themselves, based on their own goals, values, beliefs, and understanding of their situations. Maternalism undermines the autonomy of women subjected to abuse. Invoking maternalism to justify the implementation of mandatory policies is fundamentally at odds with one of the foundational goals of the battered women's movement—empowerment.

Why Empowerment Matters

If, as most scholars agree, domestic violence is characterized by a power imbalance between the parties, restoring power to women subjected to abuse should be a priority when making policies that affect these women. For that reason, empowerment has been a central, though not always well-defined, theme in the battered women's movement. In her seminal work, *Women and Male Violence: The Visions and Struggles of the Battered Women's Movement*, social work professor Susan Schechter describes empowerment as "the illusive word that embodies the sense of controlling one's life and circumstances."[35] For Schechter, empowerment is

> a process through which women, experts about their own lives, learn to know their strength. "Empowerment" combines ideas about internalizing personal and collective power and validating women's personal experiences as politically oppressive rather than self-caused or "crazy." In a feminist political context, empowerment signifies standing together as a community just as it means supportively enabling a person to take risks. Its premise is to turn individual defeats into victories through giving women tools to better control their lives and joining in collective struggle.[36]

Definitions of empowerment frequently echo the language of autonomy and agency, incorporating the ideas of controlling one's environment, self-determination, and identifying, evaluating, and making choices.

In the world of services for women subjected to abuse, however, empowerment is often defined by what service providers can give—particularly, the ability to provide choices for women whose options have been restricted by their partners.[37] Too often, though, those choices have been constrained by what service providers, advocates, and policymakers deem acceptable alternatives—particularly, separating from abusive partners and engaging the criminal justice system. In "giving" the woman options, then, certain possibilities, like engaging in mediation or dropping criminal charges, may never come up for discussion. If those options are raised, they are presented in a manner meant (consciously or unconsciously) to dissuade the woman from seeing them as viable alternatives. Certainly this is the case with mediation; while few advocates forbid women to participate in the process, many, if not most, describe mediation in a manner that makes it clear that the advocate believes the process to be detrimental to the woman's interests at best, dangerous at worst. Relying on the advocate's expertise and experience with the legal system, a woman who might otherwise be interested in attempting to mediate is easily steered toward other alternatives.

Restricting choice is congruent with a definition of empowerment that calls for "giving" women choices or "letting" women choose among the options presented; in that context, empowerment would not require that the woman be permitted to generate options for herself or that all choices be presented, only that some choice be given and that the woman be free to select from what is offered. But empowerment must mean more than simply substituting advocates or the state for the abusive partner as the arbiter of choices for women subjected to abuse. Empowerment should be read as consistent with autonomy or agency—as self-direction, self-determination, enabling the woman subjected to abuse not only to make choices, but to define and evaluate the options for herself, regardless of how others might view those options. A belief in the centrality of empowerment for women subjected to abuse should prevent advocates from embracing mandatory policies.[38]

Empowerment is a central feminist theme and was a key concept in the early battered women's movement. But as the state became more involved in the lives of women subjected to abuse, empowerment found itself competing with other goals, particularly victim safety and offender accountability. As one woman wrote many years ago,

> It has been over a decade since the battered women-mothers planted the seeds of the domestic violence movement. Something unsettling and unanticipated has occurred; a movement which began as the battered woman's is less and less hers. Rather than true empowerment for battered women, the original political ideal, we battered women could be swept away.[39]

In the case of mandatory interventions such as mandatory arrest, no-drop prosecution, and bans on mediation, empowerment has certainly taken a back seat, to the decided detriment of some women subjected to abuse.

The Law as a Disempowering Force

Noelle Mowatt is one of these women. Mowatt called police in Ontario in December 2007, alleging that her boyfriend, Christopher Harbin, punched her, grabbed her, and stabbed her feet with a knife. When she failed to appear to testify at his trial in March 2008, a warrant was issued for her arrest. In April 2008, Mowatt, nine months pregnant with Harbin's child, was jailed for a week without bail until she gave testimony. The court was well within the law in issuing the warrant, enabling prosecutors to secure Mowatt's testimony. But what did jailing Mowatt achieve? Harbin was acquitted in May 2008, largely because of questions about Mowatt's credibility after Mowatt recanted her allegations of abuse on the stand. Mowatt has vowed, "I'm never calling the police again—even if I'm dying, I'm not going to call them."[40] In seeking to hold Harbin accountable and protect Mowatt, the courts achieved neither goal. By usurping Mowatt's choice about whether to engage the criminal system to protect her, the system instead has driven her away, all but ensuring that Mowatt will avoid state intervention and any future abuse will go unpunished by the legal system.

Meredith Bell has a similar story. On July 8, 2002, police found Bell and her boyfriend, Adrian Spraggins, arguing in the parking lot of her workplace. Although Bell had not called the police for assistance, when they arrived she described how Spraggins had threatened her repeatedly, pushed her down, and forced her and her son into a car with him. Spraggins then drove her to work; when Bell grabbed the keys and left the car, Spraggins chased her and threatened to hit her. Witnesses called the police.

What precipitated this incident? Spraggins had been violent toward Bell in the past; in fact, on July 8, 2002, Bell was scheduled to testify against him in another domestic violence case, and the threats Spraggins made that day were tied to her testimony. The irony, though, is that Bell was not testifying willingly in the matter—she had been subpoenaed to appear. Bell did not testify willingly in the trial on the July 8 incident, where Spraggins was charged with witness intimidation, kidnapping, aggravated burglary, and domestic violence, either. Approximately a month before that trial, Bell sent a letter asking that the charges be dismissed, stating that "she never had any intention of testifying against Spraggins, that he did not intimidate her, and that she never wanted him to be prosecuted."[41] At trial, Bell testified that her statement to the police, in which she recounted the events of July 8, was false and that she lied to police because she was angry with Spraggins. Bell stated that she loved Spraggins, that he helped her to support her child, who was not biologically his, and that she did not want him to get into trouble. The trial judge responded acidly to the testimony that prosecutors forced Bell to give: "So let me see if I've got this all straight. We're here trying this case because you are a liar. Is that correct?"[42] Spraggins unsuccessfully appealed his conviction on the witness intimidation count, arguing that the judge's statements prejudiced the jury. While Spraggins' appeal failed, the refusal of prosecutors to allow Bell to choose whether to proceed, coupled with the judge's treatment of Bell on the witness stand, may have guaranteed that Bell will not use the legal system again.

Mandatory policies make it easy to ignore whose life will be the most affected by the state's choices, prioritizing the needs of prosecutors over the interests of the women they purport to serve. Law professor Angela Davis, a former public defender, recalls a domestic violence case in which her client's wife provided her with a statement explaining that she did not wish to prosecute; the woman told Davis that she needed her husband to keep his job and provide the family with financial support. Davis took the statement to the prosecutor, who

> was furious. She told me that she didn't care what Mrs. Jefferson wanted and that it wasn't up to Mrs. Jefferson to decide how the case was prosecuted. The prosecutor went on to say that she had a duty to fight domestic violence and that she was going to fulfill that duty, with or without Mrs. Jefferson's help. . . . Instead of viewing the victim as a person who was badly hurt and in need of assistance and compassion, the prosecutor seemed to view her as the enemy—someone standing in the path of her battle against domestic violence.[43]

After Davis provided the same statement to the judge, the prosecutor warned that she would ask for an arrest warrant for Mrs. Jefferson should she fail to appear for trial. The trial judge affirmed that she would grant the prosecutor's request. Such responses are not limited to the testimonial context. As one Colorado judge cautioned in a case where prosecutors attempted to prosecute a woman for complicity, alleging that she contacted her partner in violation of a protective order that she did not want and repeatedly and unsuccessfully asked prosecutors to dismiss, "the nature of the prosecution does not alter the victim's status as a victim nor, through some sort of legal alchemy, permit her to be exploited by a bullying prosecutor rather than a bullying spouse."[44]

Mandatory policies have led to outcomes for women that the battered women's movement could not possibly have intended. Law professor Michelle Madden Dempsey describes just such a scene from her tenure prosecuting cases in Champaign County, Illinois. Dempsey handled the first "victimless" prosecution in the county after her domestic violence prosecution unit adopted a pro-prosecution policy. David Williams was convicted of abusing his wife, who cooperated with investigators early on, but then refused prosecutors' requests that she appear at trial, and later took the witness stand, recanting her earlier story and asking the jury to acquit. Williams was convicted and sentenced to prison. Distraught and angry, his wife, Linda Williams, followed a juror to her car and

> demanded to know how she could have voted to convict David. As the juror tried to make her way past Linda to her car, Linda continued to follow her, yelling threateningly and blocking her way. A bailiff who observed these events took Linda into custody, and she was later charged with juror intimidation. Upon being convicted for this offense, Linda was sentenced to three years in prison. Her young children were now left with neither parent to care for them.[45]

Dempsey concedes that negative consequences can flow from mandatory policies, but concludes, "the risk of such consequences should not dissuade prosecutors from bringing these cases to trial,"[46] with or without the woman's assent.

The battered women's movement endorsed the policy choices that led to these results for Noelle Mowatt, Meredith Bell, Mrs. Jefferson, and Linda Williams, policies that actively prioritize safety and accountability over autonomy for every woman subjected to abuse. By championing mandatory arrest, no-drop prosecution, and mediation bans, we have contributed to the law's status as a disempowering force in the lives of women subjected to abuse. That choice is problematic on two levels: first, because it assumes that these policies will, in fact, enhance safety, despite a lack of evidence of their effectiveness at the time of their adoption and, at best, conflicting evidence today; and second, because it assumes that all women subjected to abuse would choose safety—defined as separation from an abusive partner—or accountability over autonomy.

Debates continue to rage about the efficacy of these mandatory policies. While Sherman's initial studies are still used to justify mandatory arrest, later research, including Sherman's own, paints a much more nuanced picture of the utility of arrest in domestic violence cases. Similarly, there is equivocal data on the link between prosecution and repeat violence. Although recent studies support the hypothesis that mandatory arrest laws increase the numbers of offenders arrested for violence against their partners, that research has not established a link between higher arrest rates and safety or accountability.[47] Moreover, the number of successful prosecutions did not increase in jurisdictions that implemented mandatory arrest laws; in fact, fewer cases were prosecuted in mandatory arrest jurisdictions.[48] As law professor Linda Mills argues, "At worst, the criminal justice system increases violence against women. At best, it has little or no effect."[49]

The debate about whether mediation helps or harms women subjected to abuse is similarly inconclusive. Although Kurz found that the fear of women subjected to abuse hampered their ability to mediate, another study found that women engaged in mediation who have experienced high levels of abuse are less likely to reach mediated agreements, undermining the argument that women will capitulate to their abusive partners.[50] Moreover, one study found that the agreements reached by women subjected to abuse mirrored those of other women; mothers most often retained physical custody of their children, and parties frequently agreed to joint physical and legal custody.[51] Supporters of mediation claim that women find mediation empowering, that mediation enhances women's ability to stand up for themselves, and that mediation is vastly preferable to litigating contested family cases.[52] Litigation, they argue, makes angry and hostile parents more violent, relies on attorneys (when there are actually attorneys involved, which is increasingly rare) and judges with no training in domestic violence to protect women, is costly both financially and emotionally, and undermines the self-determination of women subjected to abuse. Just as proponents of mediation have urged skeptics not to compare the best litigation with the worst mediation and find mediation wanting, mediation's champions tend to juxtapose the worst litigation against the most successful mediation. The argument assumes that one of these avenues for dispute resolution must be seen as unequivocally better for women subjected to abuse, a conclusion that cannot be drawn universally. From an autonomy perspective, what is essential is that women subjected to abuse have the opportunity to learn in an unbiased manner about all of their options and the chance to make choices about which option better serves their needs.

Assume for a moment, however, that the data about such policies were unambiguous, that mandatory policies could be clearly and causally linked to greater safety for women subjected to abuse or increased offender accountability. Would such policies then be justified? Not if we hearken back to the original goals of the battered women's movement and prioritize autonomy as we should. These policies essentialize women subjected to abuse by assuming that all women would choose state intervention if they had the unfettered ability to make that choice, and that the coercion that these women experience is keeping them from exercising the "rational" choice embodied in the mandatory policy. The emphasis on coercion in understanding the behavior of women subjected to abuse is in part responsible for these assumptions. But coercion—the pressure to make a particular decision—does not render every decision involuntary. Consider the situation of Meredith Bell. Certainly her request that prosecutors drop the criminal case against her boyfriend was coerced in the sense that she was under pressure not to testify against him. But that pressure did not necessarily prevent her from making a rational decision not to cooperate with prosecutors. Such a position assumes that, in the face of threats, women lose their abilities to consider, evaluate, and decide—that they lose their reason. It is just as possible that, in the face of a threat, a woman could look at the protection the system has offered in the past, the resources she has to draw on, her goals and priorities and relationships, and decide that not testifying could, in fact, decrease the level of danger she faces and improve her life. The operation of a mandatory policy, designed and implemented not with Meredith Bell in mind, but based on a stereotypical victim whose choices are consistent with the legal system's goals and objectives, should not deprive Meredith Bell of that choice.

Mandatory policies also ignore the profound impact that race, class, sexual orientation, immigration status, and other identities may have on women's decisions to invoke formal systems. Many women of color, for example, are profoundly ambivalent about involving the criminal system, given their negative past experiences with police and prosecutors and concerns about subjecting men of color to further control by the state. Lesbians may be reluctant to engage the criminal justice system for fear of being outed or mistreated by police and prosecutors, who assume that violence between women must be a "cat fight" or that a butch lesbian must always be the aggressor. Low-income women may not be able to afford the arrest and prosecution of their partners; the economic resources their partners provide might be more important than a cessation of abuse at a particular point in time. Immigrant women, especially those who are undocumented or whose partners are undocumented, may fear that involvement in the criminal system will lead to deportation, depriving them of economic, emotional, extended family, or community or parenting support.

How Far Is Too Far?

Advocates' willingness to justify mandatory interventions into the lives of women subjected to abuse in the name of safety and accountability is not unlimited. A look at laws requiring physicians to report evidence of domestic violence to law enforcement and/or other state agencies may be instructive. A number of states require health care professionals to report injuries resulting from criminal activity or inflicted by specific kinds of weapons to law enforcement; a smaller subset of these states requires health care professionals to report injuries resulting from violence by an intimate partner. Those laws generally mandate that physicians and other health care professionals inform police of injuries resulting from criminal acts, including domestic violence. The justification for California's physician reporting law was to ensure that all criminal activity came to the attention of police; domestic violence was specifically enumerated as a crime to be reported in 1994, at the urging of children's groups and law enforcement.[53] Kentucky's Attorney General has opined that the duty to report under Kentucky law is absolute, not alleviated by treatment, therapy, or the victim's refusal to press charges or leave the home. If the adult who is the subject of the report refuses to allow state officials to enter her home after such a report, the court may issue a search warrant permitting entry onto the premises.[54] Some laws also abrogate the physician/patient privilege in these cases and allow for the admission of statements and other information revealed during examination and diagnosis of the patient. Colorado, for example, added a domestic violence provision to its physician reporting law in 1995. The Colorado courts subsequently upheld the abrogation of the physician/patient privilege, explaining that the legislature could abrogate the privilege when an overriding public policy need for the information to be made public exists, and holding that such provisions struck an appropriate balance between the need to protect victims of domestic violence and the desire to encourage them to seek treatment free of fear or embarrassment.[55] New Hampshire's reporting law provides an exception to reporting if the victim is over the age of 18 and objects to the release of the information, unless she has been treated for a gunshot or other serious bodily injury.

These reporting laws seem to be logical extensions of the philosophy that mandatory interventions benefit women subjected to abuse because they ensure that law enforcement will have knowledge of the commission of domestic violence crimes and the opportunity to ensure that men are held accountable for their actions. Abrogating the physician/patient privilege to require reporting simply prioritizes women's safety and offender account-ability over women's privacy and autonomy—the same calculation made in the mandatory policies previously discussed. Yet advocates for women sub-jected to abuse roundly condemn such laws. Researcher Ariella Hyman has argued that "there is ample reason to believe that mandatory reporting of all injuries due to domestic violence represents a threat to the health and safety of survivors of domestic violence."[56] Hyman contends that such laws deter victims from seeking medical treatment, expose women subjected to abuse to the risk of retaliation by their partners, and undermine patient autonomy. Hyman quoted one woman involved in a support group for women sub-jected to abuse as "dismayed at being 'treated as if they were infants and not able to make up their own minds whether to report to police.'"[57] For those reasons, the Family Violence Prevention Fund, a leading voice in the move-ment against domestic violence, opposes mandatory physician reporting of domestic violence injuries.

Looking at such policies through the lens of autonomy, it is hard to discern any appreciable difference between physician reporting laws and other laws that mandate the involvement or non-involvement of the state in domestic violence matters. Yet where there is general agreement that mandatory phy-sician reporting laws are disempowering, there is no such consensus about mandatory arrest laws, even though taking the choice to engage the legal sys-tem from the hands of the victim is no different when a physician makes the phone call to police. One could argue that physician reporting laws go a step further than previous policies by usurping the woman's decision about whether to involve law enforcement at all. A woman subjected to abuse is deprived of the choice to involve the police in the first instance if her doc-tor is required to report; his duty negates any decision she might have made about whether to call the police during or after the incident. In jurisdictions embracing mandatory policies, however, the same consequences stem from a phone call made by a neighbor as from a phone call made by a doctor: man-datory arrest, victimless prosecution. While advocates have grave and war-ranted concerns about creating disincentives for women subjected to abuse to seek medical treatment, the difference between physician reporting laws and other mandatory interventions is negligible, particularly in terms of the impact on women's autonomy.

Mandatory policies are disempowering because they deprive women sub-jected to abuse of the ability to control their use of tools like arrest, prosecu-tion, and mediation. Women subjected to abuse turn to the legal system in an attempt to regain control from their partners. Researcher David Ford has described how women subjected to abuse use the threat of prosecution as a "power resource," a tool that can be deployed in order to equalize the power imbalances within the relationship. Women call police not only because they want their partners arrested, but also to interrupt an incident of abuse or to show their partners that they are willing to reach out to others and to invoke the power of the state to stop the abuse. Women participate in prosecutions against their partners not only because they want those partners punished, but also to teach them a lesson, to secure counseling for their partners, or to get support payments. Similarly, women drop charges for a variety of reasons beyond intimidation by their partners: because the abuse has stopped, he has agreed to counseling, or he has agreed to divorce. The instrumental use of arrest and prosecution empowers the woman subjected to abuse in the negotiation of the terms of her relationship with her partner. Ford warns, however, that "criminal justice options are victim power resources only if *she* can control the manner in which they are brought to bear on her mate."[58] The obvious problem with Ford's caution is that the legal system, and the police and prosecutors who work within that system, may have very different objectives for arrest and prosecution and view their role not as facilitating the woman's instrumental use of the system, but as upholding the laws against domestic violence and the societal mores reflected in those laws. The system is simply not the woman's to command—there are too many other actors with competing goals for such a practice to be possible.

Opponents of mediation justify their opposition to permitting women subjected to abuse to mediate by claiming that the goals of mediation cannot be achieved in cases involving domestic violence. But Ford's insight is important in this context as well. Whether the goals of mediation can be met in cases involving domestic violence depends on who defines those goals. If the goals are those generally articulated by the legal system—cheaper, less adversarial, more likely to promote agreement—opponents of mediation are indeed correct that the goals may be difficult to meet. But the goals of the woman subjected to abuse may be very different than those of the system. She might choose to use mediation as a space within which to express her anger at her partner, an anger that, if expressed during an adversarial proceeding, could alienate a judge and damage her case. She might choose to confront her partner with the consequences of his actions—the end of the relationship, the distribution of property and custody rights. She might use mediation to show her partner that he no longer has the ability to control her. Mediation could be a boon to the woman subjected to abuse regardless of whether any agreement is ever reached, notwithstanding that reaching an agreement is the usual measure of success for mediation. Rather than reinforcing a power imbalance between the parties, mediation could serve as a power restorative, providing a safe space within which the woman subjected to abuse could make demands and have them heard and ratified by a neutral third party, and in so doing, recapture her power. Mediation, too, could serve as a "power resource," but only if a woman has the ability to control the terms upon which it is used. Instead, though, one critic of mediation has suggested that states require women subjected to abuse to participate in therapy both before and while engaging in mediation with their partners, insinuating (in the most charitable reading) that no woman subjected to abuse can represent her own interests without therapeutic intervention.[59]

It may not be realistic to believe that women subjected to abuse will be able to control these systems. We will never know, however, if women do not have the ability to make nonconforming choices. A guiding principle for domestic violence policy that seeks to honor the autonomy of women subjected to abuse must be to only enact policies that women can control. If we truly value the empowerment of women subjected to abuse, we should not advocate for policies that operate upon women rather than at their behest, for policies that deprive them of self-determination and choice. These policies reflect the influence of dominance feminism, the idea that every woman is a victim, acted upon rather than acting, and therefore in need of the substituted judgment of the legal system. They fail to acknowledge that women can be abused and nonetheless be actors, with the ability to determine the course of their lives. These policies ignore anti-essentialist feminist thinking about women's self-definition, distilling every woman down to the stereotypical victim unable to choose, and about the diversity of choice, assuming that all women would choose safety and accountability over other priorities. Defining all women as victims allows the legal system to narrow the available options accordingly, depriving women subjected to abuse of the ability to pursue possibilities beyond those deemed acceptable by the legal system.

The choices made by women subjected to abuse will certainly have consequences, sometimes overwhelmingly negative consequences, for the women who make them. Some women who ask that their partners not be arrested will be abused again; some will die. Some offenders will be free to abuse again as a result of dismissed prosecutions. Some women will strike bad deals in mediation or experience revictimization in the process. But many other women will be empowered by the ability to make these choices for themselves, in the contexts of their own lives, rather than having the legal system impose decisions upon them based on what they "should" want, instead of what they do want. If empowerment is still the goal of the battered women's movement, we must accept that women subjected to abuse have the right to make choices that we might disagree with, dislike, or fear.

Barbara Hart has argued that

> Agency is the power to make informed decisions and implement them without interference by the batterer. . . . Agency is the power to employ the legal options, community resources, economic remedies, housing opportunities, and educational programs available in order to escape the violence and achieve lives that are free of intimidation, degradation, and violation.[60]

But agency is also the power to choose not to have an intimate partner arrested. Agency is the power to choose not to participate in a prosecution that could cause an intimate partner to go to jail, or be deported, or be removed from the family. Agency is the power to confront an intimate partner with his abuse and advocate on one's own behalf for a negotiated settlement to pending litigation. Agency is the power to see a physician to have injuries treated but to choose to have that physician maintain confidentiality about the cause of those injuries. Agency is self-direction, self-determination, the ability to identify, evaluate, and make decisions. Agency and autonomy are what women subjected to abuse lose as a result of mandatory policies.

Reframing Domestic Violence Law and Policy

Anti-Essentialist Principles

Patricia Connors, Valoree Day, Sharwline Nicholson, Dixie Shanahan, Jessica (Gonzales) Lenahan, Noelle Mowatt, Meredith Bell, Mrs. Jefferson, Linda Williams, and countless other women have been poorly served by the legal system's response to domestic violence. These failures can, in large part, be explained by the dominance feminist underpinnings of the current system. But the system need not continue to operate as it does. Just as the legal landscape was altered 40 years ago with the implementation of dominance feminism-influenced law and policy, it could again change in ways that would make it more responsive to the needs of women subjected to abuse. Shifting the theoretical lens through which the system is scrutinized can offer a blueprint for reconstructing domestic violence law and policy.

Anti-essentialist feminist legal theory provides such a lens. Anti-essentialist feminism rejects the idea that there is a unitary, overarching women's experience that can serve as the basis for making law and policy affecting women. Anti-essentialist feminists argue that the composite "woman" has simply substituted the experiences of those with power—white, heterosexual, middle-class women—for all women. An essentialist view of women elides the complexities of identity and the ways that various identities shape women's experiences. Anti-essentialist feminism focuses instead on the ways that those identities intersect, constructing and reinforcing women's oppression. Law professor Trina Grillo explains:

> Each of us in the world sits at the intersection of many categories: She is Latina, woman, short, mother, lesbian, daughter, brown-eyed, long-haired, quick-witted, short-tempered, worker, stubborn. At any one moment in time and in space, some of these categories are central to her being and her ability to act

in the world. Others matter not at all. Some categories, such as race, gender, class, and sexual orientation, are important most of the time. Others are rarely important. When something or someone highlights one of her categories and brings it to the fore, she may be a dominant person, an oppressor of others. Other times, even most of the time, she may be oppressed herself.[1]

The goal of anti-essentialist feminism is to ensure that needs and concerns of subgroups, particularly marginalized subgroups, are not lost in the rush to ascribe the common experience of oppression to gender without considering how women's multiple identities contribute to and reinforce that oppression.

In the realm of domestic violence law and policy, anti-essentialist feminism requires delving into the complexities of the lives of individual women subjected to abuse rather than reducing them to their lowest common denominator—their common experience of domestic violence. Anti-essentialist feminism stresses that being subjected to abuse is only one facet of women's identity. Women subjected to abuse are rich, poor, middle-class, African American, Latina, Asian, white, Native American, immigrant, disabled, able-bodied, gay, straight, transgendered, rural, urban, self-defensive, aggressive, frightened, and angry. They have different goals, aspirations, concerns, and priorities. All of these facets of identity shape their relationships (and the abuse that happens in those relationships), their goals, their options, and their decisions about how to handle the abuse in their lives.

Constructing an Anti-Essentialist Response to Domestic Violence

Safety and accountability are unquestionably the predominant goals of the current legal response to domestic violence. Those goals are a natural outgrowth of a dominance feminist-influenced system. Subordinated women need saving, to be made safe by those with the power to do so. In seeking accountability, the battered women's movement delegated responsibility to the state for ensuring that women are protected from men's abuse, redressing women's subjugation and rescinding the immunity that men have traditionally been offered by the state through its failure to intervene. Although the battered women's movement has acknowledged that the system might have other goals, safety and accountability are the movement's main concerns. Interventions that fail to prioritize those goals are dismissed as too risky or insufficiently punitive.

An anti-essentialist approach to domestic violence would start from a very different place. Where the dominance feminist response allocates power to the state, an anti-essentialist system prioritizes empowering the individual. An anti-essentialist system would be premised on the importance of giving individual women as much power as possible, to the greatest extent possible, to define the abuse they experience and decide how it should be addressed. Recognizing that women share one facet of identity but diverge among many other axes of identity, an anti-essentialist system would accept that women's experiences of abuse vary dramatically and must be considered contextually. No one intervention can meet the needs of all women subjected to abuse. Accordingly, an anti-essentialist system would be cognizant of the need to ensure that women's individual experiences of abuse serve as the basis for any intervention. An anti-essentialist system would also recognize that individual women are best situated to determine what form that intervention should take. Only by vesting individual women with the power to choose if, when, and how the system intervenes can the system acknowledge and accommodate the range of experiences and goals of women subjected to abuse.

To that end, an anti-essentialist system would be aware that individual women have very different goals for systemic interventions. While those goals might include safety and accountability, the meaning of those terms will be different for different women. Women will have additional goals as well and may prioritize those goals over safety and accountability. Some women may not care about safety or accountability, at least as understood in a dominance-based system, at all. An anti-essentialist system would create space for women to define their goals and enable women to pick and choose among the facets of the system that best serve their needs. An anti-essentialist system would not stereotype women as victims to be saved, but would instead view them as individuals making choices about how to deal with the difficult situations that arise in their interpersonal relationships. An anti-essentialist system would not use the experiences of white, straight, middle-class women as the default, treating women of color and other marginalized women as "white women only more so."[2] An anti-essentialist system would make public remedies available, but would not impose those remedies on women who do not want to involve the state in their relationships and would provide remedies for women who opt out of engagement with public systems.

A Woman-Centered System

Placing the relationships, needs, goals, desires, and choices of individual women at the center of the legal response to domestic violence must be the first principle of an anti-essentialist reconstruction of the legal system. The early battered women's movement recognized that self-determination was essential for women subjected to abuse; advocates understood their role as helping women to achieve whatever goals those women identified. Over the past 40 years, however, the balance of power has shifted decidedly toward the legal system, enabling the system to define acceptable goals and responses. An anti-essentialist system would place that power, to the greatest extent possible, in the hands of individual women.

Too often, the "woman-centered advocacy" made available to women subjected to abuse has been based on assumptions about what women subjected to abuse value and should want. Advocates have confined themselves to working within existing systems and offering resources that serve the legal system's goals, a constrained set of choices that are not true choices at all. Creating a woman-centered system, by contrast, means shifting the locus of power within the legal system to individual women.

In a woman-centered system, abuse would be defined by the woman's subjective experience of her partner's behavior. In both the civil and criminal systems, the law would provide redress for women who experienced a loss of autonomy, liberty, or self-direction as a result of the actions of a partner, regardless of that partner's intent and without requiring physical harm or the threat of physical harm as a predicate. In that framework, spiritual abuse or reproductive abuse would carry the same weight that physical abuse currently does, so long as a woman experiences a restraint on her liberty as a result of that abuse. Such a framework acknowledges both the complexity of women's experiences of abuse and the importance of context in determining what constitutes abuse. Defining domestic violence around the woman's experience would allow the legal system to move away from narrowly drawn categories of abuse toward a richer understanding of how myriad actions and omissions can constitute abuse. A woman-centered system, moreover, creates space for judges to explore how women's intersecting identities affect their experiences of abuse. Threatening to terminate the medical insurance of a healthy woman, for example, might seem unkind but fairly innocuous. For a low-income woman suffering from cancer or other life-threatening illness, however, the prospect of lost insurance could be sufficient to entrap her in an abusive relationship. Identity matters. Static categories of violence preclude legal system actors from considering how identity alters the experience of abuse.

Anti-essentialist domestic violence law and policy would give women the power to determine their goals, rather than ceding power to the state to make such decisions on their behalf. Women would define terms like safety and accountability within the contexts of their own lives. An anti-essentialist system would accommodate contextual definitional change, recognizing that a term like "safety," as advocate Jill Davies explains, goes beyond

> the elimination of physical violence to also include the elimination of the range of batterer and life-generated risks that most victims face. In addition to being free from the violence and control of an abusive partner, victims must be able to meet their families' basic human needs. Reducing the risk of physical and sexual violence but leaving a victim and her children with no home or means of long-range financial support is not making her safe.[3]

Expanding the definitions of terms like safety and accountability will force the state to reconsider the appropriateness of its interventions. Women struggling economically, for example, might be more interested in securing financial than penal accountability from their partners. That goal could be undermined, however, if a partner is imprisoned and unable to work. Other facets of identity similarly complicate the goal of achieving safety. For undocumented women, safety may be less about removing their partners from their homes, and more about obtaining legal immigration status. For these women, interventions that provide them with the security of that status may be more important than other types of state action.[4] Actions that might expose them to deportation, like calling the police or participating in prosecution, might not feel—or be—safe. An anti-essentialist system would work to achieve the goals that women articulate and define, rather than substituting the state's priorities.

State interventions in an anti-essentialist system would be woman-directed as well. Law professor Michelle Madden Dempsey has suggested that in a feminist response to domestic violence, the state should force women subjected to abuse to testify when the violence is serious and ongoing, when prosecution is likely to reduce the violence, when the violence reinforces patriarchy within the relationship and within society, and when strong community interests are served by compelling the victim's testimony.[5] While Dempsey's proposal is certainly consistent with a dominance feminist response, missing from that formulation is any mention of the individual woman's assessment of the risk that testifying poses to her, the potential for success of other forms of intervention, or the goals of the individual woman in pursuing or avoiding prosecution. Rather than mandating arrest or requiring prosecution, an anti-essentialist system would permit state actors to intervene only with the consent and at the behest of the woman subjected to abuse, enabling individual women to decide whether and how to deploy the criminal justice system to regulate their relationships. One of the mantras of the battered women's movement is that women subjected to abuse are best placed to determine the risk they face from their partners and the consequences of potential interventions.[6] An anti-essentialist legal system would rely on that risk assessment expertise by ceding power to women subjected to abuse to determine which interventions best meet their needs.

Many advocates have called for a return to a system that centralizes the voices of women subjected to abuse in making law and policy. But hearing women's voices is different than giving women the power to determine when systemic intervention is appropriate. An anti-essentialist system would not just listen to women subjected to abuse, but would give them the ability to use the state, in the words of researcher David Ford, as a "power resource" to be deployed if, as, and when they choose. This does not mean that advocates would have no role to play in such a system. Advocates would help women understand how the legal system works and the costs and benefits of engaging that system; assist women in articulating their goals, needs, concerns, and preferred strategies; and counsel women on the potential consequences of their decisions about using or not using the legal system. Advocates would still bring their expertise to bear in this counseling. In the end, however, the role of the advocate would be to help women decide how to use their power to effectuate those decisions, not to substitute the advocates' judgments for those of the true experts.

Avoiding Essentialism

The victim stereotype that currently shapes discourse within the legal system about how to best serve women subjected to abuse is a product of dominance feminism. The stereotypic victim is a descendant of the subordinated woman ever threatened by men's sexual violence. The manifestation of that vision in the context of domestic violence is the battered woman suffering from learned helplessness. The legal system's expectations for this paradigmatic victim have been further shaped by the strategic choice to put a white, heterosexual, middle-class face on the battered women's movement. But this meek, weak, passive, white, straight, middle-class non-actor is at odds with many of the thousands of women who seek the assistance of the legal system each year. The existence of the paradigmatic victim, and the legal structures that give substance to her myth, like battered woman syndrome, make using the legal system problematic for any woman who does not conform to that stereotype.

An anti-essentialist system would eschew that victim and eradicate the laws and policies that keep her myth alive. An anti-essentialist legal system would base its judgments on the stories of individual women, in all of their complexity and messiness, allowing women to describe what they endured without forcing them to fit within the stock narrative of the battered woman. Evidence of battered woman syndrome as currently embodied in statute and case law would be excised from the law. Women would instead be encouraged to testify about their experiences of abuse and to explain how those experiences affected them. Generalizations about how battered women act, cycles of violence, and other essentializing theories and concepts would be replaced by individualized, contextualized assessments of how abuse operated within this particular relationship to cause the specific event at issue. Expert testimony would be used to dispute myths and misinformation about women subjected to abuse, but experts would not be permitted to make assertions about typical behavior by either women subjected to abuse or their partners, to avoid perpetuating stereotypes and creating unrealistic expectations of how women subjected to abuse should act.

Eliminating battered woman syndrome and other stereotyped renderings of women subjected to abuse from the law would create space within the legal system for a variety of narratives. In the current system, stories that fail to conform to the stock battered woman narrative are difficult for legal system actors to assimilate. Women who tell such stories may find the legal system indifferent or hostile to their claims. Women who fight back against their partners, for example, frequently find it difficult to persuade police, prosecutors, and judges that their actions were justified or that they need assistance because their stories of abuse are at odds with the meek, passive stereotype of the prevailing narrative. A system unfettered by preexisting notions of who women subjected to abuse are and how they should behave would provide a forum within which women could tell a variety of stories of abuse without having to edit those stories instrumentally, a process that forces women to deny the truth of their experiences in order to secure help. Women subjected to abuse often do not recognize themselves in the paradigmatic victim; excising the stock narrative from the legal system might also enable these women to see that they, too, are entitled to the services and supports the system offers.

Some worry that moving away from an essentialized view of women subjected to abuse will weaken the battered women's movement's ability to win legislative and legal victories. As law professor Ruth Colker points out, "[F]eminist theory is often best accepted by the public . . . when it is essentialist in its portrayal of women."[7] Scholars fear that the fragmentation of women from an essentialized whole into ever smaller identity-based subgroups will prevent women from being able to wield the political power necessary to make change in the law and in the world. In the realm of domestic violence law and policy, law professor Elizabeth Schneider has framed this tension between the stories of individual women and the stock narrative of "the battered woman" as a conflict between particularity—"the particular experiences of women who are battered by men" and generality—"broader understandings of the problem of violence and gender."[8] She and other scholars suggest that the tension can be resolved by employing strategic essentialism.

Strategic essentialism, as formulated by literature professor Gayatri Spivak, involves the conscious choice to essentialize a particular community to achieve a specific political goal.[9] Schneider argues that "[t]he shared experience of women's physical abuse and pain" provides the common denominator among women's stories of abuse, allowing for strategic essentialism along those dimensions.[10] But Schneider's formulation is problematic on two fronts. First, it privileges physical violence and pain over other forms of abuse, reinforcing outdated conceptions of the nature of domestic violence. More importantly, it fails to ensure that the experiences of the paradigmatic victim will not become the default for law- and policymaking when strategic essentialism is employed. We need not discard the idea of strategic essentialism simply because it has been defined too narrowly, however. To the extent that strategic essentialism is necessary to build coalitions, exert political power, and influence the policy-making process, it may be impossible to avoid essentializing altogether. Nevertheless, acknowledging that reality should not serve as an excuse for ignoring the needs of the women who are disproportionately affected by abuse.

Studies have repeatedly established that low-income women are more likely to be subjected to abuse than other women.[11] Rates of domestic violence correlate to the financial strain felt by couples; couples feeling high strain reported domestic violence rates of 9.5 percent, as compared to 2.7 percent among couples experiencing low levels of financial strain.[12] Bernice told sociologist Jody Raphael how that dynamic played out in her relationship with her husband:

> All he wanted was to take care of his family. When he went out there and looked for jobs and couldn't get enough money, he got frustrated. He always felt he should have a better job than what he had. . . . [Billy] said, "Bernice, that was one of our biggest problems. I felt so useless as a man, because I never could have taken care of you and the kids, and here you are, out there doing it by yourself."[13]

Bernice reported that the violence and abuse in their relationship were worse when Billy was unemployed.[14] Raphael notes, "I have never met a battered woman on welfare who did not agree with Bernice's analysis of the relationship between domestic violence and the ability to support one's family."[15] Social science research supports this observation: one study found domestic violence in 4.7 percent of couples where the male partner was consistently employed, 7.5 percent of couples where the male was unemployed once, and 12.3 percent of couples where the male was unemployed twice or more.[16]

Low-income women also have fewer resources with which to respond to abuse. Higher income women can use their financial security to obtain new housing, hire lawyers, seek needed counseling or medical treatment, and put geographic space between themselves and their partners. Women in high-paying jobs are more likely to have health insurance, medical or personal leave, and autonomy in the workspace, giving them both time and crucial services and supports. Low-income women, by contrast, are more likely to become homeless as a result of abuse. They are less likely to have friends and family who can help them financially or materially. They may not have health insurance but are more likely to have physical and (at least in the short term) mental health problems related to abuse. Job loss as a result of a partner's abuse is more catastrophic for a woman surviving paycheck to paycheck than for a woman with savings. Low-income women may be so economically bound to their partners that they cannot leave their relationships and may continue to rely on economic support from their partners even after their relationships end.

Because low-income women are more likely to be subjected to abuse, and because they have fewer resources with which to address that abuse, laws and policies designed to combat abuse should be particularly attentive to their needs. Law professor Donna Coker has argued that all domestic violence law and policy should undergo a material resources test. Such a test would prioritize "those laws and policies which improve women's access to material resources."[17] Coker explains that a material resources test would focus on those women with the greatest need and argues that it is not just poor women, but poor women of color—"the women who are in the greatest need, those who are dramatically affected by the inequalities of gender, race, and class"—who should serve as the standard for determining a law or policy's impact on material resources.[18] Coker's position is based not on the prevalence of domestic violence among women of color; research shows that women of color (with the exception of Native American women, who are abused at disproportionately high rates) experience domestic violence at roughly the same rates as white women, especially when studies control for socioeconomic class.[19] Instead, her concern is with the particular vulnerability of women of color to state policies that intrude upon their privacy and their intimate relationships. Historic and continuing racism and the disproportionate intervention of the state into the lives of people of color influence how women of color experience state interventions and create barriers to accessing services. As activist Andrea Smith argues, "Women of color do not just face quantitatively more issues when they suffer violence (e.g., less supportive media attention, greater language barriers, lack of support in the judicial system), but their experience is qualitatively different from that of white women."[20] Developing laws and policies that establish the state as a gatekeeper for receiving services or mandate the intrusion of the state into the lives of women subjected to abuse ignores the context within which women of color experience abuse and may prove not only ineffective, but harmful.

Current domestic violence law and policy reflects the failure to consider how poor women and women of color view the state and the potential utility of state intervention. Creating norms around the experiences of poor women and women of color would make their needs the central focus of domestic violence law and policy. The intention is not to substitute poor women of color for white, middle-class women as "essential" women. The diversity among women of color and poor women defies such essentialization; differences of language, immigration status, culture, socioeconomic class, and religion among poor women and women of color make their experiences of abuse unique. Strategic essentialism is purely instrumental, designed to create enough commonality among women to craft law and policy, not to replace one overly simplistic view of women subjected to abuse with another. Nor is it a return to the pre-movement misunderstanding of domestic violence as a problem specific to low-income women and communities of color. Putting the needs of poor women and women of color at the forefront of advocacy efforts is instead intended to acknowledge the particular difficulties these women face when subjected to abuse and to prevent advocates and policymakers from defaulting to a white, middle-class worldview when strategic essentialism is deployed for political gain.

Humanizing Men Who Abuse Their Partners

If women are the passive, helpless victims of dominance feminism, men are its brutal aggressors. In dominance feminism, law professor Nancy Levit writes, "men subordinate, ignore, invade, harass, vilify, use and torture women. They are, quite literally, the bad guys. . . . Dominance theory opens the door to an essentialist position for the viewing of men as a uniform collective: none are better, some are worse, and all are guilty."[21] Domestic violence law and policy imported not only the paradigmatic victim from dominance feminism, but the stereotypical batterer as well. Intentionally asserting power and control over their partners using whatever tactics, however brutal, are necessary to immobilize their victims, men are undifferentiated villains within a dominance feminist framework.

But social science research suggests that men who abuse their partners are not a monolithic group. In 1994, psychologists Amy Holtzworth-Munroe and Gregory L. Stuart suggested that there were three distinct types of men who abused their partners: family only, borderline/dysphoric, and generally violent/antisocial. Men in the family only category, the researchers explained, did not generally suffer from any type of mental illness, committed the least serious violence, and were not likely to be violent outside of the family context. Dysphoric/borderline men suffered from depression and anger, were more violent than men in the family only group, were more likely to use psychological and sexual abuse than the family only men, and confined their violence largely to the family, although some committed violence and criminal behavior outside of the family. Dysphoric/borderline men were described as psychologically distressed and emotionally volatile. Generally violent/antisocial men were more likely to be substance abusers, committed the most serious violence, including psychological and sexual abuse, against their partners, and were frequently violent toward others as well. These men were most likely to be diagnosed with antisocial personality disorder or some other form of psychopathy. Based on their research, Holtzworth-Munroe and Stuart suggested that treatment for men who abused their partners would be more effective if it were specific to the type of man being treated.[22] More recently, Holtzworth-Munroe and her colleagues have found a fourth subcategory of men who abuse their partners: low-level antisocial men, who are more violent than family only and less violent than generally violent/antisocial men.[23] Further research supports the existence of these four categories.[24]

Other researchers have drawn different distinctions among classes of men who abuse their partners. Psychologists Neil Jacobson and John Gottman studied the physiological reactions of men who abused their partners during arguments and categorized the men as "pit bulls" or "cobras" based on their observations. Pit bulls responded emotionally to their partners, verbally attacking them during arguments. Cobras, by contrast, might have appeared to lose control on the outside, but were internally calm, suggesting sociopathic tendencies. Building on these studies, sociologist Michael Johnson has divided men who abuse into dependent intimate terrorists (men who are violent because they are obsessed with their partners and desperate to control them—Jacobson and Gottman's pit bulls), antisocial intimate terrorists (men who will do whatever they must to get what they want, and therefore are generally violent and willing to use violence to have their own way, at home and elsewhere—Jacobson and Gottman's cobras), and actors in situational couple violence (men who use violence in context-specific situations, not as a general pattern of control—Holtzworth-Munroe and Stuart's family only abusers).[25] Our understanding of men who abuse is not terribly deep; more "data from men to more precisely determine what motivates them to be abusive"[26] is certainly needed. It is clear from these studies, however, that there is diversity among men who abuse their partners. Law- and policymakers should be attentive to that diversity.

Identity contributes to this diversity as well. Research supports the existence of a relationship between economic stress and domestic violence; anecdotally, the media have been replete with stories about the increase in domestic violence since the economic recession began in 2009.[27] While the relationship between economics and domestic violence is nuanced,[28] it is nonetheless possible that alleviating men's financial stress may go further toward reducing domestic violence than any form of criminal justice intervention. For men of color, particularly African American men, legal system interventions to curb domestic violence occur within the context of a historically racist system that continues to punish men of color at disproportionate rates. Being ordered into batterer's treatment may have little effect when men "believe that they have been unfairly arrested, prosecuted, and convicted of a domestic violence offense by a racist criminal justice system."[29] Acknowledging the complexity of men who abuse is not meant to justify or excuse their behavior. But ignoring that complexity significantly decreases the likelihood that interventions with those men will succeed.

Dominance feminism's explanation for why men abuse their partners is similarly one-dimensional: men intentionally use physical abuse to subordinate women sexually. The reality is more complex. Men, like women, are socialized within a patriarchal system that assumes they will behave in accordance with prescribed norms. Rather than making conscious choices to perpetuate those norms, law professors Susan Williams and David Williams have argued, "many men act in ways that promote gender hierarchy without any conscious choice at all, simply because that is the way they understand their own gender identity."[30] Ellen Pence's work with men in batterer intervention groups led her to a similar conclusion—that men did not desire power and control over their partners, but rather believed that male power and control was their due in a patriarchal society.[31] That distinction has profound implications for law- and policymaking.

The legal system's response to men who abuse their partners highlights how these men are essentialized in a dominance feminist system. The legal system's preferred interventions—criminal prosecution and batterer's treatment—fail to distinguish among men who abuse their partners, and the effectiveness of these interventions is disputed. This book has already explored the limited utility of arrest and incarceration in curbing domestic violence. Exploring the growth of the batterer treatment industry further reveals the dangers of essentializing the response to men who abuse their partners.

The Duluth model, named for the Duluth Domestic Abuse Intervention Project in Minnesota, is the most widely used method of batterer's treatment. The Duluth model is a feminist, psychoeducational approach to treatment, premised upon the idea that domestic violence is a reflection of a patriarchal system in which men's use of power and control are sanctioned. The Duluth model is also "grounded in the principles of cognitive-behavioral therapy," using role playing and discussion, among other techniques, to challenge men to rewrite their cognitive scripts about male expectations and the use of abuse to ensure that their partners fulfill those expectations.[32] Equality is central to the Duluth model; the goal of treatment is to move men away from using violence and control and to help them develop egalitarian relationships with their partners.

Batterer intervention programs are among the most frequently prescribed responses to domestic violence within the legal system. Judges sentence men who abuse their partners to treatment in lieu of, or in addition to, jail time; women seek treatment for their partners in civil protection order and custody actions. This heavy reliance on batterer treatment suggests that such treatment must be effective (with effectiveness measured by a reduction in abuse or changes in men's attitudes about abuse). The research on batterer intervention programs, however, is less positive. For treatment to work, it stands to reason that men would have to participate in programs. But few men referred to batterer intervention programs actually complete those programs. As many as 50 percent of the men who contact programs for intake appointments never register with those programs.[33] Among men mandated to participate in treatment, one study found that more than half of the men attended fewer than the required 20 sessions, and almost one-third attended five or fewer.[34] As few as 25 percent of men referred to programs actually complete them.[35]

More importantly, there is significant debate about the effectiveness of these programs. As a recent Family Violence Prevention Fund/National Institute of Justice roundtable on batterer intervention programs notes, "Research findings on the effectiveness of BIPs range from little or no effect to substantial reductions in violent behavior by participants who complete the programs."[36] Sociologist Edward W. Gondolf has argued that "the vast majority of men referred to batterer counseling appear to stop their assaultive behavior and reduce their abuse in general," and that this reduction is, at least in part, attributable to participation in a batterer intervention program—although the specific aspects of the programs that produce change are not clear.[37] A 2004 meta-analysis of 22 studies evaluating Duluth and cognitive behavioral models of domestic violence treatment, however, found that such programs had only a small effect on recidivism. Men who receive treatment have a 40 percent chance of remaining successfully non-violent— but the chance of remaining successfully non-violent without undergoing treatment is 35 percent.[38] Even if men curtail their physical violence after participating in batterer's intervention programs, they often continue to use other forms of abuse. In one study of four programs, researchers found rates of continued controlling behavior of 45 percent, rates of verbal abuse of 70 percent, and rates of threats of 43 percent after treatment had ended.[39] The failure of batterer's treatment is not culturally specific; a recent study found that a South Carolina program reached "African American and Caucasian participants equally poorly."[40]

In some cases, being ordered into treatment may exacerbate an already bad situation. A rural Ohio woman described her experience with her partner's batterer treatment program:

He had to go to domestic violence counseling every Monday for six months, but sending him to that counseling meant that I got beat every Monday night for six months. Because he would come home madder than hell because he had to go to that place. . . . I told the judge, "I don't care what you do to him, but don't send him to counseling." And she sent him back there anyway. So every Monday for six more months I got beaten because he had to go for three hours and sit in class. . . . And then we meet up with a few of the guys from his class and I think they all did it. Because they were all mad every Monday night and a few of the women I talked to, they're like, "Yep, they come in extra mad because it's your fault we have to be there."

She called counseling "the worse help ever."[41]

Batterer treatment might be more effective if it distinguished among men who abused their partners.[42] There is some evidence that feminist cognitive interventions like the Duluth model are more likely to produce change in antisocial men who abuse their partners, and that psychodynamic approaches are better for dependent men.[43] Rather than creating space for a nuanced assessment of the treatment needs of men who abuse their partners, however, states have legislated standards for batterer intervention treatment, most often mandating that treatment providers employ the Duluth model. Assuming that one treatment modality will be effective with all men who abuse their partners wastes resources that could be better spent on the needs of women subjected to abuse. More disturbingly, given that women frequently return to their partners after they enter treatment, assuming that the treatment will reduce abuse, the legal system is endangering women by essentializing men.

An anti-essentialist legal system, one that appreciates the individuality and complexity of men who abuse their partners, would benefit women as well as men. Essentializing men who abuse their partners reinforces problematic stereotypes about women who have been subjected to abuse; only an "immobilized or pathologically passive" woman would remain in a relationship with the "monsters" that most assume men who abuse to be. When men are presented in a more nuanced fashion, law professor Kathryn Abrams argues, legal decision makers are able to see women who have been subjected to abuse in a different light.[44] Humanizing men who abuse their partners could open the door to a broader community response to domestic violence as well. Communities that are unwilling to engage with battered women's advocates given their loyalty to their men and "sympathy for the disadvantages they face" might be more open to partnerships if the lives of men who abuse their partners were understood in a more multifaceted way.[45]

Men who abuse their partners may be motivated to change. Change, defined as curbing a man's abusive behavior, should be a priority in state interventions, given that the behavior is what brings him to the legal system's attention in the first instance. Change, as distinguished from accountability, could be motivated by a number of factors, including immigration status, employment, the possibility of incarceration, children, or the importance of a man's relationship with his partner. Engaging men around the things that are important to them can create the kind of change that has eluded other interventions. Research has shown, for example, that men who abuse their partners can be motivated to curb abusive behavior if they understand the negative impact of their violence on their children.[46] Laws and policies that paint all men who abuse their partners with the same brush foreclose opportunities to probe what prompts individual men to change or to use that information to develop more meaningful, and more effective, responses. An anti-essentialist system, one that understands that men's identities, like women's, affect the experience of abuse, would create space for a broader range of responses to men who abuse their partners.

Maximizing Options

Given the diversity of the women subjected to abuse and the contexts in which they experience that abuse, the range of options available to them should be as broad as possible. In the current legal system, however, women are offered a fairly narrow set of choices, when they are offered choices at all. An anti-essentialist system would expand the options available to women subjected to abuse, enabling them to construct a plan based on their goals, needs, and priorities.

Maximizing options means rejecting the idea that any one strategy best meets the needs of all women subjected to abuse. For too long, as one advocate explained to psychologists Amy Lehrner and Nicole Allen, the response to a woman's concern that "[d]ivorce is not an option in my faith, I—this is the father of my children, okay, can you help me be safe in that context?" has been, "No, we don't know how to do that."[47] Instead, domestic violence law and policy has focused on separation-based strategies, for "good reason," explains advocate Jill Davies. "The violence, the danger, is clear. Broken bones, black eyes, big patches of yellowing purple bruises are images that every advocate has seen, and none will forget."[48] The legal system's reaction to those images has been to prioritize separation as the primary strategy for responding to abuse, using arrest and prosecution, orders of protection, and policies that predicate the receipt of assistance upon leaving to reinforce that preference.

As Davies argues, however, "strategies for leaving are not enough."[49] Some women will choose not to leave their partners, for whatever reason; the legal system should offer women assistance regardless of the status of their relationships. While separation-based remedies would continue to be available, legal system actors would no longer assume that such remedies should be employed in every case. Instead, separation-based remedies would be presented as one option among many for women to consider as they formulated their plans. Nor should the system "swing from an expectation of leaving to an expectation of staying."[50] The key to an anti-essentialist system is the commitment to ensuring the broadest possible range of choice for women subjected to abuse.

Autonomy and agency are key components of an anti-essentialist legal system. Mandated interventions and policies that wrest control from individual women and allocate decision-making authority to the state have no place within such a system. An anti-essentialist system would not tell women what they must do (leave their partners, cooperate with prosecution) or what they cannot do (mediate). Developing a range of voluntary policy options for women subjected to abuse reflects respect for a woman's ability and a woman's right to make choices about if, when, and how the state should intervene in her personal life. Maternalistic concerns about the potential dangers of certain options can be shared with women, but should never serve as the basis for denying a woman the opportunity to take any course of action that she deems appropriate. Women should not be told that an option is foreclosed because the professionals involved lack sufficient understanding of and expertise in domestic violence to make that option viable; instead, legal system actors dedicated to the creation of an anti-essentialist system should provide those services themselves. We must become the mediators, the counselors, the police officers, the prosecutors.

Allocating decision-making power to women would be the norm in an anti-essentialist legal system—not just in the criminal system, but in the civil system as well. Although originally envisioned as a tool for women to control, civil protection orders are increasingly being used by the state in ways that undermine women's autonomy. Linguist Shonna Trinch has documented how the state has usurped the power of women applying for protective orders by requiring that a woman report abuse to the police before she can receive help, by controlling women's access to needed services, and by determining which stories women should tell to convince judges of their need for assistance.[51] Protective orders are also being used in the criminal system. Prosecutors seek and obtain protective orders at initial arraignments and use protective orders in plea-bargaining. This use of protective orders in the criminal system amounts to a type of "state-imposed de facto divorce," law professor Jeannie Suk has argued.[52] Defendants agree to the imposition of final protective orders in lieu of jail time or further prosecution; by doing so, they give up any right to contact or share homes with their partners, effectively severing the relationship for the duration of the order. Women subjected to abuse are essentially bystanders in this transaction. They are powerless to prevent prosecutors from seeking the orders or their partners from taking the plea deals that might keep them out of jail or get a case dismissed altogether. Judges refuse to dismiss protective orders upon the woman's request, prioritizing their own concerns about the woman's safety over her stated wishes. Women have been prosecuted for violating the orders that they went to court to obtain,[53] orders that were not intended to restrain their behavior. An anti-essentialist legal system would return to women the power that the creators of the civil protective order intended them to have, removing state-sanctioned gatekeepers from the process and precluding the state from using orders in ways that are inconsistent with the wishes of women subjected to abuse.

Maximizing options also means using creative legal advocacy to develop remedies for women subjected to abuse that are responsive to the harms that women seek to redress. The current system is a two-sizes-fit-all system: criminal prosecution and/or civil protective orders are the remedies it offers. But many women have no desire to invoke the criminal system, and not every woman needs a civil protective order. If a woman's primary goal is financial restitution rather than court enforced separation, a tort claim for damages based on assault, battery, or intentional infliction of emotional distress might better meet her needs. Lynn Feltmeier brought just such a case after enduring years of abuse during her marriage, abuse that did not cease after the couple's divorce. The Supreme Court of Illinois found that Roger Feltmeier's actions could constitute the continuing tort of intentional infliction of emotional distress and allowed the case to go forward.[54] But such actions, according to law professor Sarah Buel, are rare, both because lawyers are reluctant to bring them and judges are unwilling to consider them. Buel argues for the creation of a tort of domestic violence to provide women subjected to abuse with a clear legal remedy for tortious conduct. California created such a law in 2002, and in *Pugliese v. Pugliese*, a California appeals court held that the continuing tort doctrine applied to the law, enabling Michele Pugliese to bring an action for damages based on her husband's abuse throughout their 13-year marriage and subsequent to her filing for divorce.[55] Tort remedies will not benefit all women. But they are an example of an underutilized tool for helping some women subjected to abuse become more financially stable, and of the kind of creative lawyering necessary to expand the legal options for women subjected to abuse.

In an anti-essentialist system, all of a woman's options should be on the table, giving her the broadest possible range of responses to assess. Remedies involving state intervention should be at the disposal of women subjected to abuse, but should not be imposed upon them. The legal system should work at the behest of women subjected to abuse, not against their will or in opposition to their goals. Legal options beyond criminal prosecution and civil protective orders must be explored, and there must be options for those women who are not interested in using the legal system at all.

Looking Beyond the Law

Despite the reservations of some within the battered women's movement, the primary societal response to domestic violence undeniably has been legal. The battered women's movement spent immense amounts of political capital on enacting law and policy responses within the legal system: civil protection orders, mandatory arrest, no-drop prosecution, immigration reform, and custody and visitation laws. VAWA firmly established the legal system's primacy by channeling billions of dollars into the provision of legal services, training, technical assistance, and equipment for law enforcement, courts, and lawyers. The choice the battered women's movement made to focus its efforts on making the legal system responsive to women's claims of abuse made sense at the time; the most visible and graphic abuse that women endure violates the criminal law, and systems already existed to punish those violations. Using those systems gave the movement a way to promote its twin goals of safety and accountability. Given the lack of understanding of why men abuse their partners and how women experience that abuse, and without the hindsight that 40 years of experience with legal interventions provides, turning to the legal system seemed to provide a way both to protect individual women and to change societal perceptions about abuse within families.

For some women, the system has kept its promise—criminal law and criminally enforceable civil law have worked in tandem to safeguard women from further abuse and to send the message, both to the individual perpetrator and society as a whole, that abuse of women is unacceptable. But the legal system has not been nearly as successful in stopping abuse as the battered women's movement must have hoped. Rates of violence against women have not dramatically declined since the inception of legal reforms; they have, instead, kept pace with the declining crime rate in the United States.[56] The only group that is markedly safer as a result of 40 years of domestic violence law and policy is men. Fewer men are being killed by their abused partners today,[57] likely because other options, like shelter, social services, and legal services, are available to their partners. Empirical evidence on the effects of arrest and prosecution on recidivism among men who abuse their partners is equivocal at best. Coordinated responses among criminal justice professionals, the civil legal system, and community members, a major VAWA initiative, have, according to one recent study, a "minimal impact on changing offender attitudes and behavior."[58] Although the legal system increased "offender accountability," the study concluded, those gains "did not translate into significantly lower rates of repeat violence reported by victims in both sites or by the offenders themselves."[59] In other words, the legal system processed the men, but did little to stop abuse against their partners.

Significant numbers of women are still choosing not to use the legal system. A 2000 report analyzing data from the National Violence Against Women survey found that only 27 percent of women who were assaulted by their partners reported their abuse to police. The vast majority of those who decided against reporting said that they did not believe the police would do anything or that the police would not believe them. One-third of the women interviewed stated that they did not want the police or courts involved in their relationships. Only 7 percent of the women who were physically assaulted reported that their partner was prosecuted; of those men, fewer than half were convicted.[60] As sociologist Evan Stark has written, the odds that a given act of abuse will result in incarceration are still infinitesimal, "better than the odds of winning a lottery, but not by much."[61] Some have argued that low rates of arrest, prosecution, and incarceration militate in favor of increased funding and training for police, prosecutors, and courts; if legal system professionals were better trained, the theory goes, the system would work more effectively. But millions of dollars have already been poured into the legal response, with minimal success. Tying policy to the hope that legal system actors will change their beliefs, become more enlightened, and improve their handling of abuse cases is naïve, particularly in the absence of research establishing that VAWA monies spent on training and education have caused the rates of abuse of women to decrease.

Intervention by the legal system has harmed rather than helped some women subjected to abuse. Involvement in the legal system can further traumatize women who have already been subjected to abuse. As psychiatrist Judith Herman writes,

> Victims need social acknowledgment and support; the court requires them to endure a public challenge to their credibility. Victims need to establish a sense of power and control over their lives; the court requires them to submit to a complex set of rules and bureaucratic procedures that they may not understand and over which they have no control. Victims need an opportunity to tell their stories in their own way, in a setting of their choice; the court requires them to respond to a set of yes-or-no questions that break down any personal attempt to construct a coherent and meaningful narrative. Victims often need to control or limit their exposure to specific reminders of the trauma; the court requires them to relive the experience. Victims often fear direct confrontation with their perpetrators; the court requires a face-to-face confrontation between a complaining witness and the accused. Indeed, if one set out intentionally to design a system for provoking symptoms of traumatic stress, it might look very much like a court of law.[62]

Policies specifically designed to help women subjected to abuse have instead worked to their detriment. Since the inception of mandatory arrest, for example, arrest rates for women and dual arrests in abuse cases have significantly increased, particularly among women of color.[63] Men who abuse their partners have learned to use the system to their advantage; as one woman explained, "He always called the police for them to take me away and they were willing to do what he wanted."[64] Arrest and prosecution increase the abuse some women experience. Mandatory interventions by the legal system deprive women of autonomy. Reporting domestic violence to police raises the possibility that mothers will be flagged for investigation by child protective services. One mother explained her decision not to call police:

> What the . . . police had been doing is taking both people to jail, and so I was terrified of calling the police because I didn't know what would happen to my children because I had nobody to take them, so if I had called the police on him, they would have taken both of us to jail, they would have taken my children to CPS, and in foster care, and it would've turned into a nightmare.[65]

Even those tools designed for women to control, like civil protection orders, have been co-opted by state actors, taking power out of women's hands.

Reliance on the law to address domestic violence is problematic on a number of levels. The law is reactive, responding to incidents of abuse that have already occurred. Law does little to reveal why men abuse their partners and how to prevent that abuse. As law professor Martha Albertson Fineman has written, "Law is a very crude instrument with which to fashion and further social policy—much better at fashioning prohibition and determining punishment than it is at creating affirmative incentives for behavior."[66] Law does not fundamentally alter the structural conditions that create the context for abuse. Defining abuse as primarily a criminal justice problem sends the message that "a distinct group of wicked people commit domestic violence and that once these persons are managed, the problem is solved."[67] Reliance on the law has preempted creative thinking about other ways to assist women subjected to abuse and diminished the possibility of partnership with communities who are unwilling to increase state intervention into their members' lives. Enacting laws and legal system policy allows us to believe that we have done something about domestic violence, but it is not clear what we have actually accomplished,[68] particularly for those women who are unwilling or unable to deploy the state against their partners.

Law does not, and cannot, meet all of the needs of women subjected to abuse. Social work professor Susan Schechter warned in 1982, "[L]egal solutions have not provided battered women with the economic and social resources—jobs, child care, housing, and safe communities—that they need to free themselves from dependence on violent men."[69] Women report that material services and supports (day care, housing, education, food banks, and job training, for example) are the most useful resources they are offered; civil legal assistance ranked near the bottom ("22 out of 24 possible services") in terms of perceived helpfulness of services.[70] In 2009, the National Network to End Domestic Violence surveyed 83 percent of the local domestic violence programs in the United States. That survey revealed that on a given day during that year, programs were unable to meet 9,280 requests for services; 60 percent of those requests were for emergency shelter or transitional housing. The report documented how the recession has stressed the safety net for women subjected to abuse and their families: "Food banks are empty, financial assistance is exhausted, and services such as mental health and housing assistance are no longer available." A Wisconsin advocate explained, "It used to be that nearly everyone who came to shelter was able to leave after 30 days. Now they are almost always going beyond 60 days. Survivors can't find affordable housing or jobs." Keeping women in shelter longer has a domino effect; the longer a woman stays, the longer it takes for a shelter bed to become available for another. Alternatives to shelter are few; an advocate in Oregon reported, "A caller asked me today if I knew of a safe bridge she could sleep under." Most of the women who contacted the programs lacked health insurance, forcing them to choose between remaining in abusive relationships and receiving necessary treatment. A Texas program, for example, has "a client who is battling breast cancer but her health insurance is covered through her abusive husband, and she's not eligible for free or low-cost health care. She feels trapped because without his medical insurance she'll die, but if she returns to him, she fears she'll die from the abuse instead."[71] It is hard to see why allocating billions of dollars to police, prosecutors, and courts should be the priority when women subjected to abuse sleep under bridges, cannot feed their children, and are forced to decide between death by abuse and death by cancer.

The legal system will never be a viable alternative for some women. The goals of the legal system do not match the goals of some women subjected to abuse. The system is unreceptive to some kinds of claims and some kinds of women. It cannot address all of the needs that keep women in abusive relationships. Alternatives to using the legal system must be available for women subjected to abuse. As law professor Renée Römkens writes, "Law can have a beneficial effect, but only for a limited number of women and at a considerable price."[72] There must be options for those women that the law cannot serve.

Developing non-legal alternatives for women subjected to abuse could actually improve the system for those women who choose to use it. Police and prosecutors complain that women subjected to abuse are uncooperative and change their stories, making it more difficult to successfully hold men who abuse accountable. Women who refuse to testify or recant on the witness stand anger judges. One judge described his practice in recantation cases: "[I]f the victim recants in court, she can then be held criminally liable for making a false filing. Typically, if I find a false statement was made, I will hold her to time served that he did on false charges—for example, if he did 2 days, so will she."[73] These frustrations lead police, prosecutors, and judges to stereotype women subjected to abuse as dishonest and not credible. If women had options beyond the legal system, the cases coming through the system would more likely be cases that women were committed to prosecuting. Rates of recantation and perjury would likely decrease, helping to change the perceptions of system actors about women subjected to abuse.

We should not turn our backs on the last 40 years of domestic violence legal system reform. Creating a legal framework was an essential step in developing a societal response to domestic violence and expanding the options available to women subjected to abuse. The existence of that framework has given women who seek to address abuse without state intervention a powerful tool as well; in his study of women's responses to abuse, sociologist Lee Bowker found that "[t]he most potent personal strategy used by the wives [who did not leave their relationships], threatening to contact the police or a lawyer, gained at least some of its potency by association with these powerful caretakers of social sanctions."[74] Simply because the law can reach a problem does not mean that the law should be the only mechanism used to address a problem, however. Women subjected to abuse need options beyond the law and the legal system.

Forty years into the legal revolution, the time for tinkering around the edges of the system has passed. As one anti-violence advocate noted, "What we [the anti-violence movement] asked for was 'police, police, police' and now that's what we have. There's no room for the community. There's no room for what the woman wants."[75] Feminists created this system; feminists must now undo the harm caused by the system that we created.[76] The theoretical underpinnings of the legal system must change to make the system work more effectively for women subjected to abuse. An anti-essentialist framework would produce a very different, and vastly more responsive, system.

A Reconstructed Legal System

The night of June 23, 2010, was cool and clear. Karen Anderson and her boyfriend, Corbin Jones, decided to open the windows to let the air into the apartment they shared with their son, Daniel, who was seven. Around 10:00 that evening, Corbin began teasing Karen about her Facebook use and insisted upon seeing her friends list. The playful teasing turned to an abusive outburst, however, when Corbin found that Karen's ex-boyfriend was among her many Facebook friends. Corbin berated Karen, calling her a slut and demanding to see all of the communications between Karen and her former partner. Karen refused and attempted to pull the computer away. Corbin grabbed the computer, slammed it to the ground, and screamed at Karen, "You fucking whore, I'll kill you before I let you make a fool of me with that asshole. You'll never see your son again." Karen tried to placate Corbin as he continued to rage and to throw and break plates, vases, and the porcelain figures Karen's mother had given her as a child. Karen begged Corbin to stop before someone called the police. Corbin responded that if Karen had him arrested, he would expose Karen's infidelity to the members of their church. Before long, there was a knock at the door. Karen opened the door to find two police officers, looking concerned. One officer escorted her outside of the apartment; the other remained in the apartment with Corbin.

So begins Karen's journey through the legal system. The account that follows is a worst-case scenario—at every turn, Karen's wishes will be thwarted and her appeals for assistance ignored. While it is certainly unlikely that her every contact with the legal system would unfold quite so badly, it is absolutely possible, and even probable, that any one or more of these interactions could play out just as they are described here. For a woman like Karen, who wants to control how the system intervenes in her relationship with her partner, what is about to happen is a nightmare.

Karen first asks why the police have come. The police tell her that a neighbor called after hearing the shouting from the apartment. Karen tells the police what has happened: that she and Corbin were arguing about her ex-boyfriend, that Corbin threatened to kill her, and that he destroyed the property in the apartment. She also tells the police, however, that she does not want to press charges. Corbin and Karen have been together for nine years. Although he is occasionally verbally abusive, he has never been physically abusive. Karen does not believe that he will harm her physically. Karen cannot afford to keep the apartment without Corbin's income, and she believes that it is important for Daniel to have his father in the home. The police explain that notwithstanding her wishes, they are required to arrest if they have probable cause to believe that an act of domestic violence has occurred. Corbin's threat to kill and his destruction of property qualify as such acts. The police address her economic concerns by counseling Karen to seek a civil protection order to secure child support from Corbin. They also tell Karen that they must conduct a danger assessment with her. Karen responds that she wants to check on Daniel and is not interested in talking with the police further. The police insist, citing the department's policy of reviewing every domestic violence case for future risk. The police ask her a series of questions about prior incidents of abuse, Corbin's jealousy, his use of drugs and alcohol, his access to weapons, his threats to kill her and Daniel, and whether Corbin has ever been suicidal. Based on the information Karen provides, particularly as to Corbin's jealousy and threats to kill her and Daniel, the police advise Karen that she is at serious risk of further abuse, possibly life-threatening abuse, and tell her that she must speak to a domestic violence counselor. When Karen explains that she is not interested in seeking any assistance, the police pressure her to talk with the counselor. The counselor reiterates what the police have said about the potential danger to her and Daniel. Karen believes that they are mistaken, but tells the counselor and the police that she will seek a civil protection order. Corbin is arrested and taken to central booking. The police cannot tell her when he will be arraigned.

The next day, with Daniel in tow, Karen goes to the courthouse to file for a civil protection order. She fills out the petition and is led to the courtroom, where ten other women are waiting to be heard. Karen tries to keep the fidgety Daniel quiet. The bailiffs glare at her when Daniel asks, a little too loudly, for a snack. Finally, Karen's case is called. The judge, without looking up from the file, asks Karen why she is there. Karen responds, "The police told me to come so that I could get child support." The judge snaps, "We don't do that here. If you need child support, file a child support case. It says that you were threatened. What did he say?" Karen repeats Corbin's threat to kill her and Daniel as well as his threat to expose her to their church. "Are you afraid he's going to hurt you?" the judge responds. "No," says Karen, "I can take care of myself." "Well, under our law, you've got to show me fear of bodily harm. If you're not afraid of him, then you don't have grounds for a protective order," the judge tells Karen and dismisses her petition.

Karen is back in court the following day for Corbin's arraignment. Bail and conditions of release are set. One of the conditions of release is the entry of a criminal protective order barring Corbin from any contact with Karen or Daniel pending trial. No one asks Karen if these conditions are acceptable to her or whether she wants the order entered. Despite the criminal protective order, Corbin calls Karen that night, asking her to let him come home. Karen agrees, and Corbin's defense attorney arranges for all of them to return to court to have the criminal protective order lifted. Over the objections of the state's attorney, the judge asks to speak with Karen. The judge asks Karen whether she is afraid of Corbin or has concerns about him being around Daniel. Karen answers that she is not afraid and that she wants to make her relationship work. The judge is skeptical of Karen's claim that she is not afraid of Corbin and asks whether anyone has pressured or coerced her into asking that the protective order be rescinded. Karen denies any pressure or coercion. The judge threatens to report her to child protective services for failing to protect Daniel from exposure to abuse if any further incidents of violence occur, and tells her that she would be better off keeping her distance from Corbin and his violent temper. The judge refuses to rescind the protective order based on his concerns about Daniel's well-being.

Several weeks later, Karen is struggling financially and emotionally. Daniel has been acting out, screaming for his father and fighting with Karen. Karen fears that she will lose her apartment if Corbin is incarcerated. Checking the mail after work, Karen finds a subpoena for her to appear at Corbin's trial for misdemeanor domestic violence. Karen calls the prosecutor and explains that she does not want to testify at the trial. She asks the prosecutor to dismiss the case. The prosecutor refuses, citing the office's no-drop prosecution policy. Karen is told that if she refuses to come to court, a warrant will be issued for her arrest. Faced with the prospect of jail, Karen reluctantly agrees to appear. She testifies for the prosecution, but is not forthcoming in her testimony. She does not repeat Corbin's threat to kill her and Daniel and tells the prosecutor that the destroyed items documented by the police were broken accidentally. The judge admonishes Karen that her prior sworn statement to police is inconsistent with her testimony and warns her that she could be prosecuted for perjury or making false statements if she fails to tell the truth on the stand. Again, fearing for Daniel's stability and her own freedom, she eventually testifies to what happened on the night of June 23. Corbin is convicted of misdemeanor domestic violence.

The story could develop in a number of different ways from this point, all equally bad for Karen. Corbin is incarcerated, leaving Karen with an apartment she cannot afford, an angry child, and no financial or emotional support. Corbin, an Irish citizen in the United States without documentation, is deported after serving his jail sentence. Or, more likely, Corbin is not incarcerated and is furious with Karen for seeking a protective order and cooperating with prosecutors. Corbin's abuse increases and intensifies after their separation. Corbin files for custody of Daniel, accusing Karen of being financially incapable of caring for the child and using Daniel's out of control behavior during Corbin's absence from the home as proof that Karen is not a fit parent. Karen asks whether she can avoid yet another court appearance by negotiating with Corbin. She believes that they can come to some agreement about Daniel's care if she can talk to him, and she cannot afford to take additional time away from work. Karen is told that the court will not permit the case to be mediated given Corbin's conviction for domestic violence. Karen asks her lawyer whether she and Corbin can share custody of Daniel. Her lawyer tells her that joint custody is not appropriate in cases involving domestic violence and strongly advises her against seeking such an arrangement. Fearing that her lawyer will not represent her if she continues to press for joint custody, Karen does not raise the issue again. During the custody trial, Karen is stoic and unemotional. Corbin makes good on his threat to report her friendship with her ex-boyfriend to the church; members of the church come to testify on Corbin's behalf. The judge questions Karen's credibility. She appears particularly skeptical about the post-separation incidents of domestic violence Karen reluctantly describes, asking why Karen has not called the police and why she recanted at trial. The judge cites concerns about Karen's stability and truthfulness in her ruling that Corbin, despite his domestic violence conviction, should have custody of Daniel.

At every point in the legal system's process, Karen is deprived of choice. Her perceptions of the threat to her are disregarded. Her preferences for addressing Corbin's abuse are ignored. Her experiences are assessed under a narrow and static definition of abuse, one that deprives her of the opportunity to explain how Corbin's abuse affected her. The legal system's interventions, intended to safeguard her or to hold Corbin accountable, only make Karen less safe and less stable. Again, this is a worst case rendering of one woman's experiences with the legal system. Sociologist Neil Websdale notes that some women have positive experiences with police and prosecutors, warning, "We discount the stories of these women at our peril. If we write off these apparently 'good' experiences as mere 'false consciousness,' we perpetuate that patriarchal style of reasoning that discounts the voices of the subordinate."[1] But variations on Karen's story are playing out every day in the current legal system. The harm the legal system causes cannot be ignored.

An Anti-Essentialist Retelling

How could Karen's story unfold in an anti-essentialist legal system? When the police arrive at Karen's apartment, their mandate would be different: after investigating the neighbor's complaint to determine whether domestic violence was, in fact, occurring, the police would be required to consult with Karen to determine whether she wants Corbin arrested. This consultation would take place out of Corbin's hearing, in a space where Karen could safely share her concerns with police and receive counseling about her options. That discussion could include a description of the police arrest procedure, how long Karen could expect Corbin to be out of the home until his arrest is processed, and the demands that will be placed on Karen if she chooses to have Corbin arrested. The goal of the intervention would be to help Karen come to an informed decision about whether arrest is a good choice for her on this occasion. The police would assure Karen that her decision not to ask for Corbin's arrest this time will not preclude her from having the option of contacting police and seeking his arrest should Corbin's abuse resume.

The police would also offer Karen the option of participating in a danger assessment, explaining that while there is not conclusive social science evidence establishing that danger assessments are a valid predictor of future violence, the assessment might give her a better sense of the common risk factors for future danger and where she scores relative to other women who have been screened. If Karen declines the danger assessment, the police would not pursue it further. If Karen engages in the danger assessment, the police would offer her the option of speaking with a counselor, stressing that participation in the program is voluntary and that she is not expected to seek services or take any particular action as a result of the conversation. Again, if Karen decides not to speak with the counselor, the police would offer her information to be used at another time, but would not require that she take that information. The police could also advise Karen to seek a protective order, explaining that the basis for granting a protective order is Karen's experience of abuse, which she would have to describe to a judge before receiving the order. Only if a judge finds that abuse has occurred, the police would explain, would she be able to seek other remedies, like custody and child support.

Reinstating a permissive arrest regime will not return the legal system to the bad old days of unfettered police discretion, when all power resided in the hands of police and police declined to intervene in family matters. That impetus to refrain from intervention sprung from a desire to protect family privacy and men's patriarchal entitlements to govern their families as they saw fit. An anti-essentialist arrest policy instead grows from a determination to empower women subjected to abuse. It places the power in the hands of individual women to decide whether they want police to intervene, a radically different proposition. The police serve as consultants in an educational and counseling process designed to help women make informed decisions about arrest. But the ultimate decision maker is the person with the most at stake and the most knowledge about her risk and what she hopes to achieve through the choice she makes about arrest—the woman subjected to abuse. The police arrest if, but only if, the woman wants them to arrest.

Assume that Karen chooses to pursue a protective order. The protective order statute provides relief for acts of abuse; the definition of abuse would now include coercion, defined as any threatened or intentional action or course of action that materially limits the petitioner's ability to exercise her liberty or autonomy. In addition to determining whether Corbin's actions fell under a preexisting category of crime, like assault, the judge would scrutinize Karen's allegations to determine whether Karen experienced a loss of freedom as a result of Corbin's actions. The judge would make that determination by listening to Karen's story and probing the impact of Corbin's actions on her to ascertain whether Corbin's threats and violence prevented Karen from exercising her ability to continue a friendship with a former partner, to use her computer, to safely remain in her home. Because doctrines like battered woman syndrome will have been removed from state law, judicial expectations about appropriate victim behavior and responses to abuse will be less likely to color how judges view women subjected to abuse. The judge in Karen's case would no longer necessarily expect to find that Karen is afraid of Corbin; nor would he be legally required to find that fear existed, because fear of harm would not be the applicable standard. Instead, the judge could find that Karen's freedom was limited when Corbin intentionally damaged her computer and other property and threatened her life and her son's life, whether she feared Corbin would physically harm her or not.

The judge would also be permitted and encouraged to probe how Karen's identity affected her experiences on the night of June 23, given this new definition of abuse. What the judge might learn in Karen's case, for example, is that the threat to expose her to the members of her church would have been sufficient to entrap her in her relationship with Corbin. Karen relies on the members of the church for social and emotional support, and a great deal of her social life is conducted through the church. Karen credits the church with having saved her life during a particularly difficult time and cannot imagine living outside of its ambit. Karen's church deals strictly with allegations of infidelity, and Karen fears that, although she has done nothing wrong, some church members might agree with Corbin that her contact with a former partner was inappropriate and sufficient cause to cast her out of the community. For Karen, Corbin's threat to accuse her of infidelity was more credible, and more abusive, than his threat to kill. In a system that treats coercion seriously, and looks not at what the abuser intended but how the woman subjected to abuse was affected, Karen's perception of Corbin's threat, and the impact of that threat on her behavior, would be sufficient to justify the issuance of a protective order. That order could contain any number of provisions, but would allow her the option of continuing her relationship or contact with Corbin while under its protection, an option that is forbidden by law in at least one state and as a matter of judicial practice in many others.[2]

The interchange about the entry of a criminal protective order at Corbin's arraignment would be very different in an anti-essentialist system. Prior to the arraignment, the prosecutor, or a victim advocate from the prosecutor's office, would have spoken with Karen about her desire to have such an order entered. The prosecutor's office would explain why an order might be beneficial to Karen and what the drawbacks would be. They would discuss the terms that the order could contain and decide which, if any, of those terms were acceptable to Karen. After their discussion, the prosecutor might seek an order that simply barred Corbin from re-abusing Karen pending trial, allowing him to remain in their apartment. In the alternative, the prosecutor might have sought to address Karen's concerns about Daniel's contact with his father and Karen's financial issues by requesting provisions governing visitation and support in Corbin's conditions of release. The prosecutor would not, however, act on the assumption that separation was best for Karen by unilaterally deciding to request the imposition of a criminal protective order or by seeking such an order over Karen's objections. A similar conversation with the state would take place prior to the request to rescind the criminal protective order. The state would not object to vacating the order if, after that conversation, Karen still wanted to go forward.

The judge's decision about rescinding the protective order would be reached differently as well. The judge would understand that separation is not necessarily the best option for every woman subjected to abuse. In lieu of assuming that Karen should be kept separate from Corbin for her own good and for Daniel's, the judge could probe the reasons for Karen's request that the order be vacated and Karen's assessment of the danger posed by Corbin's return to the home. The judge would consider how removing Corbin from the home could harm Karen and Daniel as well as any potential benefit removal might offer. The judge would credit Karen's assertion that her decision was not coerced. Rather than warning Karen, "You can't just open the door to the state, getting the state involved, and then think that you can shut it at any time,"[3] the judge would honor Karen's decision to use prosecution instrumentally and facilitate her request. Again, judges in an anti-essentialist framework would not simply be returning to the minimally interventionist stance that existed before the battered women's movement. Instead, they would be honoring a woman's right to self-determination and her knowledge of her needs, goals, and priorities by placing the power in her hands to make decisions about how the state should intervene.

Prior to making the decision to proceed with prosecution, a representative of the state would contact Karen to determine whether she was still interested in pursuing the case. What prosecution would require of Karen, the prosecutor's assessment of the likelihood of conviction, and the sentence Corbin could receive if convicted would be discussed. Sociologist David Ford's research suggesting that women use prosecution instrumentally for purposes other than incarceration of their partners would inform that conversation, as Karen and the prosecutor confer about what Karen hopes to achieve through prosecution. Ideally, Karen would decide whether prosecution should proceed; if her goals diverged from the state's goal of offender accountability, Karen's desire would trump. Placing the decision in Karen's hands does not, as some have argued, simply cede the power to prosecute to Corbin. Instead, it recognizes that Karen may have strong reasons for deciding not to seek state intervention and places some faith in her ability to make that determination for herself, although the basis for that decision may not be transparent to prosecutors. Giving Karen the power to decide whether prosecution should proceed enables her to weigh the benefits of prosecution against any concerns she may have about Corbin being deported, the loss of his income, the impact of his conviction on Daniel, her concern about state intervention into her community, and her desire to make her relationship with Corbin work. Karen would retain the option to prosecute any future abusive incident and is more likely to do so if her choices are honored; depriving women of the power to make such decisions may deter them from seeking state intervention following recidivist episodes of abuse.[4] Even if, however, prosecutors decide to pursue the matter without Karen's cooperation, in no event would prosecutors subpoena or otherwise coerce Karen to testify against Corbin. Moreover, services like crime victim compensation monies, which are currently denied to those who refuse to seek or cooperate with state intervention against their abusive partners in some states, would be available to Karen regardless of whether she assisted law enforcement or prosecutors.

If Karen chooses to prosecute, the state would proceed against Corbin for committing the crime of coercive control. Prosecutors would seek to prove that Corbin intentionally engaged in or threatened a course of conduct that operated to materially deprive Karen of her liberty, freedom, or autonomy. Sociologist Evan Stark has argued that casting coercive control as a violation of liberty "links broad social inequities to individual acts of victimization; explains why obstructing, monitoring, regulating, and exploiting women's personal activities constitute discrimination; and shows how these acts compromise women's personhood and their rights as citizens."[5] The standard for determining whether Karen had, in fact, suffered such a deprivation would be an individualized objective standard, assessing whether a reasonable person standing in Karen's shoes, with Karen's intersecting identities, would have experienced Corbin's abuse as a denial of freedom or autonomy.

An anti-essentialist system would ensure that Corbin was treated equitably in the legal process—which would not only honor his personhood, but might also keep Karen safer. Men who abuse their partners are less likely to commit subsequent violence when they believe that they have been treated fairly by state actors. Being attentive to men when they tell their side of the story and treating them with dignity and respect, the research suggests, can have "important crime-reduction effects." In fact, the perception of fair treatment may be "as important as the substantive outcomes [men] eventually experience."[6] From initial investigation through trial, then, an anti-essentialist system would treat men who abuse not as monsters, but as individuals whose stories must be heard before any decision can be rendered. Men who abuse should receive full due process and fair and respectful treatment by the courts, regardless of what they are alleged to have done.[7]

Allowing for a jury trial option in civil protection hearings, law professor Melissa Breger has suggested, might provide a form of procedural justice. Juries may be perceived as less biased than judges, who may have multiple contacts with families involved in domestic violence cases. Additionally, Breger argues, when litigants are able to choose their finders of fact, they may be more likely to accept the outcome of the proceedings, increasing compliance with court orders.[8]

The legal system should see men who abuse not as a monolith, but as individuals whose behavior could potentially change if approached correctly. If Corbin is convicted, such individualized treatment would mean seeking an appropriate sanction for his behavior. Using the available social science research, pre-sentencing investigators might attempt to determine which type of batterer intervention program (if any) might best serve Corbin and what might motivate Corbin to change his behavior. If, like some men, Corbin could be motivated to change his behavior toward Karen by understanding the impact of his violence on his son, sentencing options could include conditioning visitation upon successful completion of an appropriate program, one that includes a responsible fatherhood component.

In lieu of traditional prosecution, Karen might opt to use restorative justice methods. Law professor Quince Hopkins and public health experts Mary Koss and Karen Bachar define restorative justice as "a philosophy that places emphasis on repairing harm, empowering a victim-driven process, and transforming the community's role in addressing crime. It approaches offender accountability through making reparations and undergoing rehabilitation rather than punishment."[9] Commonly used restorative justice practices include victim-offender mediation, which involves a face-to-face meeting facilitated by a trained mediator, intended to empower victims, hold offenders accountable, and determine reparations; conferencing, which brings together family members, friends, service providers, and other stakeholders to achieve the same goals; and circles, including peacemaking circles, sentencing circles, and what law professor Linda Mills calls "intimate abuse circles," again intended to engage the community in empowering victims and holding offenders accountable. Restorative justice practices occur both within and outside of state systems, and cooperation with the criminal system, particularly in ensuring offender accountability, is common.

Restorative justice has the potential to increase victim participation, voice, and validation, which could help to restore the victim to her place within the community. Increasing victim voice and the victim's role within the process may also help to right power imbalances between the victim and offender. As restorative justice practitioner Kay Pranis explains, "Listening respectfully to someone's story is a way of giving them power—a positive kind of power. . . . Listening respectfully to a person's story gives that person dignity and worth."[10] Restorative justice encourages offenders to admit guilt, prompting them to take greater responsibility for their actions, and, in turn, making the community more likely to welcome the offender back. Being involved in a practice that encourages offender participation also increases the likelihood that the offender will perceive it as just and, as a result, make him more likely to comply with any sanction. Including the community in seeking solutions could disrupt social support for abuse and expand the community response.

For women subjected to abuse, restorative justice provides an alternative to the separation-based focus of the traditional criminal justice system, allowing for relationship repair in those cases where the woman seeks reconciliation. Community-based solutions can allow both victims and offenders to avoid the racism of the criminal justice system and, for women subjected to abuse, sidestep the coercion of the criminal justice system's response to domestic violence. Restorative justice practices may make material resources, in the form of reparations and other community supports, more available to women subjected to abuse.

Research has found high levels of victim satisfaction with restorative justice practices. Victims who participate in restorative justice programs report decreased levels of fear and anxiety and positive effects on victim dignity, self-respect, and self-confidence. The few studies examining the use of restorative justice in domestic violence cases report that women felt empowered and satisfied, although the impact on men was limited.[11] Restorative justice may be an alternative to what some see as an ineffectual criminal justice system. As sociologist Lawrence Sherman points out, "Since there is no evidence that standard justice is any more effective than doing nothing in response to an incident of domestic violence, the only challenge to restorative justice is to do better than doing nothing."[12]

Notwithstanding these potential benefits, advocates for women subjected to abuse have been wary of restorative justice practices, fearing that restorative justice is unsafe and subject to manipulation by offenders. Restorative justice's focus on forgiveness may prompt women to take some responsibility for their partner's abuse, prevent women from being permitted to express anger, and encourage reconciliation in relationships that cannot be safely resumed. Restorative justice practices, critics argue, provide little impetus for offenders to change their behavior; some believe that they are too lenient or amount to nothing more than a form of "cheap justice."[13] Detractors believe that women will be coerced into participating and into agreeing to resolutions that may be harmful. Community participants, like family and friends, may have mixed loyalties, preventing them from acting to protect women from further abuse. Communities may not condemn abuse, decreasing their ability to provide accountability, or may not have the resources to support women. Cultural context may make restorative justice inappropriate or ineffective. Law professor Rashmi Goel, for example, argues that the Indian feminine ideal of self-sacrifice, which prompts women to place the needs of their husbands and communities before their own, renders restorative justice useless in cases involving Indian women subjected to abuse.[14] Restorative justice practices are seen as a form of reprivatization of abuse, threatening the gains made by the battered women's movement to bring abuse into the public sphere. Despite the shared principles of the battered women's and restorative justice movements—the interests in restoring victims of crime and preventing recidivism among offenders, promoting the community's role in crime prevention, and addressing the social context of crime[15]—the battered women's movement has been overwhelmingly opposed to the use of restorative justice practices.

That opposition is tempered, however, when restorative justice projects are created and run by feminists attentive to the needs of women subjected to abuse. The RESTORE project, for example, facilitates post-arrest, pre-conviction community conferences involving women who have been raped or sexually assaulted, their community support networks, the alleged offenders, and their support networks. In these conferences, women describe the event that precipitated prosecution and the harm that act caused to them and to their relationships with others. Offenders acknowledge the wrongs committed and harms done. Supporters for both women and alleged offenders describe how they have been affected by the abuse. All participants work together to develop a "redress agreement" detailing what the alleged offender will do to right the wrong both for the woman and for the wider community. A Community Accountability and Reintegration Board monitors compliance with the agreement. Charges are dropped if the agreement is successfully completed; if not, the case is referred back to the prosecutor.[16]

Social work professor Joan Pennell has created two feminist restorative justice projects addressing family violence: The Family Group Decisionmaking Project (FGDMP) in Canada, and safety conferencing, in conjunction with advocacy groups for women subjected to abuse, in North Carolina. FGDMP brought families involved with the child welfare system together to develop plans to address partner and child abuse within the family. An evaluation of FGDMP found that no violence occurred during the conferences and that partner and child abuse—both physical and emotional—decreased significantly post-conference.[17] Safety conferencing brings women subjected to abuse and their supporters together to develop safety plans for women; conferences can involve women's partners if the women so desire.

Feminist restorative justice projects put power into the hands of women subjected to abuse: the power to determine whether a matter is appropriate for restorative justice, to confront her partner, to be heard and validated, to have her partner admit responsibility for his actions, to choose participants in conferencing and circles, to develop a plan going forward, to recommend a sentence. They are woman-centered, deployed only at the behest of the woman subjected to abuse and only in ways that she approves. They address the desire that women have for community acknowledgment and denunciation of the abuse they experience. They focus on women's needs for reintegration into their communities after abuse, community sanction of abuse, and material support. They create options beyond the traditional legal system for women who fear the system's racism and coercion and reject the system's emphasis on separation.

These are the kinds of restorative justice projects that an anti-essentialist feminist legal system would house—projects that law professor Donna Coker might call "transformative" rather than "restorative." Transformative justice projects create communities that support women's autonomy, and while the reintegration of the man who abuses is a goal, it is secondary to enhancing his partner's autonomy. Transformative justice projects are open to considering how oppression in a man's life relates to his abuse, but do not excuse his actions as caused by economics, racism, substance abuse, child abuse, or other conditions of oppression. Transformative justice programs are attentive to cultural context; transformative justice, Coker writes, "helps women build a community that supports women's autonomy without forcing women to choose between their ethnic/racial communities and safety."[18]

A transformative justice project might give Karen and Corbin the opportunity to engage in victim-offender mediation, enabling Karen to tell Corbin how his abuse affected her and Daniel, to have Corbin take responsibility for his actions, and to collaboratively develop an agreement to repair the damage Corbin has done. Through safety conferencing, Karen could work with supporters, including members of her church, and service providers to develop a plan to safeguard herself and Daniel, incorporating Corbin only if it addressed her goals for the conference. She might have input into Corbin's sentence through a sentencing circle, preventing him from being incarcerated and, as a result, losing his income and influence on Daniel.

Making restorative or transformative justice practices available in cases involving domestic violence is not necessarily an either/or choice. Restorative justice practices can run parallel to criminal justice interventions, providing another option for women subjected to abuse. Law professor Laurie Kohn has suggested that restorative justice could provide an alternative to the civil justice system as well. Women seeking protective orders, or those whose abuse does not yet meet the standard for receiving a protective order, could opt instead to engage in conferences with their partners. Those conferences would involve members of the community and be fashioned around the woman's goals and concerns. A broad range of remedies, some of which the court cannot award through protective orders, would be available to women through the resolution process. The offender's resolutions could be enforceable by court order, but judges would not be empowered to modify agreements reached in the conferences.[19]

That restorative justice may not be well suited to the needs of some women does not justify rejecting it out of hand. Restorative justice is simply another option for women who want some level of state involvement without the trappings and intrusion of the traditional justice system. An anti-essentialist system would offer that option.

Karen's custody case would also play out differently in an anti-essentialist system. Karen might choose to engage in a collaborative law process, where she and Corbin and their lawyers would work together to attempt to come up with a viable custody agreement. Although collaborative law advocates have generally been unwilling to use the process in cases involving domestic violence, for many of the same reasons offered by opponents of mediation, the collaborative law process should be available to Karen so long as her informed consent is obtained.[20] Mediation would also be available to Karen, at her discretion. Court systems would permit women subjected to abuse to opt out of mediation, but would also provide mediation for any woman who wanted it, regardless of a history of domestic violence. Mediators trained in domestic violence and committed to facilitating autonomous decision making by women subjected to abuse would be available to mediate Karen and Corbin's custody case. Mediators would discuss any concerns that Karen had about engaging in mediation with her prior to the first session and would tailor the mediation to address those concerns. Mediation between Karen and Corbin could take a number of forms: face-to-face discussions facilitated by a mediator, with or without lawyers present, at Karen's request; relay mediation, in which the parties would remain in separate rooms throughout the proceedings, with the mediator shuttling between Karen and Corbin but not requiring them to speak directly; or mediation through counsel, with Karen available to provide feedback to her attorney as options are suggested. Mediation could even take place online, conducted via methods ranging from emails and chat sessions to video conferencing, with a neutral third party able to reinforce the ground rules for mediation and block inappropriate, threatening, or abusive exchanges.[21] Mediation could involve Daniel as well;

social work professor Amanda Hart has suggested that involving children in mediation gives children a voice in deciding the family's future, something children very much desire, and can enhance their coping capacity.[22] Hart calls the exclusion of children from decision making "the oppression of children . . . not the protection of children."[23]

Joint custody would be one of Karen's options. Some mothers subjected to abuse want to co-parent children post-separation.[24] In an anti-essentialist system, mothers would be free to seek such arrangements, understanding that courts would have to find that those arrangements are in their children's best interests. In this case, if Karen believes that co-parenting Daniel will defuse some of the tension created by the state's intervention and benefit Daniel by keeping his father actively involved in his life, joint custody might be an option that might benefit her and make Daniel happier. Despite common concerns about the level of interaction required to successfully share decision-making authority, Karen might seek joint legal custody of Daniel (recognizing that many of the major decisions in Daniel's life, including religion and education, have already been made, decreasing the opportunities for conflict) or offer to share physical custody of Daniel, enabling her to increase her hours at work to better support them both. Joint custody would not be presumed in an anti-essentialist system, but neither would it be foreclosed as an option.

If the custody case proceeds to trial, Karen's stoicism and lack of emotion—her failure to present as a stereotypical victim—would not undermine her credibility. The judge would recognize that Karen's decision not to involve the police further in her dealings with Corbin neither proves nor disproves her allegations of separation-related violence and would probe those allegations fully and uncritically. Understanding coercive control, the judge would recognize that Corbin's allegations of infidelity and his use of witnesses from their church are still operating to control Karen's behavior.

An anti-essentialist system would have more realistic expectations of mothers subjected to abuse. Such a system would not hold mothers responsible for "exposing" their children to domestic violence by virtue of having been abused by their partners. But an anti-essentialist system would not assume that women subjected to abuse are perfect mothers, either. Stereotypes pitting blameless victims against monstrous abusers have operated to create judicial expectations that mothering by women subjected to abuse will be above reproach. The failure of women subjected to abuse to live up to these unrealistic standards has had disastrous consequences for those women whose mothering simply does not measure up. Statutory presumptions against awarding custody to men who abuse their partners have been overcome on the trial court level by evidence that mothers suffered from low self-esteem and eating disorders, had used drugs in the past, or smoked around their children.[25] Research by the Wellesley Centers for Women found that mothers subjected to abuse are held to higher parenting standards than their partners; as Janice, a mother in Massachusetts, told the Battered Mothers' Testimony Project,

> I had to prove myself all those years. He was just, you know, the perfect dad. The judge had no concerns over him. And it's like, they wanted me to do so many things, they wanted me to go to school, they wanted me to do this and that, but they weren't asking him to do anything.[26]

Some women subjected to abuse are simply not good mothers, because of what they have suffered or for some other reason. An anti-essentialist system would weigh the impact of domestic violence on children, assess responsibility for any damage caused as a result of that exposure, and factor that assessment into its determination of the child's best interests, without imposing unreasonable standards or expectations on mothers subjected to abuse.

Statutory presumptions against awarding custody to perpetrators of domestic violence assume that all men who abuse their partners are necessarily bad fathers, absent evidence to the contrary. Batterer's counselor Lundy Bancroft and psychologist Jay Silverman make this argument in their book, *The Batterer as Parent*, documenting the parental failings common to men who abuse their partners: authoritarianism, underinvolvement, neglect, and irresponsibility; undermining of the mother, both overtly and through his use of violence against her; self-centeredness; manipulativeness.[27] While some men who abuse their partners may, in fact, exhibit just such behaviors, painting all fathers with the same brush is problematic in an anti-essentialist system. Instead of presuming that domestic violence renders a father unfit to parent, a judge would ask how this man's behavior in this family affected the children, not only directly but also in terms of the mother's freedom to function as a parent. In this case, Corbin's violence, and the consequences of that violence (Corbin's exclusion from the home), created Karen's difficulty in handling Daniel. Karen's inability to control Daniel would not be considered a parenting deficit on her part, but a result of Corbin's actions that hampered Karen's ability to parent effectively.

Karen might be dissuaded from seeking a protective order or custody judgment by the prospect of multiple court appearances requiring her to take time away from work or by the thought of describing Corbin's abuse in front of a crowded courtroom. Wealthy individuals in some jurisdictions use private judging as an alternative to overcrowded public adjudication systems with lengthy backlogs and delays. Private judges are often (in some states, by law) former judges who hear the parties' arguments and make binding rulings. In states like California and Colorado, private judges are subject to the same rules of evidence and procedure as public judges and are bound by state case law and statutes. Private judges can make quicker rulings in more confidential settings than public judges and can accommodate the scheduling concerns of the parties.

Private judging can cost hundreds of dollars per hour, making it inaccessible to most litigants. But just as retired judges serve as private judges for pay, they could also serve as private judges pro bono. Partnering with battered women's organizations, private judges could offer their services in protective order and custody proceedings, sparing women like Karen the necessity of multiple trips to public courts and public airings of the intimate details of their lives. Organizations could research judges' records on domestic violence cases or engage them in training before providing them as a resource to the community to ensure that only judges with an understanding of domestic violence are being utilized. Karen would be less likely to encounter skepticism about her claims of abuse and less likely to lose her job as a result of repeated returns to court. Because private judicial decisions are binding and enforceable through public courts, the use of private judges provides women subjected to abuse with an option that enables them to keep some parts of the legal process private without forfeiting the power of the state. While some will argue that privatizing any aspect of domestic violence law risks a return to the days when domestic violence was considered a private matter, private judging maintains state involvement in adjudicating cases of domestic violence, albeit in a different setting. Private judging blends the needs of women subjected to abuse for flexibility, privacy, and expedited decision making with the invocation of state power on their behalf.

Karen would be able to look to other parts of the legal system for relief as well. If Corbin had resources, Karen might bring an action against him for intentional infliction of emotional distress. For a remedy more closely tailored to the harm Karen has suffered, states could create a tort of coercive control, awarding damages for loss of liberty or autonomy proximately caused by a partner's intentional or threatened actions. Such a tort would enable Karen to allege harms based on Corbin's threats of physical harm as well as his destruction of property and threats to denounce her as an adulterer. To protect herself in the future, Karen might be able to contract with

Corbin, establishing new terms for their relationship through a private but enforceable agreement that might give her greater financial leverage.

The description of how Karen's case would proceed in an anti-essentialist system admittedly replaces a worst-case scenario with an ideal one. Certainly, an anti-essentialist system would put more power in the hands of women subjected to abuse, avoid the stereotypes that permeate the current system, eliminate policies that assume what is best for women, be attentive to the individual characteristics of both women subjected to abuse and men who abuse, and consider how those characteristics affect their experiences with abuse and with the legal system. Nonetheless, it is extremely unlikely that a case would move this seamlessly through even an anti-essentialist legal system. Police, prosecutors, and judges would still be influenced (as we all are) by their biases and would still require training to understand concepts like coercive control and processes for maximizing women's freedom. That training might not reap all of the desired results, as has been true of the judicial and law enforcement training conducted over the last 40 years. Courts would still be flooded with cases. The overburdened system would still have little time to spend on the stories of individual women subjected to abuse. Judicial demeanor would still vary widely. Women subjected to abuse would still be exposed to the judges that sociologist James Ptacek labels "bureaucratic," "harsh," and "condescending."[28] Experiencing those styles of judging might weigh more than any change in law or policy on a woman's willingness to engage the system. Women would still need representation to ensure that their stories were fully told. Lawyers for women subjected to abuse might still be in short supply, even if VAWA funds were diverted from criminal interventions to civil legal solutions. An anti-essentialist framework is more likely to create a system that protects women's individuality and autonomy and treats men and women with dignity and respect. But, anthropologist Mindie Lazarus-Black notes, "when domestic violence survivors choose to pursue rights and protections offered by domestic violence law, they face significant obstacles intrinsic to law and the legal process itself. Law is literal and it is unforgiving."[29] Those intrinsic obstacles will continue to exist, regardless of the theoretical orientation of the system, making it ill-suited to meet the goals and objectives of some women subjected to abuse. Even if cases did move this perfectly through the system, the legal system still could not provide some of what women subjected to abuse need: long-term economic stability, fundamental changes in men who abuse their partners, and a society that rejects domestic violence. For that reason, anti-essentialist domestic violence law and policy must create options outside of the legal system as well.

Beyond the Law

Reconstructing the legal response to domestic violence will make the legal system a more viable alternative for many women. For other women, however, redress from within the justice system will continue to prove elusive, because the justice system cannot provide them with what they need or because they are unwilling to invite state intervention into their lives. Those women need a remedy beyond the law. Justice beyond the justice system, economic stability, meaningful engagement with men who abuse their partners, and community accountability: these are the central elements of the extra-legal anti-essentialist system.

Finding Justice Beyond the Justice System

"For your own peace of mind, be prepared to throw any illusions about 'justice' you might have had out the window," abuse survivor Mary Walsh warned other women considering criminal prosecution of their partners.[1] What does justice mean to women subjected to abuse? For some, justice is criminal punishment, a goal well suited to the retributive criminal justice system. But other women define justice differently. Psychiatrist Judith Herman found that women subjected to abuse often equate justice with validation (from families and communities of their abuse and the harm caused by that abuse) and vindication (through the community's condemnation of the abuse).[2] Punishment is not as important to some women as the ability to reclaim their places within the community and to heal relationships within the community that were damaged by the abuse. Justice may also mean breaking free of the continued emotional hold that their partners have over their lives, even after the abuse has ended. Law professor Brenda Smith asked her mother how she could forgive her father for years of serious physical and sexual abuse. Her mother replied, "I forgave . . . for me and for you. I could not continue to hold on to my anger . . . and do what I needed to do for myself or for you."[3] This "state of mind in which the offender and his offense no longer dominated their thoughts. . . . this very limited sense of letting go of resentment and moving on with life,"[4] can be called forgiveness. Forgiveness returns power to women subjected to abuse. Forgiveness can also create accountability, argues Smith, by focusing on the offender's conduct, not on the offender as a person. This narrow conception of forgiveness can be a form of justice. An anti-essentialist system would help women achieve validation, vindication, and forgiveness without state intervention. Such a system would enable women to define what justice means for them and provide a variety of avenues to help them achieve it.

Restorative (or transformative) justice practices, for example, can be accessed without state intervention and might provide a pathway to justice for some women. Hillsboro, Oregon's Domestic Violence Surrogate Dialogue program allows women subjected to abuse to seek validation, vindication, and forgiveness by engaging with men who abuse—but not the men who abused them. The program pairs women subjected to abuse with men in prison who have accepted responsibility for the abuse they perpetrated against their partners and are involved in batterer intervention counseling. The program seeks to foster understanding between women subjected to abuse and men who abuse their partners, give women an outlet for their anger, and enhance women's understanding of men who abuse. The program also hopes to build empathy in men who abuse their partners, allowing them to understand the impact of their actions from the perspective of women subjected to abuse. Women involved in the dialogues have reported empowerment, increased healing, and satisfaction from the sense that they have claimed voice not only for themselves, but also on behalf of the men's partners.[5] Men involved with the program report that the dialogues allow them to hear what they could not hear from their own partners—how destructive their behaviors were and how much courage it took for women to recover from abuse. The men found it humbling to reexamine their actions in light of the dialogues.[6]

Community-based truth commissions might provide another pathway to justice for women subjected to abuse. Described as "a radically new kind of justice,"[7] truth commissions have been created throughout the world in the aftermath of conflicts involving human rights abuses. Truth commissions provide public space for both victims and perpetrators of violence to share their stories and to be heard by other participants and their communities. Unlike trials, during which story-telling is constrained by the rules of evidence and procedure and feelings and harms are deemed irrelevant, truth commissions allow the community to decide how stories should be told, allowing victims to "ramble, cry, and scream."[8] Through truth commissions, communities can unearth and confront how violence affected the lives of those who experienced it; as law professor Teresa Phelps argues, "These settings can reveal the truth about what oppression did to people—not just the recitation of events, but what oppression *felt* like, how it changed and destroyed lives, even lives not touched by a specific crime."[9] Truth commissions seek reconciliation, but reconciliation is a complicated concept, as law professor Roslyn Myers explains:

> Truth and reconciliation commissions are founded on the principle that neither individual victims nor entire communities can move beyond violent criminal events without the public recognition of suffering, the collaborative effort of understanding the complete story of what happened, and gestures of remorse from the ones who caused it. The records of the commission become a repository, in perpetuity, for the stories of those affected by the crimes. Speaking truth leads to reconciliation—but not necessarily between victims and perpetrators. The change is not utopian. . . . There is no happily ever after.[10]

Phelps believes that truth commissions can help restore victim voice and validation after violence. Victims of torture, Phelps explains, lose their voices, the stories that they have constructed about their own lives. Those stories are replaced by the story of the perpetrator, which becomes "the dominant and only narrative."[11] Truth commissions create space within which victims can reshape and share their narratives, restoring voice. As Myers states, "[V]ictims heal through the act of testifying."[12]

Truth commissions provide victims with a pathway to reintegrate themselves in their communities, particularly when the community's perception of the victim has been negatively affected by violence. Being subjected to torture, Phelps argues, communicates a false message about the victim's worth, depicting the victim of torture as somehow less than human and therefore worthy of abuse. Hearing the stories of victims gives the community the opportunity to validate the victim's experiences, thereby welcoming the victim back into the community. Narratives, political science professor James Gibson maintains, are the most effective and compelling way of communicating victim experiences to the public.[13] The truth commissions' public hearings provide the community with the opportunity to "share in the experiences and empathize with the speakers. . . . Thus, losses and grief that once belonged to individuals become experienced collectively."[14]

Critics of truth commissions argue that they are a poor substitute for the "real" justice of a criminal prosecution, that telling stories is simply not a form of justice. Others have argued that encouraging reconciliation between victim and offender is inconsistent with achieving justice or, in the alternative, that truth commissions have not brought about promised reconciliations between victims and offenders or victims and communities. Some have questioned whether the truth commission process has served women well. Writing about women's experiences with South Africa's Truth and Reconciliation Commission, government professor Tristan Anne Borer argues that the truth commission was unable to ascertain the truth about women's experiences of sexual violence in apartheid-era South Africa, in part because of how the truth commission defined its mandate and in part because of women's reticence about discussing sexual abuse in a public forum. Borer notes that the commission later adopted a series of policies intended to facilitate women's testimony, including allowing statements to be made confidentially, enabling women to testify in closed sessions, and permitting women to request that their statements be taken by or testimony be given only to other women. The Commission even organized a set of women's hearings, including only female commissioners, with psychologists and social workers available for assistance. Treating men and women differently, however, drew criticism as well.[15] Notwithstanding these critiques, Phelps concludes that the South African hearings

> were a public enactment of a radical kind of justice, justice that returns dignity to those who have been victimized; justice that gives back the power to speak in one's own words and to shape the experience of violence into a coherent story of one's own, thereby allowing for a renewed (or new) sense of autonomy and sense of control; justice that allows victims, in hearing stories from other victims, to locate their personal stories in a larger cultural story.[16]

Community-based truth commissions could provide women subjected to abuse with the justice that they seek without requiring them to use the legal system. Truth commissions could help women subjected to abuse regain voice by providing a forum in which they are free to tell their stories of abuse however they choose to do so, without the restrictions of the courtroom: as stories of pain, suffering, strength, anger, resilience. Constructing and sharing abuse narratives gives a woman "control and distance from the traumatic event and empowers the victim to get on with . . . her life."[17] Truth commissions are open to stories of abuse and victimization; in fact, they exist to hear those stories. In South Africa, Myers notes, "the needs of the victims drove the proceedings . . . their need to have their suffering acknowledged by the wider community; their desire to hear perpetrators admit to their abuses; and their hope to have the local and international community react with indignation and empathy."[18] Women subjected to abuse share many of these needs: the need to be heard, to have their experiences validated, to be reintegrated into their communities. Truth commissions could provide a forum for meeting these needs.

Truth commissions would not force or pressure women subjected to abuse to forgive or reconcile with their partners. Forgiveness is a choice. As Phelps writes of a woman in the context of the South African Truth and Reconciliation Commission, "In this space, she is given the opportunity to forgive, forgiveness is offered as an option. She freely turns it down—she cannot forgive—not yet. But this moment manifests a state in which her dignity is acknowledged, her voice counts, her opinion matters, her mind and heart are free."[19] Forgiveness in the broader sense of absolving a partner for his actions is not expected, but having the opportunity to tell her story could provide a woman subjected to abuse with the narrower version of forgiveness as freedom that many victims seek. For women who plan to remain in relationships with their partners or who seek some form of reconciliation, the truth commission model could provide an opportunity to share their stories with their partners in safe public spaces in the hopes that doing so might elicit their partners' empathy and understanding and prevent further abuse.

Truth commissions could also provide a forum for men who abuse their partners to examine their behavior. Many truth commissions provide amnesty to perpetrators of violence in exchange for an honest accounting of the perpetrator's actions. Amnesty enables a perpetrator to discuss his past abuse without fear of prosecution, making men who abuse more likely to share their stories as well. Amnesty can even serve as a form of accountability, argues Borer; being granted amnesty means being certified as a perpetrator of violence to both the individual subjected to abuse and the community. By coming forward, telling their stories, and accepting responsibility for their actions, men who abuse could begin to be reconciled with their communities as well. The truth commission process should not allow men to make excuses for or justify their behavior. But it can give their partners and the community some insight into their actions and help men who abuse develop the kind of empathy that is necessary to understand how their actions have affected their partners and communities. Rehumanization of the other, Jodi Halpern and

Harvey Weinstein have argued, is a necessary precondition for reconciliation;[20] the truth commission process can provide a venue for that to occur.

Creating truth commissions could increase the community's sense of responsibility for abuse of women. Community in this context is defined narrowly, as those affected by the abuse and those who will be affected by the proceedings—family members, friends, and professionals working with the family, for example.[21] Justice cannot be achieved without the involvement of the community, particularly if the community has previously been complicit, actively or passively, in the abuse.[22] The community must bear witness to the stories of women subjected to abuse and, having heard those stories, acknowledge that the community is responsible for safeguarding women against further abuse and helping them achieve justice, however each woman defines that term.

A community-based domestic violence truth commission would provide a forum within which women subjected to abuse and men who perpetrate abuse could share their stories with their communities. The commission would have an explicitly woman-centered mandate: to examine how abuse of women operates on the individual, community, and systemic levels. The commission's governing policies would enable women to share their stories safely and, if necessary, confidentially, and provide a variety of options (giving written or oral testimony, delivering testimony privately or publicly) designed to facilitate the collection of the widest range of stories. Men would be required to admit to abusing their partners and to agree to curtail that abuse before offering testimony. Commissions would be grassroots efforts, staffed in partnership with organizations serving women subjected to abuse and men who abuse their partners, providing a broad range of experience and perspective and the potential for referrals to needed services for those who give testimony. As law professor Brenda Smith has suggested, hearings could be held in shared community spaces, including child care centers, schools, churches, recreation centers, barbershops, and hair salons.[23]

The truth commission would examine not only individual experiences of abuse, but how existing legal and economic structures serve to perpetuate abuse of women and the community's complicity in failing to prevent or redress abuse. The truth commission would collect the stories of women and men in order to document the extent and nature of abuse of women within the community and to make recommendations about appropriate reparations, both to individuals and community-wide. To ensure that the commission is perceived as legitimate, as political science professor James Gibson has suggested, the process would be open for community participation, allowing all community members to voice their ideas and concerns. Decision making would be transparent and all commission recommendations would be supported by facts that would be publicly available through the commission's record.

Advocates for women subjected to abuse have used the structure of human rights reporting, relying on the narratives of individual women and system actors, to unearth violations of local, national, and international laws in the courts that adjudicate the claims of women subjected to abuse. The Battered Mothers' Testimony Project created by the Wellesley Centers for Women provides one example of how powerful the first-person narratives of women subjected to abuse can be in highlighting system failures. A truth commission would go several steps further, engaging perpetrators of abuse as well as their victims, enlisting community members in soliciting and gathering stories and determining appropriate reparations.

Reparations could take a number of forms: women subjected to abuse could be awarded monetary reparations;[24] communities could agree to provide services and supports for women subjected to abuse that are not currently available; communities and perpetrators could offer apologies for their abuse and/or their failure to respond to abuse. While the community would have some role to play in determining reparations, power would ultimately rest with the woman subjected to abuse to determine what type of reparations she is willing to accept. If a woman subjected to abuse does not want an apology from her perpetrator, an apology will not be forced upon her, particularly if that apology is offered in lieu of monetary or other types of support. Too often reparations focus on what the perpetrator is willing to give, rather than what the victim wants or needs. Involving women in the process of determining and implementing reparations is therefore essential, argues law professor Carlton Waterhouse:

> Victims' participation in the design of reparations enables them to see themselves healing and to articulate the steps needed to see that healing accomplished. . . . [V]ictims' involvement in designing reparations also helps elevate their status in the reparations process in the initial stages, increasing the likelihood that they will be included as equal partners throughout.[25]

Achieving justice for women subjected to abuse does not require a formal structure or process. Asian and Pacific Islander groups in the United States have sought justice for women subjected to abuse using public naming to expose men's abuse of their partners to their communities. After her husband burned her, Syeda Mohsin asked Sakhi, an organization serving South Asian women, to help her publicize his crime and create community support for her. Anti-violence advocate Mimi Kim describes Sakhi's efforts on Mohsin's behalf, organizing volunteers and supporters to march at Mohammed Mohsin's home, researching the legal requirements for a public protest, notifying the local police, and ultimately protesting outside of his home, shouting "outrage at this act of violence." At her request, Syeda Mohsin's name was changed for confidentiality purposes during the organizing work and the demonstration itself. Kim describes neighbors as "shocked," but states that they "supported the demonstrators." Their support was crucial, since Mohsin's husband and his family had attempted to turn community members against her. Syeda Mohsin was not present, "but felt that this community act would be supportive in its public demonstration that she, too, had community members on her side." The demonstration was widely publicized in the South Asian and mainstream press. Although Sakhi was threatened with lawsuits and other repercussions of the demonstration, the organization ultimately went ahead with the protest, determining that "it was more critical to act than to be silent." Sakhi supporters maintained their presence through the husband's criminal trial, and Sakhi continued to work with Syeda Mohsin for eight years after the protest.[26]

Kim warns that public naming may not be appropriate in less serious cases of abuse: "Had his crimes been less sensational, community support for Sakhi and the survivor may have been significantly reduced and may have made this shaming ritual a less obvious community-based strategy."[27] But advocates from the Asian and Pacific Islander community in the United States have expressed support for the concept of publicly naming abusers and seeking public acknowledgment of wrongdoing. Advocates believe, for example, that men should be barred from cultural events, rather than forcing women to stay away in order to avoid meeting their partners at such events. Some organizations have explored the use of public amends in engaging the community on the side of the woman subjected to abuse, requiring the man to appear before his family, his counselors, and his community to say, "I'm not going to do this anymore."[28] Research shows that what men who abuse their partners fear most, more than criminal punishment or loss of employment, is stigma and social disapproval.[29] Public naming is a particularly powerful response in those communities that highly value public standing and family honor and among those who fear bringing shame and notoriety to themselves or their families.

Each woman should have the opportunity to define justice for herself and to seek justice as she defines it. This is the guiding philosophy for the work that

Mimi Kim does through her organization, Creative Interventions. Creative Interventions provides women subjected to abuse with "greater access to options than those conventionally available." Creative Interventions asks each woman

> What does she value? What are her goals? In what ways can she take leadership in attaining these goals? How can she organize her intimate network and other accessible resources to help her attain these goals or initiate others to take this role? If engagement with the perpetrator is a possibility, who can participate? Is this strategy feasible?[30]

The organization works with women to define and actualize their goals, developing plans that can be carried out within their homes and communities, exploring collective responses, and engaging community members for support. Creative Interventions does not assume that safety is a woman's ultimate goal, nor does it pressure women to separate from their partners. Providing women with "[t]he space to explore and co-create more meaningful goals allows for more creative strategies and actions more aligned with the broader principle of self-determination at the level of the individual and community."[31] Justice can be attained without engaging formal systems; organizations like Creative Interventions provide women subjected to abuse with the tools they need to seek justice on their own terms.

The primacy of the legal response to domestic violence has stunted the growth of community-based justice approaches and deluded women into believing that the legal regime can deliver what women seek. As Mimi Kim writes, "[W]e have created a system outside of community . . . to protect us from violence, complete with a qualified set of experts to manage our way toward that mirage called safety."[32] This lack of community-based justice has inured to the detriment of those women who are not willing to engage with the state and those who are not able to access the legal system. Programs like the ones described in this section arose because of the alienation communities felt from the dominant systemic response. Only by returning the ability to seek justice to the community and developing community-based and community-centered mechanisms will many women find the justice that will otherwise elude them.

Establishing Economic Security

Throughout 2009–2010, the media was replete with stories about the link between rising domestic violence rates and the economic recession. Domestic violence seems to increase in times of economic distress for at least two reasons. First, the stress of economic downturns exacerbates tensions within relationships that can lead men to abuse their partners. Women have reported to domestic violence agencies that financial pressures have made their partners quicker to anger and abuse;[33] research has found that unemployment is the most significant demographic risk factor for intimate partner femicide.[34] Second, women may be less willing to leave abusive relationships in a weak economy. Establishing economic freedom, lawyer and anti-violence advocate Barbara Hart explains, requires economic resources including emergency and transitional financial assistance, housing, child support, education, employment skills, and jobs and the ability to maintain those jobs[35]—all scarce during an economic downturn.

Although exacerbated in a recession, economic obstacles to leaving abusive relationships exist even in a more robust economy. For that reason, organizations serving women subjected to abuse have created a variety of financial literacy and economic support programs designed to help women obtain education and develop employment skills, find housing and child care, and learn to manage their money. Those programs, and the resources associated with those programs—transitional and permanent housing, legal services, education, and job training—are essential components in establishing economic freedom. What few of these programs do, however, is put money directly into the hands of women subjected to abuse, enabling them to secure economic freedom by building businesses and establishing credit.

Microfinance can give women that security. Microfinance involves extending loans (also known as microcredit) and providing other financial services, including savings and insurance, to those who would otherwise be unable to access them because of their poverty—making "very small loans to very poor people for very small businesses."[36] The poor are frequently unable to borrow money because mainstream banks lack the ability to assess their creditworthiness and because the poor lack collateral to guarantee their loans. But, as economics professor Charlotte Lott explains, "Microcredit programs solve these two problems with two primary innovative institutional structures: peer group lending with public repayment and progressive lending with early and frequent repayment."[37] Peer group lending requires that a group of borrowers come together to seek loans. Each member of the group is responsible for the repayment of loans made to any member of the group, and members cannot borrow additional funds until all loans are repaid. Because group members are more likely to know the capacity of their friends and neighbors to repay loans, the group selection process weeds out those who are less able to repay and serves as a public statement of a member's creditworthiness by the group. Loans are repaid during group meetings, enabling the community of borrowers to monitor members' repayments. Using the risk of public shaming and the fear of loss of group support as well as the encouragement and approbation that come from timely repayment of loans, public repayment and peer group pressure ensure that members repay their loans. Progressive lending programs start with very small loans with very short terms, making the loan less risky and repayment more likely. After developing a relationship with the borrower over time, loans become bigger and can be repaid more slowly, creating an incentive to repay the early loans. The efficacy of these practices is borne out in the high repayment rates among microborrowers; microlending organization Acción USA reports that since 1991, its historic repayment rate is close to 90 percent.[38]

Women have been at the center of microfinance since the Grameen Bank, founded by Nobel Prize winner Muhammad Yunus, first began making microloans in Bangladesh in 1977. Economics professor Lott explains that microlending is particularly well suited to women in three important ways. First, because they frequently lack collateral or control over family resources, women have less access to borrowing through traditional financial structures. Second, women are more likely to comply with the conditions of microlending, like attendance at group meetings and training, either because of this lack of access to capital or because they see the benefits of such services. Finally, women work in the types of small-scale enterprises that microlending capitalizes, possibly because they are excluded from other types of labor or because they need or want to remain in the home.[39] Microcredit organizations have targeted women, in turn, because they have learned that lending money to women has a greater positive impact on poor families. Research establishes that "women have a different spending pattern than men. Increases in women's income results in larger household expenditures on both food and non-food items than similar increases in income to men, and women spend more income on the health and education of children in the household." Women also tend to reinvest profits in their businesses. Men, by contrast, are more likely to spend increased income on alcohol, tobacco, and other items for personal consumption.[40] For these reasons, some microlending organizations, like Grameen Bank, loan primarily to women; a 2009 report of the Microcredit Summit Campaign found that 71 percent overall, and 83.4 percent of the microloans made to the poorest clients, went to women.[41] Nearly 100 percent of the borrowers involved in Grameen America are women.[42]

Microlending can help women escape poverty. A March 1993 study found that of the women who borrowed from Grameen for eight or more years, 46 percent had crossed the poverty line and were unlikely to fall back, 34 percent were close to coming out of poverty, and 20 percent remained in extreme poverty, usually because of a chronic illness. By contrast, only 4 percent of non-Grameen families had escaped poverty during the same period.[43] The Women's Initiative in California, which serves only low-income women, reports that annual household income for graduates of its program grows from $14,000 prior to receiving business training and microloans to over $37,000 two years after training.[44] Lott concludes, "[W]omen are the key reason why microcredit works and why microcredit is beneficial."[45]

Microfinance is often thought of as a strategy for helping the poorest of the poor in third world countries. But microcredit programs are working with low-income Americans to escape poverty and establish themselves as entrepreneurs. Organizations like Acción USA and the Women's Initiative have been making domestic microloans since the late 1980s and early 1990s. Kiva, best known for its online service connecting potential microlenders to borrowers throughout the world, began partnering with microlenders in the United States in 2009. Kiva's president, Premal Shah, explains,

> Most people think of microfinance as something that helps people in the developing world alone, but the impact of microfinance can be felt in any community that supports creative, industrious entrepreneurs. . . . Kiva's micro-loan model is extremely relevant to low– to moderate-income, U.S. based entrepreneurs, especially given the current economic conditions which makes access to credit a very real problem.[46]

Microfinance is already providing women subjected to abuse with the resources they need to establish economic freedom from their partners. Twenty-five percent of the women who work with the Women's Initiative report past or present domestic violence.[47] In a twist on traditional microlending, the Kentucky Domestic Violence Association, in conjunction with the Credit Builders Alliance, provides women subjected to abuse with microloans of between $200 and $800 to meet immediate needs—transportation or rent, for example. Women must contribute to individual development accounts for up to six months prior to receiving the loans; those accounts serve as collateral for the microloans and remain available to the women after their loans are repaid. Repayment of the loans is monitored by two of the three major credit agencies, which enables women to establish credit histories and boost their credit ratings as they repay the loans.[48]

Microfinance is empowering, giving women a greater degree of influence over home and community decision making and more control over their lives. Studies suggest that women who receive microloans are significantly more likely to be empowered than non-borrowers, with empowerment defined as the ability to make or influence household decisions and to engage with the community.[49] The relationship between receipt of microloans and domestic violence is somewhat more complicated. Numerous anecdotal reports support the idea that receipt of microloans can help to stop abuse of women. Journalists Nicholas Kristof and Sheryl WuDunn describe how the husband of Saima Muhammad, a Pakistani woman living outside Lahore, regularly beat her until she used a microloan to start an embroidery business that eventually employed 30 families—and her husband—and brought economic prosperity to their family.[50] A Grameen bank worker described how the husband of one borrower, who had in the past beaten his wife regularly, virtually stopped for the first time since their marriage because he depended upon her for investment capital.[51] A 1996 study of women who received microloans in Bangladesh showed that women who received loans were less likely to be physically abused by their spouses.[52] Decreases in domestic violence may be attributable to lessened economic tensions within the home, the woman's own sense of empowerment, or the presence of a supportive community around the woman subjected to abuse. In a study by the Working Women's Forum in India, 40.9 percent of borrowers who had been subjected to abuse reported that they were able to stop the abuse through personal empowerment, and 28.7 percent were able to curtail abuse through group action.[53]

But microlending could also increase violence against women, at least in the short term; putting capital into women's hands challenges traditional gender roles, which could spur their partners to reassert control through violence.[54] This concern squares with sociologist Jody Raphael's observations of the behavior of the partners of women on welfare, who increased their violence when the women sought education or training to keep them from achieving sufficient economic security to leave their relationships.[55]

Microfinance has the potential to enable women subjected to abuse to become economically free of their partners and to increase economic stability and lessen tensions in families that choose to remain intact. Given the possibility of increased violence attributable to both separation and the assertion of economic power, women will need to consider carefully whether microfinance makes sense for them. But certainly microfinance can be a powerful means of giving women, particularly low-income women, one of the tools they need to extract themselves from abusive relationships or to decrease or stop the abuse within relationships they choose to maintain.

Microfinance is just one example of the kind of creative solution to increase women's economic strength that is possible in an anti-essentialist system. By focusing on giving women what they need, rather than what the system has made available, an anti-essentialist system can help women achieve the power and economic stability that can free them from abuse.

Engaging Men Who Abuse

Providing justice and resources to women subjected to abuse is crucial, but will not eliminate abuse. Men's abuse of women can only be stopped if men stop abusing women. The casting of men who abuse their partners as irredeemable monsters has prevented the battered women's movement from thinking strategically and creatively about ways to work with men to end their abuse. But some men who abuse can change and want to change. Looking at the needs and motivations of individual men across a variety of dimensions of their lives—as earners, as partners in relationships, as fathers, and as members of cultural communities—may be the key to helping men achieve that change.

Giving men access to economic opportunity is a crucial anti-abuse strategy. A recent study of court-involved men in Albuquerque, New Mexico, found that more than half of the men lacked high school diplomas, 36 percent were unemployed at the time they came into contact with the court, 61 percent made less than $20,000 per year, and 88 percent earned less than $30,000 per year.[56] Although economic stress does not excuse abuse, it certainly correlates; recall Bernice's observation that Billy's abuse became worse when Billy was unemployed, and sociologist Jody Raphael's confirmation that the women on welfare with whom she had worked tied their abuse to their partners' inability to support their families.[57] Ensuring that men who abuse are engaged in educational programs and helping men to find and keep employment may do more to change their abusive behavior than any batterer intervention program.

Men may be motivated to change in order to maintain relationships with their partners, and some women want to repair those relationships. Couples counseling may help them to do so. Sociologist Richard Gelles describes the prevailing attitude toward couples counseling as "*verboten* . . . [the] great third rail of violence against women." [58] Advocates for women subjected to abuse have argued that couples therapy is inappropriate in relationships involving abuse because it encourages both partners to share responsibility for the problems in their relationship, suggesting that the woman is in some way culpable for the abuse. Nonetheless, for couples experiencing low-level or situational couple violence, there is some evidence that couples counseling can prompt men to change abusive behavior. A few studies have found that therapy for couples experiencing low levels of abuse can be as effective as individual, gender-based therapy in reducing or eliminating that abuse. A 2004 study of couples engaged in treatment found that multi-couple group therapy was more effective than individual couples therapy in increasing marital satisfaction, increasing negative attitudes about violence against women among both men and women, and decreasing levels of aggression within the family. The study specifically excluded men who had engaged in "battering" or coercively controlling behavior. Men who participated in either individual or group couples therapy were less likely to recidivate than men in the control group, but the group process was particularly helpful for the couples. Couples noted the importance of hearing from other couples struggling with violence in their relationships, learning from others, and "'vicarious communication' . . . hav[ing] difficult issues broached by others as a way of communicating with their own spouse without the discomfort of doing so directly." The study's authors conclude, "[C]onjoint treatment can be a safe and useful way to help couples that have a history of mild-to-moderate partner violence and that freely choose to stay together."[59] The importance of distinguishing among types of abuse and types of abusers is evident in this context; assuming that all men who abuse their partners are engaging in coercive control forecloses what could be a promising option for couples experiencing lesser levels of abuse.

Men who abuse can be reached through their children. Understanding how their abuse affects their children can motivate men to change their behavior. Moreover, many women subjected to abuse want their partners to have relationships with their children; as one study found, "Respondents did not struggle with the question of 'if' contact should take place but, rather, 'how' and 'when.'"[60] Interventions around fatherhood benefit children who want relationships with their fathers, women who co-parent with them, and men who have ended or who are trying to curtail their abuse and want to strengthen relationships with their children that may have been damaged by abuse.

Most programs focus on helping men to understand how abuse affects their children and use that understanding to motivate men to change, balancing condemnation of the harm caused by men's abusive behavior with support for their efforts. The Family Violence Prevention Fund's Fathering After Violence Program, for example, works with fathers to stop using any form of abuse; to model constructive non-abusive behavior for their children; to stop denying, blaming others for, or justifying their abusive behavior; to accept the consequences of their behavior, including the loss of trust, love, and contact with their children; to acknowledge the damage they have done; to support and respect the mother's parenting; to listen to and validate their children's feelings of hurt, anger, sadness, fear, and rejection; and to accept that change in their relationships with their children will occur at the children's pace and on their terms. The Fathering After Violence Program uses exercises that help men develop empathy for their children, give them an opportunity to model good and bad parenting behaviors, and brainstorm ways that a father could improve his relationship with his children. Not all men will make the connection between their abuse and their impaired relationships with their children; after completing the Fathering After Violence Program, some men still did not see the link or understand the challenges in building or rebuilding relationships with their children. But others clearly recognized how their violence affected their children and were more realistic about their relationships with their children after participating in the program.[61]

Fatherhood interventions must acknowledge the variation among men who abuse their partners and incorporate culturally specific, community-based values. El Circulo (The Circle), a program designed for Latino men, is centered on four components: conocimiento (acknowledgment); entendimento (understanding); integración (integration); and movimento (movement). These four stages allow men to share their stories, find purpose and dignity, understand how false images of fatherhood and masculinity are undermining their relationships with their partners and children, and learn the importance of fathers in child development. Other men in the group provide guidance, advice, and support. Ultimately, El Circulo allows participants to become part of a network of men who have rededicated their lives to their children and provides them with "a support system that helps them to maintain accountability."[62]

Like El Circulo, the Pacific Islander Men's Program in Hawaii engages men through their ties to their cultural community. Founder Sharon Spencer focuses on Maori culture to help men who abuse their partners change their behavior. Spencer stresses the Maori concepts of male and female power and family relational values to help men see the importance of gender equity and nonviolence. Spencer also creates opportunities for men to work within the community, harvesting taro, making ukeleles, and restoring eroded seashores, providing hands-on experiences of nurturing and creation. Anti-violence advocate Mimi Kim notes, "This is not a standard men's curriculum with added cultural elements. Rather, deep cultural values and historical, political context underlie the causal assumptions for violence and the seeds of transformation."[63]

Engaging men who abuse their partners is simply acknowledging the obvious: abuse of women will not stop if men who abuse women do not change. Work with men who abuse their partners is not meant to supplant the crucial services, supports, and resources that women who are subjected to abuse receive. Instead, these efforts supplement work with women subjected to abuse by going to the root of the problem—the men who abuse them. Providing services to men who abuse benefits not only women who want to maintain their relationships with their partners, but also women who would otherwise be subjected to separation-related abuse, women who are co-parenting with former partners, and the future partners of men who have abused women in the past. Such efforts should not excuse men's abusive behaviors, but condemnation alone is not sufficient to stop abuse. Men need motivation and assistance to stop using abuse in their relationships. An anti-essentialist system must provide pathways for men to access these services without shame or stigma—and without requiring legal system involvement.

Developing Community Accountability

One oft-expressed concern about adopting community-based strategies for addressing domestic violence is the fear that the community will not sufficiently condemn the abuse or support women subjected to abuse. As law professor Ruth Busch argues in the context of restorative justice, community-based strategies rely on the assumption that there is some "uniform community view of right and wrong," some core consensus among members of the community that abuse of women is unacceptable, that does not attribute some responsibility for the abuse to the woman or condone abuse in certain circumstances.[64] Without that kind of shared understanding, critics worry, community-based responses will be ineffective at best and harmful at worst.

Community accountability is intended to help the community develop that shared consensus. As restorative justice practitioner Kay Pranis writes,

> We have few places in our current social structure for community dialogue about expected standards of behaviour—few places for making the case for behaviour based not on legal constraint but moral imperative. . . . We now have an urgent need for forums in which we can explore our shared values, the implications of those values for behaviour, and ways to be accountable to one another for our behaviour.[65]

Community accountability strategies enhance the community's capacity to recognize and intervene in abusive situations; support women subjected to abuse; confront men who abuse; create processes for ensuring offender accountability, reparation, and transformation; and articulate non-abusive norms to the wider community. The goals of community accountability include developing community-wide norms supporting intervention and prevention of abuse, creating "accessible, effective and just interventions" by decreasing reliance on state systems, and establishing collective respect and responsibility within communities.[66] That sense of responsibility can lead community members to intervene actively on behalf of women subjected to abuse, as the families of Grass Valley, California did when their women's shelter closed. Rather than waiting for the shelter to reopen, families in the community volunteered to take women subjected to abuse and their children into their own homes. As community member Harry Bailey explains, "You did it just because it was what needed to be done."[67]

Anti-violence advocate Mimi Kim, who is engaged in community accountability work through her organization, Creative Interventions, distinguishes community accountability from community education that purports to explain how to "end violence," but that in actuality relies on resources that may not be accessible to community members or requires them to rely on systems, like the legal system, that they would rather avoid.[68] Community accountability, by contrast, enhances the ability of the community to end and prevent abuse by providing community resources—family, friends, neighbors, co-workers, and others—with tools and models for intervention. Kim explains, "This focus on the front lines of intimate and family violence raises the possibility of intervention at early stages of abuse, offers more accessible and sustainable resources, and builds intervention and prevention strategies into the very spaces and places where violence occurs—homes, streets, and communities."[69] Creative Interventions works with community members to collectively address abuse, helping them to identify problems, find allies, establish common goals, and coordinate a plan of action, based on the goals and values of the woman subjected to abuse. In so doing, Kim argues, "communities in their various formations can create a new set of norms, practices, and relationships to not only end violence but to build community health."[70]

Men have a key role to play in changing community norms around abuse of women. Men influence each other's actions; research suggests that male peer groups can create conditions that support the use of abuse in relationships.[71] But men can have a positive impact on the behavior of others as well. Research shows that many men are uncomfortable with prevailing notions of manhood and with other men's sexism and inappropriate behavior and are more likely to intervene to prevent abuse when they believe that other men will also be willing to intervene.[72] Men can be partners in stopping abuse by helping other men to reject harmful stereotypes about masculinity and by condemning and intervening against abusive behaviors. Men need to hear these messages from other men "because it empowers men who want to help and provides them with visible allies." For that reason, research suggests that all-male groups with male facilitators are most effective in changing attitudes about woman abuse. Such messages are also more effective when delivered with attention to culture, ethnicity, and race.[73] Programs for men should strive to help men develop empathy for women subjected to abuse and teach them skills both to change their own behavior and to confront men who are abusive.[74]

Such programs have the potential to change the way that men interact with the women in their lives. An evaluation of Hombres Unidos contra la Violencia Familia (Men United Against Family Violence), a program for migrant Latino men in the United States, facilitated by men, demonstrated that the program helped men improve their understanding of the definition and causes of abuse and debunked some myths about abuse. Participants said that the program gave them the language to talk about abuse, an understanding of the harm caused by emotional abuse, a basis for redefining how a man should act, and a sense of the importance of teaching other men about abuse.[75]

Groups like A Call To Men have also taken up the challenge of changing community norms among men. A Call To Men offers trainings, workshops, and other educational programs designed to help men change the way that they view women as well as the way they view themselves. The organization works with community groups to shift societal norms regarding what it means to be a man. A Call To Men stresses the need for "well meaning men"—men who do not abuse women, who treat women respectfully—to reexamine their own marginalization and objectification of women, to recognize their privilege and entitlement, and to engage men who use that privilege and entitlement to justify their abuse.[76] Other men are finding creative ways to hold their peers accountable. In Australia's Northern Territory, for example, the Santa Teresa football club has announced that men who abuse their partners will not be permitted to play, but would be given support from teammates and counseling resources.[77] All of these programs and actions send a crucial message from men to men—that abuse is not synonymous with manhood, that other men will not tolerate woman abuse, and that men will not stand silently by when women are being abused. Such messages can transform community norms about woman abuse.

Lawyers can also help to develop community accountability for woman abuse. Community organizing among those who Kim describes as "most affected by the problem . . . including women and children survivors of violence; [and] family, friends, and social networks impacted by intimate and family violence" is an essential community accountability strategy. Community organizing helps to build a collective identity and power that can be used to challenge systemic and institutional norms about abuse. There is a role for lawyers to play in such organizing, suggests law professor Sameer Ashar. Ashar argues that public interest lawyers could be more effective change agents if they supported the efforts of those "working to change the social order."[78] Client collectives and lawyers could work together to define the goals of the collective and determine what options exist for achieving those goals. Lawyers would not dominate the discourse within the community attempting to eradicate woman abuse. Instead, lawyers would provide information and assistance in generating options based on their expertise and use their skills and knowledge to help the collective fulfill its goals—a role that could range from helping the collective navigate the legal requirements for protesting outside an abusive partner's home to working to create or change systemic practices in ways that benefit the community. Even without engaging the state, lawyers could serve as partners in the development of community accountability.

Rather than continuing to pour money into a legal system that has not proven effective in stopping woman abuse, we should explore and support options that enable women to access justice, leverage economic resources, and engage men and communities in the effort to prevent woman abuse. Not every strategy discussed here will be appropriate for every community. Each community must decide where its resources are best spent, guided by the voices of women subjected to abuse within that community. Those who believe that an anti-essentialist response to domestic violence is the way to serve women subjected to abuse must deploy their knowledge, skills, and experience to commit to, create, build, and monitor these community-based enterprises. The justice system is simply one tool, and not always the best tool, among the many available to respond to domestic violence. Those who want to eradicate woman abuse must channel their energy, creativity, and passion into constructing multiple pathways for women to live autonomous lives free of abuse.

Notes

INTRODUCTION

1. This book will use the phrase "women subjected to abuse" to describe the individuals others have called "abused wives," "battered wives," "victims of domestic violence," "survivors of domestic violence," "battered women," or "victims of intimate partner violence." I take this phrase from Margaret E. Johnson, "Redefining Harm, Reimagining Remedies and Reclaiming Domestic Violence Law," *UC Davis Law Review* 42, no. 4 (2009): 1107–64 (2009). A woman who is subjected to abuse is not necessarily a victim, a survivor, or a battered woman, though she may be any or all of these at various times. These terms—victim, survivor, battered woman—have all been used to describe the women who are the subject of this book, and all are limited. Victim conjures up visions of a stereotype, a passive, meek, cowering (and, as will be discussed in chapter 3, white, heterosexual) woman consistent with the early domestic violence literature. Survivor, a term intended to cast off that stereotype and instead portray women as active agents struggling against their oppressors to ensure their own survival, is similarly limited; not all women do, in fact, survive domestic violence, and not all women take action on their own behalf (however inclusive that term might be). The term battered woman is problematic because it reduces the woman to her experience of battering, and assumes that all women who are abused experience battering, as opposed to other forms of non-physical abuse. A woman so described can only be understood within the context of the battering in her relationship; she has no existence independent of that one facet of her life. All of these terms reflect the same type of reductionism that plagues so much of domestic violence law and policy. Using the term "women subjected to abuse," by contrast, is intended to call attention to the circumstances these women have faced without describing them solely as a product of those circumstances, defining the action rather than the woman herself. Moreover, using the words "subjected to" rather than "experiences" calls attention to an often invisible figure: the partner who is abusive. This construction is intended to provide the freedom within which to see women subjected to abuse as individuals, with different values, capacities, goals, and visions for their future and to suggest principles for policymaking consistent with this conception. This book will refer to the "battered women's movement," however, in part because the movement self-identifies using that term, and in part because the use of the term highlights some of the problems within the movement that the book seeks to address. And although "domestic violence" is a similarly limited term, focusing on the home and thereby excluding partners who do not share a home and violence that occurs in public spaces and focusing on violence to the exclusion of other forms of abuse, the term is so entrenched that I have chosen to use it as well.

2. Martha Chamallas, *Introduction to Feminist Legal Theory*, 3rd ed. (New York: Aspen Publishers, 2003), 46.

3. Barbara J. Hart, "Arrest: What's the Big Deal?" *William & Mary Journal of Women and the Law* 3, no. 1 (1997): 207–9.

CHAPTER 1

1. Catharine A. MacKinnon, "Feminism, Marxism, Method, and the State: An Agenda for Theory," *Signs: Journal of Women in Culture and Society* 7, no. 3 (1982): 529, 535.

2. Catharine A. MacKinnon, *Toward a Feminist Theory of the State* (Cambridge, MA: Harvard University Press, 1989), 113.

3. Catharine A. MacKinnon, *Feminism Unmodified: Discourses on Life and Law* (Cambridge, MA: Harvard University Press, 1987), 170–71.

4. MacKinnon, *Toward a Feminist Theory of the State*, 163.

5. Ibid., 161–62.

6. Ibid., 114.

7. Ibid., 244.

8. Ellen C. Dubois et al., "Feminist Discourse, Moral Values, and the Law—A Conversation," *Buffalo Law Review* 34, no. 1 (1985): 72.

9. MacKinnon, *Feminism Unmodified*, 104.

10. Ibid., 116.

11. Kathryn Abrams, "Sex Wars Redux: Agency and Coercion in Feminist Legal Theory," *Columbia Law Review* 95, no. 2 (1995): 304.

12. MacKinnon, *Feminism Unmodified*, 220.

13. Martha R. Mahoney, "Whiteness and Women, In Practice and Theory: A Response to Catharine MacKinnon," *Yale Journal of Law and Feminism* 5, no. 2 (1993): 217.

14. Angela P. Harris, "Race and Essentialism in Feminist Legal Theory," *Stanford Law Review* 42, no. 3 (1990): 585.

15. MacKinnon, *Feminism Unmodified*, 76.

16. Harris, "Race and Essentialism," 591–92.

17. Wendy Brown, *States of Injury: Power and Freedom in Late Modernity* (Princeton, NJ: Princeton University Press, 1995), 170.

18. Ibid., 173.

19. MacKinnon, *Toward a Feminist Theory of the State*, 178.

20. Kersti Yllo, "Through A Feminist Lens: Gender, Diversity, and Violence: Extending the Feminist Framework," in *Current Controversies on Family Violence*, eds. Donileen R. Loseke, Richard J. Gelles, and Mary M. Cavanaugh (Thousand Oaks, CA: Sage Publications, 2005), 22.

21. MacKinnon, *Toward a Feminist Theory of the State*, 177.

22. Abrams, "Sex Wars Redux," 345.

23. Melanie F. Shepard and Ellen L. Pence, "An Introduction: Developing a Coordinated Community Response," in *Coordinating Community Responses to Domestic Violence: Lessons from Duluth and Beyond*, eds. Melanie F. Shepard and Ellen L. Pence (Thousand Oaks, CA: Sage Publications, 1999), 9.

24. Ibid., 10.

25. Janet Halley, *Split Decisions: How and Why to Take a Break from Feminism* (Princeton, NJ: Princeton University Press, 2006), 20, 22.

26. Ibid., 29.

27. Aya Gruber, "The Feminist War on Crime," *Iowa Law Review* 92, no. 3 (2007): 792.

28. William L. Hart et al., *Attorney General's Task Force on Family Violence: Final Report* (Washington, DC: Department of Justice, 1984), 11.

29. G. Kristian Miccio, "If Not Now, When? Individual and Collective Responsibility for Male Intimate Violence," *Washington and Lee Journal of Civil Rights and Social Justice* 15, no. 2 (2009): 412–13.

30. Elizabeth Pleck, *Domestic Tyranny: The Making of American Social Policy against Family Violence from Colonial Times to the Present* (New York: Oxford University Press, 1987), 197.

31. Garrine P. Laney, *Violence Against Women Act: History and Federal Funding* (Washington, DC: Congressional Research Service, 2005), 4.

32. Catherine Pierce, *The American Recovery and Reinvestment Act of 2009: A Message from OVW Acting Director Catherine Pierce* (Washington, DC: Office on Violence Against Women, 2009).

33. Laney, *Violence Against Women Act*, 6.

34. *2006 Biennial Report to Congress on the Effectiveness of Grant Programs Under the Violence Against Women Act* (U.S. Department of Justice Office on Violence Against Women, 2006), 143.

35. Ibid., 144.

36. 140 Cong. Rec. H5177-01 (daily ed. June 28, 1994).

37. 140 Cong. Rec. H8957-02 (daily ed. August 21, 1994).

38. 140 Cong. Rec. H8575-01 (daily ed. August 17, 1994).

39. G. Kristian Miccio, "A House Divided: Mandatory Arrest, Domestic Violence, and the Conservatization of the Battered Women's Movement," *Houston Law Review* 42, no. 2 (2005): 290.

40. Susan Schechter, *Women and Male Violence: The Visions and Struggles of the Battered Women's Movement* (Boston, MA: South End Press, 1982), 186–87.

41. Katharine T. Bartlett, "Family Law and American Culture: Feminism and Family Law," *Family Law Quarterly* 33, no. 3 (1999): 498.

42. Harris, "Race and Essentialism," 588.

43. Lenore E. Walker, *The Battered Woman* (New York: Harper Perennial, 1979), 19.

44. Beth E. Richie, "A Black Feminist Reflection on the Antiviolence Movement," in *Domestic Violence at the Margins: Readings on Race, Class, Gender, and Culture*, eds. Natalie J. Sokoloff with Christina Pratt (New Brunswick, NJ: Rutgers University Press, 2005), 52–53.

45. Barbara Fedders, "Lobbying for Mandatory-Arrest Policies: Race, Class and the Politics of the Battered Women's Movement," *New York University Review of Law and Social Change* 23, no. 2 (1997): 296.

46. Shepard and Pence, "Introduction," 7.

47. Ibid.

48. Pleck, *Domestic Tyranny*, 194.

49. Miccio, "A House Divided," 292–93.

50. Schechter, *Women and Male Violence*, 96.

51. "Interview with Cathryn Curley," *Power and Control: Domestic Violence in America*, April 20, 2010, http://www.powerandcontrolfilm.com/the-topics/founders/cathryn-curley/.

52. Amy Lehrner and Nicole E. Allen, "Still a Movement After All These Years? Current Tensions in the Domestic Violence Movement," *Violence Against Women* 15, no. 6 (2009): 668.

53. Neil Websdale, *Rural Woman Battering and the Justice System: An Ethnography* (Thousand Oaks, CA: Sage Publications, 1998), 209–10.

54. Angela Moe Wan, "Battered Women in the Restraining Order Process: Observations on a Court Advocacy Program," *Violence Against Women* 6, no. 6 (2000): 626, 629.

55. Shonna L. Trinch, *Latinas' Narratives of Domestic Abuse: Discrepant Versions of Violence* (Amsterdam: John Benjamins Publishing Company, 2003), 72.

56. Pleck, *Domestic Tyranny*, 199.

57. Lehrner and Allen, "Still a Movement," 665–66.

58. Miccio, "If Not Now, When?" 439.

59. Leah Lakshmi Piepzna-Samarasinha, "What It Feels Like When It Finally Comes: Surviving Incest in Real Life," in *Yes Means Yes: Visions of Female Sexual Power and a World Without Rape*, eds. Jaclyn Friedman and Jessica Valenti (Berkeley, CA: Seal Press, 2008), 103.

CHAPTER 2

1. This name has been changed to protect the identity of the woman described.

2. Elizabeth M. Schneider, "Particularity and Generality: Challenges of Feminist Theory and Practice in Work on Woman-Abuse," *New York University Law Review* 67, no. 3 (1992): 536.

3. Walker, *The Battered Woman*, 59.

4. Using basic statistics, Faigman estimated that between 23 percent and 58 percent of Walker's subjects had experienced all three phases of the cycle. David L. Faigman, "The Battered Woman Syndrome and Self-Defense: A Legal and Empirical Dissent," *Virginia Law Review* 72, no. 3 (1986): 640n108.

5. Holly Johnson, "The Cessation of Assaults on Wives: A Study of Domestic Violence Against Women," *Journal of Comparative Family Studies* 34, no. 1 (2003): 75.

6. Melanie Randall, "Domestic Violence and the Construction of 'Ideal Victims': Assaulted Women's 'Image Problems' in Law," *Saint Louis University Public Law Review* 23, no. 1 (2004): 122.

7. See, e.g., Jennifer Gentile Long, "Prosecuting Intimate Partner Sexual Assault," *The Prosecutor* 42, no. 2 (2008).

8. See, e.g., *State v. Drew*, No. 07AP-467, 2008 WL 2349649, at *12–13 (Ohio Ct. App. Jun. 10, 2008); *People v. Byrd*, 855 N.Y.S.2d 505, 508 (N.Y. App. Div. 2008).

9. *I.J. v. I.S.*, 744 A.2d 1246, 1249 n.1 (N.J. Super. Ct. Ch. Div. 1999).

10. See, e.g., *State v. B.H.*, 870 A.2d 273, 279 (N.J. 2005) (citing *State v. Kelly*, 478 A.2d 364, 370–73 (N.J. 1984)).

11. See, e.g., *State v. Worrall*, 220 S.W.3d 346, 349–50 (Mo. Ct. App. 2007).

12. "Interview with Ellen Pence," *Power and Control: Domestic Violence in America*, April 20, 2010, http://www.powerandcontrolfilm.com/the-topics/founders/ellen-pence/.

13. See, e.g., *State v. Drew*, No. 07AP-467, 2008 WL 2349649 (Ohio Ct. App. Jun. 10, 2008); *Borchgrevink v. Borchgrevnik*, 941 P.2d 132 (Alaska 1997); *State v. Maelega*, 907 P.2d 758 (Haw. 1995).

14. Some iterations of the Wheel deemphasize the centrality of physical and sexual abuse by equating physical and sexual violence with isolation, emotional and economic abuse, and the other controlling behaviors that comprise the spokes of the wheel. These edited versions are not the norm, however, and are not produced by DAIP. See, e.g., "Abuse in Intimate Relationships— 'The Wheel,'" London Abused Women's Centre, accessed October 17, 2010, http://www.lawc.on.ca/PDF_Files_Reports/Power%20and%20 Control%20Wheel.pdf.

15. Michael P. Johnson, *A Typology of Domestic Violence: Intimate Terrorism, Violent Resistance, and Situational Couple Violence* (Boston: Northeastern University Press, 2008), 9.

16. Evan Stark, *Coercive Control: How Men Entrap Women in Personal Life* (Oxford: Oxford University Press, 2007), 228–29.

17. Ibid., 255.

18. Ibid., 260.

19. Ibid., 271.

20. Ibid., 367.

21. Mary Ann Dutton and Lisa A. Goodman, "Coercion in Intimate Partner Violence: Toward a New Conceptualization," *Sex Roles* 52, no. 11/12 (2005): 746–47.

22. Tamara L. Kuennen, "Analyzing the Impact of Coercion on Domestic Violence Victims: How Much Is Too Much?" *Berkeley Journal of Gender Law and Justice* 22, no. 1 (2007): 11–12.

23. 725 Ill. Comp. Stat. 5/112A-3 (5) (2010).

24. Mo. Rev. Stat. § 565.074.1(6) (2010). "A person commits the crime of domestic assault in the third degree if the act involves a family or household member or an adult . . . and . . . (6) The person knowingly attempts to cause or causes the isolation of such family or household member by unreasonably and substantially restricting or limiting such family or household member's access to other persons."

25. See, e.g., *In re Joseph L.*, 939 A.2d 16, 26–27 (Conn. App. Ct. 2008).

26. Johnson, *Typology*, 11.

27. See, e.g., Victoria Frye et al., "The Distribution of and Factors Associated with Intimate Terrorism and Situational Couple Violence Among a Population-Based Sample of Urban Women in the United States," *Journal of Interpersonal Violence* 21, no. 10 (2006): 1286–1313; Joseph H. Michalski, "Explaining Intimate Partner Violence: The Sociological Limitations of Victimization Studies," *Sociological Forum* 20, no. 4 (2005): 613–40.

28. Ellen Pence and Shamita Das Dasgupta, *Re-Examining "Battering": Are All Acts of Violence Against Intimate Partners the Same?* (Duluth, MN: Praxis International, 2006), 3.

29. Ibid., 11.

30. Johnson, "Redefining Harm," 1133.

31. Richard M. Tolman, "The Validation of the Psychological Maltreatment of Women Inventory," *Violence and Victims* 14, no. 1 (1999): 26.

32. Mo. Rev. Stat. § 565.074.1(6) (2010) ("A person commits the crime of domestic assault in the third degree if . . . (6) The person knowingly attempts to cause or causes the isolation of such family or household member by unreasonably and substantially restricting or limiting such family or household member's access to other persons, telecommunication devices, or transportation for the purpose of isolation"; Nev. Rev. Stat. § 33.018 ("Domestic violence occurs when a person commits one of the following acts . . . (e) A knowing, purposeful or reckless course of conduct intended to harass the other person."

33. Del. Code Ann. 10 § 1045(1) (2010); Haw. Rev. Stat. § 586-1 (2010); 750 Ill. Comp. Stat. 60/103 (2010); N.M. Stat. Ann. § 40-13-2(D) (2010).

34. Heather Stark and Emilee Watturs, *Why Doesn't She Just Leave: Real Women, Real Stories. A New Perspective on Domestic Violence* (Woodinville,WA: MidPacifik Publishing, 2008), 112.

35. Adrienne E. Adams et al., "Development of the Scale of Economic Abuse," *Violence Against Women* 14, no. 5 (2008): 564.

36. Ibid., 567.

37. Jody Raphael, *Saving Bernice: Battered Women, Welfare, and Poverty* (Boston: Northeastern University Press, 2000), 5, 31.

38. Adams et al., "Development," 580.

39. Jody Raphael, "Battering Through the Lens of Class," *American University Journal of Gender, Social Policy and the Law* 11, no. 2 (2003): 368.

40. Mich. Comp. Laws § 600.2950(1)(g), (4) (2010).

41. Jean Chang et al., "Homicide: A Leading Cause of Injury Deaths Among Pregnant and Postpartum Women in the United States, 1991–1999," *American Journal of Public Health* 95, no. 3 (2005): 471–77; but see Rae Taylor and Erin L. Nabors, "Pink or Blue . . . Black and Blue? Examining Pregnancy as a Predictor of Intimate Partner Violence and Femicide," *Violence Against Women* 15, no. 11 (2009): 1287 (arguing that studies are mixed on whether intimate partner violence increases or decreases during pregnancy).

42. Stark, *Coercive Control*, 292.

43. Elizabeth Miller et al., "Pregnancy Coercion, Intimate Partner Violence and Unintended Pregnancy," *Contraception* 2010, no. 4 (2010): 1–2; see also Heike Thiel de Bocanegra et al., "Birth Control Sabotage and Forced Sex: Experiences Reported by Women in Domestic Violence Shelters," *Violence Against Women* 16, no. 5 (2010): 601.

44. Sarah Kliff, "Coerced Reproduction: Experts Are Studying a Phenomenon that Brings a Whole New Meaning to the Term 'Unwanted Pregnancy,'" *Newsweek*, January 26, 2010, http://www.newsweek.com/id/232542/output/print.

45. Yolanda R. Davila, "Influence of Abuse on Condom Negotiation Among Mexican-American Women Involved in Abusive Relationships," *Journal Association of Nurses in AIDS Care* 13, no. 6 (2002): 52.

46. Kliff, "Coerced Reproduction," 2.

47. Nicole Dehan and Zipi Levi, "Spiritual Abuse: An Additional Dimension of Abuse Experienced by Abused Haredi (Ultraorthodox) Jewish Wives," *Violence Against Women* 15, no. 11 (2009): 1300.

48. Ibid., 1302.

49. Ibid., 1305.

50. Beth Kiyoko Jamieson, *Real Choices: Feminism, Freedom, and the Limits of Law* (State College: Pennsylvania State University Press, 2001), 210.

51. Johnson, "Redefining Harm," 1107–08.

52. Deborah Tuerkheimer, "Recognizing and Remedying the Harm of Battering: A Call to Criminalize Domestic Violence," *Journal of Criminal Law and Criminology* 94, no. 4 (2004): 1019–23.

53. Alafair Burke, "Domestic Violence as a Crime of Pattern and Intent: An Alternative Reconceptualization," *George Washington Law Review* 75, no. 3 (2007): 556.

54. Jeffrey R. Baker, "Enjoining Coercion: Squaring Civil Protection Orders with the Reality of Domestic Abuse," *Journal of Law and Family Studies* 11, no. 1 (2008): 59.

55. Burke, "Domestic Violence," 571n106.

56. "Interview with Ellen Pence."

57. Mary Ann Dutton, Lisa Goodman, and R. James Schmidt, *Development and Validation of a Coercive Control Measure for Intimate Partner Violence: Final Technical Report, Prepared for National Institute of Justice, Office of Justice Programs* (Washington, DC: U.S. Department of Justice, 2005), 2.

58. Ellen Pence, "Some Thoughts on Philosophy," in *Coordinating Community Responses to Domestic Violence: Lessons from Duluth and Beyond* (Thousand Oaks, CA: Sage Publications, 1999), 29.

59. Cheryl Hanna, "The Paradox of Progress: Translating Evan Stark's Coercive Control into Legal Doctrine for Abused Women," *Violence Against Women* 15, no. 12 (2009): 1467–68.

60. Jane C. Murphy, "Lawyering for Social Change: The Power of the Narrative in Domestic Violence Law Reform," *Hofstra Law Review* 21, no. 4 (1993): 1275.

61. MacKinnon, *Feminism Unmodified*, 90.

62. Sue Osthoff, "But, Gertrude, I Beg to Differ, a Hit Is Not a Hit Is Not a Hit: When Battered Women Are Arrested for Assaulting Their Partners," *Violence Against Women* 8, no. 12 (2002): 1540.

63. Md. Code Ann., Family Law § 7-103(a)(7), (8) (LexisNexis 2010); Wash. Rev. Code § 26.09.060 (2010).

64. Leigh Goodmark, "From Property to Personhood: What the Legal System Should Do For Children in Family Violence Cases," *West Virginia Law Review* 102, no. 2 (1999): 254–59; Nancy K.D. Lemon, "Statutes Creating Rebuttable Presumptions Against Custody to Batterers: How Effective Are They?" *William Mitchell Law Review* 28, no. 2 (2001): 610–15.

65. Julie Goldscheid and Robin Runge, *Employment Law and Domestic Violence: A Practitioner's Guide* (Chicago: American Bar Association, 2009), 6–8. [online at http://new.abanet.org/domesticviolence/PublicDocuments/ABA_CDV_Employ.pdf]

66. Ibid., 8.

67. Or. Rev. Stat. § 90.449 (2010); Wash. Rev. Code §§ 59.18.575, 59.18.580 (2010).

68. D.C. Code § 42-3505.01(c-1)(2010); N.M. Stat. Ann. § 47-8-33(J) (2010).

CHAPTER 3

1. Minouche Kandel, "Women Who Kill Their Batterers Are Getting Battered in Court," *Ms.* (July/August 1993): 89.

2. Elizabeth A. Waites, "Female Masochism and the Enforced Restriction of Choice," *Victimology: An International Journal* 2, no. 3–4 (1977–78): 536.

3. Christine E. Rasche, "Early Models for Contemporary Thought on Domestic Violence and Women Who Kill Their Mates: A Review of the Literature from 1895 to 1970," *Women and Criminal Justice* 1, no. 2 (1990) 41 (describing A. A. Kurland, J. Morgenstern, and C. Sheets, "A Comparative Study of Wife Murderers Admitted to a State Psychiatric Hospital," *Journal of Social Therapy* 1 (1955): 7).

4. John E. Snell, Richard J. Rosenwald, and Ames Robey, "The Wifebeater's Wife: A Study of Family Interaction," *Archives of General Psychiatry* 11, no. 2 (1964): 111.

5. Natalie Shainess, "Vulnerability to Violence: Masochism as Process," *American Journal of Psychotherapy* 33, no. 2 (1979): 178.

6. Schechter, *Women and Male Violence*, 71.

7. Lenore E. A. Walker, "Politics, Psychology and the Battered Woman's Movement," *Journal of Trauma Practice* 1, no. 1 (2002): 96.

8. Charles Patrick Ewing and Moss Aubrey, "Battered Woman and Public Opinion: Some Realities about the Myths," *Journal of Family Violence* 2, no. 3 (1987): 260–62. Interestingly, women were much more likely than men to label a woman who stayed as masochistic (34% to 49.5%).

9. Schechter, *Women and Male Violence*, 55 (citing communication with battered woman's advocate Candace Wayne).

10. Elaine Hilberman, "Overview: The "Wife-Beater's Wife" Reconsidered," *American Journal of Psychiatry* 137, no. 11 (1980): 1343.

11. Walker, *The Battered Woman*, 46.

12. Edward W. Gondolf and Ellen R. Fisher, *Battered Women as Survivors: An Alternative to Treating Learned Helplessness* (Lexington, MA: Lexington Books, 1988), 13.

13. Walker, *The Battered Woman*, 49–50.

14. Lenore E. A. Walker, *The Battered Woman Syndrome* (New York: Springer Publishing, 1984), 87. The same language appears in the third edition, published in 2009. Lenore E. A. Walker, *The Battered Woman Syndrome*, 3rd ed. (New York: Springer Publishing, 2009), 72.

15. Walker, *The Battered Woman*, xvii.

16. See, e.g., *State v. Borelli*, 629 A.2d 1105 (Conn. 1993).

17. In the Interest of N.S.E., 651 S.E.2d 123, 126 (Ga. Ct. App. 2007).

18. Gondolf and Fisher, *Battered Women as Survivors*, 3.

19. Walker, *The Battered Woman Syndrome*, 3rd ed., 69.

20. Ibid., 42.

21. Elizabeth M. Schneider, *Battered Women and Feminist Lawmaking* (New Haven, CT: Yale University Press, 2000), 23–24.

22. Alafair S. Burke, "Rational Actors, Self-Defense, and Duress: Making Sense, Not Syndromes, Out of the Battered Woman," *North Carolina Law Review* 81, no. 1 (2002): 221.

23. Anne M. Coughlin, "Excusing Women," *California Law Review* 82, no. 1 (1994): 81–82; Gondolf and Fisher, *Battered Women as Survivors*, 18.

24. Randall, "Domestic Violence and the Construction of 'Ideal Victims,'" 124.

25. Gondolf and Fisher, *Battered Women as Survivors*, 11.

26. bell hooks, *Feminist Theory: From Margin to Center*, 2nd ed. (Cambridge, MA: South End Press, 2000), 46.

27. Walker, *The Battered Woman Syndrome*, 2nd ed., 40.

28. Sharon Lamb, "Constructing the Victim: Popular Images and Lasting Labels," in *New Versions of Victims: Feminists Struggle with the Concept*, ed. Sharon Lamb (New York: New York University Press, 1999), 126.

29. Evan Stark, "Framing and Reframing Battered Women," in *Domestic Violence: The Changing Criminal Justice Response*, eds. Eve S. Buzawa and Carl G. Buzawa (Westport, CT: Auburn House, 1992), 277.

30. Stark, *Coercive Control*, 165–66.

31. Shamita Das Dasgupta, "A Framework for Understanding Women's Use of Nonlethal Violence in Intimate Heterosexual Relationships," *Violence Against Women* 8, no. 11 (2002): 1378.

32. Shamita Das Dasgupta, "Just Like Men? A Critical View of Violence by Women," in *Coordinating Community Responses to Domestic Violence: Lessons from Duluth and Beyond*, eds. Shepard and Pence (Thousand Oaks, CA: Sage Publications, 1999), 214.

33. Kathleen J. Ferraro, "The Words Change But the Melody Lingers: The Persistence of Battered Woman Syndrome in Criminal Cases Involving Battered Women," *Violence Against Women* 9, no. 1 (2003): 116.

34. Carrie Cuthbert et al., *Battered Mothers Speak Out: A Human Rights Report on Domestic Violence and Child Custody in the Massachusetts Family Courts* (Wellesley, MA: Wellesley Centers for Women, 2002), 36.

35. *Nicholson v. Williams*, 203 F. Supp. 2d 153, 170 (E.D.N.Y. 2002).

36. Deborah M. Weissman, "Gender-Based Violence as Judicial Anomaly: Between 'The Truly National and the Truly Local,'" *Boston College Law Review* 42, no. 5 (2001): 1122.

37. Judge Susan Scott, "Panel Discussion: Advocating for Victims of Domestic Violence (Oct. 7, 1998)," *Women's Rights Law Reporter* 20, no. 1 (1999): 76–77.

38. Joan S. Meier, "Domestic Violence, Child Custody, and Child Protection: Understanding Judicial Resistance and Imagining the Solutions," *American University Journal of Gender, Social Policy and the Law* 11, no. 2 (2003): 686.

39. Merle H. Weiner, "The Potential and Challenges of Transnational Litigation for Feminists Concerned About Domestic Violence Here and Abroad," *American University Journal of Gender, Social Policy and Law* 11, no. 2 (2003): 784.

40. Shelby A. D. Moore, "Battered Woman Syndrome: Selling the Shadow to Support the Substance," *Howard Law Journal* 38, no. 2 (1995): 324.

41. See, e.g., Adele M. Morrison, "Queering Domestic Violence to 'Straighten Out' Criminal Law: What Might Happen When Queer Theory and Practice Meet Criminal Law's Conventional Responses to Domestic Violence," *Southern California Review of Law and Women's Studies* 13, no. 1 (2003): 139.

42. Beth E. Richie, *Compelled to Crime: The Gender Entrapment of Battered Black Women* (New York: Routledge, 1996), 119.

43. For a review of the literature on African American women, see Leigh Goodmark, "When Is a Battered Woman Not a Battered Woman? When She Fights Back," *Yale Journal of Law and Feminism* 20, no. 1 (2008): 96–104.

44. Leslye E. Orloff et al., "Battered Immigrant Women's Willingness to Call for Help and Police Response," *UCLA Women's Law Journal* 13, no. 1 (2003): 83.

45. See Hilary N. Weaver, "The Colonial Context of Violence: Reflections on Violence in the Lives of Native American Women," *Journal of Interpersonal Violence* 24, no. 9 (2009): 1552–63.

46. Donna H. Lee, "Next Steps: Intimate Partner Violence Against Asian American Women" (discussion draft, CUNY School of Law, Flushing, NY, 2009), 19.

47. Orloff et al., "Battered Immigrant Women's Willingness to Call," 71.

48. Margot Mendelson, "The Legal Production of Identities: A Narrative Analysis of Conversations with Battered Undocumented Women," *Berkeley Women's Law Journal* 19, no. 1 (2004): 139.

49. Shankar Vedantam, "Call for Help Leads to Possible Deportation for Hyattsville Mother," *Washington Post*, November 1, 2010, http://www.washingtonpost.com/wp-dyn/content/article/2010/11/01/AR2010110103073_pf.html.

50. Maia Ingram et al., "Experiences of Immigrant Women Who Self-Petition Under the Violence Against Women Act," *Violence Against Women* 16, no. 8 (2010): 859–60.

51. Websdale, *Rural Woman Battering*, 185n9.

52. Laurie E. Powers et al., "Interpersonal Violence and Women with Disabilities: Analysis of Safety Promoting Behaviors," *Violence Against Women* 15, no. 9 (2009): 1041.

53. Websdale, *Rural Woman Battering*, 8.

54. Ibid., 105.

55. Walter S. DeKeserdy and Martin D. Schwartz, *Dangerous Exits: Escaping Abusive Relationships in Rural America* (New Brunswick, NJ: Rutgers University Press, 2009), 85.

56. Websdale, *Rural Woman Battering*, 179.

57. Lisa R. Pruitt, "Toward a Feminist Theory of the Rural," *Utah Law Review* 2007, no. 2 (2007): 449. Pruitt notes the need to be cognizant of the diversity among rural women, citing rural sociologist Daryl Hobbs: "If you've seen one rural place, you've seen *one* rural place." Lisa R. Pruitt, "Place Matters: Domestic Violence and Rural Difference," *Wisconsin Journal of Law, Gender and Society* 23, no. 2 (2008): 388.

58. Adele M. Morrison, "Changing the Domestic Violence (Dis)Course: Moving From White Victim to Multi-Cultural Survivor," *UC Davis Law Review* 39, no. 3 (2006): 1083.

59. This exchange occurred on a day in 2008 when I was in the District Court for Baltimore City, watching the proceedings. Unfortunately, I failed to record the exact date, but jotted it down in the notebook I was carrying because I was so struck by it.

60. Jamieson, *Real Choices*, 206.

61. Leigh Goodmark, "Telling Stories, Saving Lives: The Battered Mothers' Testimony Project, Women's Narratives, and the Law," *Arizona State Law Journal* 37, no. 3 (2005): 741–42.

62. Trinch, *Latinas' Narratives of Domestic Abuse*, 115.

63. Ibid., 277.

64. Renée Römkens, "Law as a Trojan Horse: Unintended Consequences of Rights-Based Interventions to Support Battered Women," *Yale Journal of Law and Feminism* 13, no. 2 (2001): 284.

65. Kimberlé Crenshaw, "Mapping the Margins: Intersectionality, Identity Politics, and Violence Against Women of Color," *Stanford Law Review* 43, no. 6 (1991): 1245–46.

66. Jeannie Suk, *At Home in the Law: How the Domestic Violence Revolution Is Transforming Privacy* (New Haven, CT: Yale University Press, 2009), 72.

CHAPTER 4

1. Transcript of Trial at 728, *State v. Shanahan*, No. FECR006475 (Iowa Dist. Ct. Shelby County, Apr. 28, 2004).

2. Ibid., 717.

3. Christine A. Littleton, "Women's Experience and the Problem of Transition: Perspectives on Male Battering of Women," *University of Chicago Legal Forum* 1989 (1989): 29.

4. Callie Marie Rennison and Sarah Welchans, *Intimate Partner Violence* (Washington, DC: U.S. Department of Justice, 2001), 1, 5.

5. Renée Römkens, "Protecting Prosecution: Exploring the Powers of Law in an Intervention Program for Domestic Violence," *Violence Against Women* 12, no. 2 (2006): 160.

6. Ruth E. Fleury, Cris M. Sullivan, and Deborah I. Bybee, "When Ending the Relationship Does Not End the Violence: Women's Experiences of Violence by Former Partners," *Violence Against Women* 6, no. 12 (2000): 1381.

7. Martha R. Mahoney, "Legal Images of Battered Women: Redefining the Issue of Separation," *Michigan Law Review* 90, no. 1 (1991): 6.

8. DeKeserdy and Schwartz, *Dangerous Exits*, 85.

9. Raphael, *Saving Bernice*, 63–64.

10. David Owens, "West Hartford Man Arrested Three Times on Domestic Violence Charges," *Hartford Courant*, June 1, 2010, http://www.courant.com/news/domestic-violence/hc-westhartford-arrested-tree-times-020100531,0,1352850,print.story.

11. Laura Isensee et al., "Gunman's Rage Over Estranged Wife Leaves 5 Dead at Hialeah Restaurant: Gerardo Regalado, 38, of Coral Gables, Took His Own Life Just Blocks Away from the Shootings, Police Say," *Miami Herald*, June 8, 2010, http://www.sun-sentinel.com/sports/fl-hialeah-restaurant-shootings-20100607,0,5238568,print.story.

12. Lisa A. Goodman and Deborah Epstein, *Listening to Battered Women: A Survivor-Centered Approach to Advocacy, Mental Health, and Justice* (Washington, DC: American Psychological Association, 2008), 74.

13. Patricia Tjaden and Nancy Thoennes, *Extent, Nature and Consequences of Intimate Partner Violence* (Washington, DC: National Institute of Justice, 2000), 52; but see generally Joel H. Garner and Christopher D. Maxwell, "Prosecution and Conviction Rates for Intimate Partner Violence," *Criminal Justice Review* 34, no. 1 (2009) (arguing that arrest and conviction rates in domestic violence cases are higher than previous studies have recognized, but still finding conviction rates of only 16.4 percent).

14. Suzanne Le Breton, "Man Sentenced After Fifth Domestic Violence Conviction," *St. Tammany News*, May 19, 2010, http://www.thesttammanynews.com/articles.2010/05/19/news/doc4bf315981614c395906231.txt.

15. Robert E. Pierre and Clarence Williams, "Woman Had Lived in Fear of Former Boyfriend: D.C. Victim Slain After Calling Police," *Washington Post*, November 25, 2008, http://www.washingtonpost.com/wp-dyn/content/article/2008/11/24/AR2008112402763.html.

16. Charles L. Diviney, Asha Parekh, and Lenora M. Olson, "Outcomes of Civil Protective Orders: Results from One State," *Journal of Interpersonal Violence* 24, no. 7 (2009): 1211.

17. Adele Harrell and Barbara E. Smith, "Effects of Restraining Orders on Domestic Violence Victims," in *Do Arrests and Restraining Orders Work*, eds. Eve S. Buzawa and Carl G. Buzawa (Thousand Oaks, CA: Sage Publications, 1996), 218.

18. Diviney et al., "Outcomes of Civil Protective Orders," 1209–21.

19. Kathleen J. Ferraro, *Neither Angels Nor Demons: Women, Crime, and Victimization* (Boston: Northeastern University Press, 2006), 51.

20. Mary Owen and Steve Schmadeke, "Police: Attorney Beat Wife Outside Joliet Courtroom," *Chicago Tribune*, November 20, 2010, http://www.chicagotribune.com/news/local/southsouthwest/ct-met-joliet-lawyer-beating-1121-20101120.0.2346242.story.

21. Jane C. Murphy, "Engaging with the State: The Growing Reliance on Judges and Lawyers to Protect Battered Women," *American University Journal of Gender, Social Policy, and Law* 11, no. 2 (2003): 511–12.

22. Alesha Durfee, "Victim Narratives, Legal Representation, and Domestic Violence Civil Protection Orders," *Feminist Criminology* 4, no. 1 (2009): 24, 27.

23. Murphy, "Engaging with the State," 509–10.

24. TK Logan et al., "Protective Orders: Questions and Conundrums," *Trauma, Violence, and Abuse* 7, no. 3 (2006): 184; see also Ann Malecha et al., "Applying for and Dropping a Protection Order: A Study with 150 Women," *Criminal Justice Policy Review* 14, no. 4 (2003): 492.

25. D.C. Code Ann. § 16-1005 (c)(11) (2001).

26. Jennifer McMenamin, "Abuse Victim, Children to Return Home After Appeal," *Baltimore Sun*, October 24, 2008, http://articles.baltimoresun.com/2008-10-24/news/0810230170_1_bisnath-lamdin-judge.

27. Logan et al., "Protective Orders," 191.

28. Sally F. Goldfarb, "Reconceiving Civil Protection Orders for Domestic Violence: Can Law Help End the Abuse Without Ending the Relationship?" *Cardozo Law Review* 29, no. 4 (2008): 1516; see also Diviney et al., "Outcomes of Civil Protective Orders," 1209–21 (finding weak enforcement of protective orders in Utah courts).

29. *Town of Castle Rock v. Gonzales*, 545 U.S. 748, 752 (2005).

30. Ibid., 760.

31. Families in Transition: A Follow-Up Study Exploring Family Law Issues in Maryland (Towson, MD: Women's Law Center of Maryland, 2006), iii.

32. Cuthbert et al., *Battered Mothers Speak Out*, 3

33. Stark and Watturs, *Why Doesn't She Just Leave?* 56.

34. Megan Twohey, "One Woman's Struggle to Escape Abuse," *Chicago Tribune*, November 11, 2008, http://www.chicagotribune.com/news/local/chi-regan_tue-nov11,0,389866.story.

35. Stark and Watturs, *Why Doesn't She Just Leave?* 95.

36. Phyllis L. Baker, "And I Went Back: Battered Women's Negotiation of Choice," *Journal of Contemporary Ethnography* 26, no. 1 (1997): 58.

37. Donna Coker, "Shifting Power for Battered Women: Law, Material Resources, and Poor Women of Color," *UC Davis Law Review* 33, no. 4 (2000): 1019.

38. Lynn Ingrid Nelson, "Community Solutions to Domestic Violence Must Address Cultural Roots and Beliefs, *Assembling the Pieces* 3, no. 2 (2002): 2.

39. Subadra Panchanadeswaran et al., "Profiling Abusive Men Based on Women's Self-Reports: Findings from a Sample of Urban Low-Income Minority Women," *Violence Against Women* 16, no. 3 (2010): 315.

40. Ibid., 313–27.

41. Raymond M. Bergner, "Love and Barriers to Love: An Analysis for Psychotherapists and Others," *American Journal of Psychotherapy* 54, no. 1 (2000): 1.

42. Molly Chaudhuri and Kathleen Daly, "Do Restraining Orders Help? Battered Women's Experience with Male Violence and Legal Process," in *Domestic Violence: The Changing Criminal Justice Response*, eds. Eve S. Buzawa and Carl G. Buzawa (Westport, CT: Auburn House, 1992), 238.

43. Richie, *Compelled to Crime*, 70.

44. Lee H. Bowker, *Beating Wife-Beating* (Lexington, MA: Lexington Books, 1983), 63.

45. Jacquelyn C. Campbell et al., "Relationship Status of Battered Women Over Time," *Journal of Family Violence* 9, no. 2 (1994): 105.

46. Ibid., 107.

47. Littleton, "Women's Experiences," 47.

48. Coughlin, "Excusing Women," 60–61.

49. Ibid., 61.

50. Lora Bex Lempert, "Women's Strategies for Survival: Developing Agency in Abusive Relationships," *Journal of Family Violence* 11, no. 3 (1996): 284.

51. Lori A. Zoellner et al., "Factors Associated with Completion of the Restraining Order Process in Female Victims of Partner Violence," *Journal of Interpersonal Violence* 15, no. 10 (2000): 1095–96.

52. Sascha Griffing et al., "Domestic Violence Survivors' Self-Identified Reasons for Returning to Abusive Relationships," *Journal of Interpersonal Violence* 17, no. 3 (2002): 315.

53. Baker, "And I Went Back," 63.

54. Victims of Trafficking and Violence Protection Act of 2000 § 1513 (a)(2)(A) (2000).

55. Alice Davis, "Unlocking the Door By Giving Her the Key: A Comment on the Adequacy of the U-Visa as a Remedy," *Alabama Law Review* 56, no. 2 (2004): 569.

56. Nina W. Tarr, "Employment and Economic Security for Victims of Domestic Abuse," *Southern California Review of Law and Social Justice* 16, no. 2 (2007): 375.

57. Littleton, "Women's Experience," 52.

CHAPTER 5

1. Elizabeth M. Schneider, "The Violence of Privacy," *Connecticut Law Review* 23, no. 4 (1991): 984–85.

2. Lawrence W. Sherman et al., "Crime, Punishment, and Stake in Conformity: Legal and Informal Control of Domestic Violence," *American Sociological Review* 57, no. 5 (1992): 680.

3. For a comparison of mandatory arrest laws across the United States, see April M. Zeoli, Hannah Brenner, and Alexis Norris, "A Summary and Analysis of Warrantless Arrest Statutes for Domestic Violence in the United States," *Journal of Interpersonal Violence* 26 (forthcoming).

4. See, e.g., *State v. Hancock*, No. C-030459, 2004 WL 596103 (Ohio Ct. App. Mar. 26, 2004) (upholding conviction in domestic violence case where witness impeached with written and videotaped statements to police); *State v. Spraggins*, No. 82170, 2003 WL 22971050 (Ohio Ct. App. Dec. 18, 2003) (affirming conviction in domestic violence case where witness impeached with sworn statement).

5. Cheryl Hanna, "No Right to Choose: Mandated Victim Participation in Domestic Violence Prosecutions," *Harvard Law Review* 109, no. 8 (1996): 1891.

6. Tara Lea Muhlhauser and Douglas D. Knowlton, "Mediation in the Presence of Domestic Violence: Is It the Light at the End of the Tunnel or Is a Train on the Track?" *North Dakota Law Review* 70, no. 2 (1994): 267.

7. Allen M. Bailey and Carmen Kay Denny, "Attorneys Comment on Mediation and Domestic Violence," *Alaska Bar Rag* 27, no. 4 (2003): 16.

8. Sarah Krieger, "The Dangers of Mediation in Domestic Violence Cases," *Cardozo Women's Law Journal* 8, no. 2 (2002): 235.

9. Karla Fischer, Neil Vidmar, and Rene Ellis, "The Culture of Battering and the Role of Mediation in Domestic Violence Cases," *SMU Law Review* 46, no. 5 (1993): 2162.

10. Ibid., 2168.

11. Joan Zorza, "Protecting the Children in Custody Disputes When One Parent Abuses the Other," *Clearinghouse Review* 29, no. 12 (1996): §V (B).

12. Nancy Thoennes, Peter Salem, and Jessica Pearson, "Mediation and Domestic Violence: Current Policies and Practices," *Family and Conciliation Courts Review* 33, no. 1 (1995): 10–11.

13. Jane C. Murphy and Robert Rubinson, "Domestic Violence and Mediation: Responding to the Challenges of Crafting Effective Screens," *Family Law Quarterly* 39, no. 1 (2005): 63.

14. Thoennes et al., "Mediation and Domestic Violence," 20–21.

15. Demie Kurz, "Separation, Divorce, and Woman Abuse," *Violence Against Women* 2, no. 1 (1996): 76.

16. Del. Code Ann. 13 § 711A (2008).

17. Md. Rule 9-205 (b)-(c) (West 2008).

18. Diana T. Meyers, *Self, Society, and Personal Choice* (New York: Columbia University Press, 1989), 76.

19. See generally Joel Feinberg, "Autonomy," in *The Inner Citadel: Essays on Individual Autonomy,* ed. John Christman (New York: Oxford University Press, 1989), 27–53.

20. John Christman, "Feminism and Autonomy," in *"Nagging" Questions: Feminist Ethics in Everyday Life,* ed. Dana E. Bushnell (Lanham, MD: Rowman & Littlefield, 1995), 18.

21. Margaret E. Johnson, "Balancing Liberty, Dignity and Safety: The Impact of Domestic Violence Lethality Screening," *Cardozo Law Review* 32, no. 2 (2010): 522.

22. Christman, "Feminism and Autonomy," 30.

23. See, e.g., Grace Clement, *Care, Autonomy, and Justice: Feminism and the Ethic of Care* (Boulder, CO: Westview Press, 1996), 22; Misha Strauss, "The Role of Recognition in the Formation of Self-Understanding," in *Recognition, Responsibility, and Rights: Feminist Ethics and Social Theory,* eds. Robin N. Fiore and Hilde Lindemann Nelson (Lanham, MD: Rowman & Littlefield, 2003), 46–47.

24. Susan Wendell, "Oppression and Victimization: Choice and Responsibility," in Bushnell, *"Nagging" Questions,* 43.

25. Morwenna Griffiths, *Feminisms and the Self: The Web of Identity* (London: Routledge, 1995), 135.

26. Kathryn Abrams, "From Autonomy to Agency: Feminist Perspectives on Self-Direction," *William & Mary Law Review* 40, no. 3 (1999): 824.

27. Jamieson, *Real Choices,* 7.

28. Griffiths, *Feminism and the Self*, 142.

29. Ruth Jones, "Guardianship for Coercively Controlled Battered Women: Breaking the Control of the Abuser," *Georgetown Law Journal* 88, no. 4 (2000): 628.

30. Marilyn Friedman, *Autonomy, Gender, Politics* (New York: Oxford University Press, 2003), 150.

31. Ibid., 151.

32. Ibid., 155.

33. Christman, "Feminism and Autonomy," 35.

34. Abrams, "From Autonomy to Agency," 832.

35. Schechter, *Women and Male Violence*, 320.

36. Ibid., 109.

37. M. Joan McDermott and James Garofalo, "When Advocacy for Domestic Violence Victims Backfires: Types and Sources of Victim Disempowerment," *Violence Against Women* 10, no. 11 (2004): 1248.

38. Jane Aiken and Katherine Goldwasser argue that empowerment-based strategies are problematic for women subjected to abuse because they place the onus for ending the abuse on individual women rather than on the state. They argue instead for norm-changing strategies that shift responsibility for ending violence to communities. Jane Aiken and Katherine Goldwasser, "The Perils of Empowerment," *Cornell Journal of Law and Public Policy* 20, no. 1 (2010): 141–43. While I agree that communities have a crucial role to play in ending abuse of women, I see Aiken and Goldwasser's definition of empowerment, which links empowerment to utilization of state-provided remedies like protective orders, as excessively narrow.

39. Merle H. Weiner, "From Dollars to Sense: A Critique of Government Funding for the Battered Women's Shelter Movement," *Law and Inequality: A Journal of Theory and Practice* 9, no. 2 (1991): 237 (citing *Reclaiming Our Movement: A Focus on Formerly Battered Women*).

40. Michele Henry, "Pregnant Woman 'Never Calling the Police Again,'" *Toronto Star*, April 8, 2008, http://www.thestar.com/printArticle/411222.

41. *State v. Spraggins*, No. 82170, 2003 WL 22971050, at *2 (Ohio Ct. App. Dec. 18, 2003).

42. Ibid.

43. Angela J. Davis, *Arbitrary Justice: The Power of the American Prosecutor* (New York: Oxford University Press, 2007), 67–68.

44. *People v. Caldarella*, No. 07CV174 (Dist. Ct. Colo. 2007). One study found that 92 percent of prosecutors' offices use subpoenas to secure victim testimony. Donald J. Rebovich, "Prosecution Response to Domestic Violence: Results of a Survey of Large Jurisdictions," in *Do Arrests and Restraining Orders Work?* eds. Eve S. Buzawa and Carl G. Buzawa (Thousand Oaks, CA: Sage Publications, 1996), 186.

45. Michelle Madden Dempsey, *Prosecuting Domestic Violence: A Philosophical Analysis* (Oxford: Oxford University Press, 2009), 219–20.

46. Ibid., 220.

47. David Hirschel et al., "Domestic Violence and Mandatory Arrest Laws: To What Extent Do They Influence Police Arrest Decisions," *Journal of Criminal Law and Criminology* 98, no. 1 (2007): 255; Carla Smith Stover et al., "The Efficacy of a Police-Advisory Intervention for Victims of Domestic Violence: 12 Month Follow-Up Data," *Violence Against Women* 16, no. 4 (2010): 411 (discussing studies on effectiveness of mandatory arrest).

48. Tarr, "Employment and Economic Security," 389.

49. Linda G. Mills, *Insult to Injury: Rethinking Our Responses to Intimate Abuse* (Princeton, NJ: Princeton University Press, 2003), 6.

50. Connie J.A. Beck, Michele E. Walsh, and Rose Weston, "Analysis of Mediation Agreements of Families Reporting Specific Intimate Partner Abuse," *Family Court Review* 47, no. 3 (2009): 411.

51. Ibid., 411.

52. See, e.g., Mary Adkins, "Moving Out of the 1990s: An Argument for Updating Protocol on Divorce Mediation in Domestic Abuse Cases," *Yale Journal of Law and Feminism* 22, no. 1 (2010).

53. 36 Ops. Cal. Attorney General 200 (1960); Mia M. McFarlane, "Mandatory Reporting of Domestic Violence: An Inappropriate Response for New York Health Care Professionals," *Buffalo Public Interest Law Journal* 17, no. 1 (1999): 13–14.

54. Ops. Kentucky Attorney General 83-187 (1983); Ky. Rev. Stat. Ann. § 209.030(8) (West 2010).

55. *People v. Covington*, 19 P.3d 15, 22 (Colo. 2001).

56. Ariella Hyman, *Mandatory Reporting of Domestic Violence by Health Care Providers: A Policy Paper* (San Francisco: Family Violence Prevention Fund, 1997), 14.

57. Ibid., 6n5. The American Medical Association also opposes mandatory reporting of intimate partner abuse among adults, stating that such policies "violate basic tenets of medical ethics." *AMA Data on Violence Between Intimates* (American Medical Association, 2000), http://www.ama-assn.org/ama/no-index/about-ama/13577.shtml.

58. David A. Ford, "Prosecution as a Victim Power Resource: A Note on Empowering Women in Violent Conjugal Relationships," *Law and Society Review* 25, no. 2 (1991): 318.

59. Krieger, "The Dangers of Mediation," 257.

60. Hart, "Arrest: What's the Big Deal,"209.

CHAPTER 6

1. Trina Grillo, "Anti-Essentialism and Intersectionality: Tools to Dismantle the Master's House," *Berkeley Women's Law Journal* 10, no. 1 (1995): 17.

2. Harris, "Race and Essentialism," 595.

3. Jill Davies, *When Battered Women Stay . . . Advocacy Beyond Leaving* (Harrisburg, PA: National Resource Center on Domestic Violence, 2008), 7.

4. Mendelson, "The Legal Production of Identities," 199–201.

5. Dempsey, *Prosecuting Domestic Violence*, 208. It is, of course, impossible to determine whether any particular prosecution will reduce the violence within that relationship at the time of prosecution, given that the outcome of the case is unknown and the likelihood of incarceration for any appreciable period of time slight.

6. See, e.g., D. Alex Heckert and Edward W. Gondolf, "Battered Women's Perceptions of Risk Versus Risk Factors And Instruments in Predicting Repeat Assault," *Journal of Interpersonal Violence* 19, no. 7 (2004): 778–800; A. Weisz, R. Tolman, and Daniel Saunders, "Assessing the Risk of Severe Domestic Violence: The Importance of Survivors' Predictions," *Journal of Interpersonal Violence* 15, no. 1 (2000): 75–90; Panchanadeswaran et al., "Profiling Abusive Men," 323.

7. Ruth Colker, "Abortion and Violence," *William & Mary Journal of Women and the Law* 1, no. 1 (1994): 98–99.

8. Schneider, "Particularity and Generality," 527.

9. Gayatri Chakravorty Spivak, "Subaltern Studies: Deconstructing Historiography," in *Selected Subaltern Studies*, eds. Ranajit Guha and Gayatri Chakravorty Spivak (New York: Oxford University Press, 1988), 13, 15.

10. Schneider, *Battered Women and Feminist Lawmaking*, 64–65.

11. Claire M. Renzetti, *Economic Stress and Domestic Violence* (VAWNet Applied Research Forum, 2009), 1.

12. Ibid. (citing M. L. Benson and G. L. Fox, *When Violence Hits Home: How Economics and Neighborhood Play a Role* (Washington, DC: U.S. Department of Justice, National Institute of Justice, 2004)).

13. Raphael, *Saving Bernice*, 140–41.

14. Ibid., 141.

15. Ibid., 143.

16. Renzetti, *Economic Stress and Domestic Violence*, 3 (citing Benson and Fox).

17. Coker, "Shifting Power for Battered Women," 1009.

18. Donna Coker, "Addressing Domestic Violence Through a Strategy of Economic Rights," *Women's Rights Law Reporter* 24, no. 3 (2003): 189.

19. Patricia Tjaden and Nancy Thoennes, *Prevalence, Incidence and Consequences of Violence Against Women: Findings From the National Violence Against Women Survey* (Washington, DC: National Institute of Justice, Center for Disease Control and Prevention, 1998), 6 (citing high rates of victimization among Native American women).

20. Andrea Smith, "Beyond Restorative Justice: Radical Organizing Against Violence," in *Restorative Justice and Violence Against Women*, ed. James Ptacek (New York: Oxford University Press, 2010), 255–56.

21. Nancy Levit, "Feminism for Men: Legal Ideology and the Construction of Maleness," *UCLA Law Review* 43, no. 4 (1996): 1048–49.

22. Amy Holtzworth-Munroe and Gregory L. Stuart, "Typologies of Male Batterers: Three Subtypes and the Differences Among Them," *Psychological Bulletin* 116, no. 3 (1994): 481–82.

23. Amy Holtzworth-Munroe et al., "Testing the Holtzworth-Munroe and Stuart Typology," *Journal of Consulting and Clinical Psychology* 68, no. 6 (2000): 1000.

24. Matthew T. Huss and Jennifer Langhinrichsen-Rohling, "Assessing the Generalization of Psychopathy in a Clinical Sample of Domestic Violence Perpetrators," *Law and Human Behavior* 30, no. 5 (2006): 571; Panchanadeswaran et al., "Profiling Abusive Men," 313–27.

25. Johnson, *Typology*, 31.

26. DeKeseredy and Schwartz, *Dangerous Exits*, 96.

27. See, e.g., Natalie Bedell, "'Economic Control' Up 40 Percent As Local Domestic Violence Cause," *Falls Church* (Virginia) *News-Press*, September 22, 2010, http://www.fcnp.com/news/7394-economic-control-up-40-percent-as-local-domestic-violence-cause.html; Michael Lollar, "Economy, Technology Feed Rising Domestic Violence Rates," (Memphis, Tennessee) *Commercial Appeal*, October 11, 2010, http://www.commercialappeal.com/news/2010/oct/10/economy-technology-feed-rising-domestic-02/; Rebecca L. White and James J. Postl, "Domestic Violence Spikes Amid Financial Stress," *Houston Chronicle*, October 16, 2010, http://www.chron.com/disp/story.mpl/editorial/outlook/7250193.html.

28. Claire M. Renzetti, "Economic Issues and Intimate Partner Violence," in *Sourcebook on Violence Against Women*, 2nd ed., eds. Claire M. Renzetti, Jeffrey L. Edleson, and Raquel Kennedy Bergen (Thousand Oaks, CA: Sage Publications, 2011), 174.

29. Frederick P. Buttell and Michelle M. Carney, "Do Batterer Intervention Programs Serve African American and Caucasian Batterers Equally Well? An Investigation of a 26 Week Program," *Research on Social Work Practice* 15, no. 1 (2005): 27.

30. Susan H. Williams and David C. Williams, "A Feminist Theory of Malebashing," *Michigan Journal of Gender and the Law* 4, no. 1 (1996): 68.

31. "Interview with Ellen Pence."

32. Edward W. Gondolf, "Theoretical and Research Support for the Duluth Model: A Reply to Dutton and Corvo," *Aggression and Violent Behavior* 12, no. 6 (2007): 647.

33. Edward Gondolf, "Mandatory Court Review and Batterer Program Compliance," *Journal of Interpersonal Violence* 15, no. 4 (2000): 428 (citing Edward Gondolf and Robert Foster, "Pre-program Attrition in Batterer Programs," *Journal of Family Violence* 6, no. 4 (1991): 337).

34. Jennifer E. Daly, Thomas G. Power, and Edward W. Gondolf, "Predictors of Batterer Program Attendance," *Journal of Interpersonal Violence* 16, no. 10 (2001): 985.

35. Gondolf, "Mandatory Court Review," 428; see also Greg Barnes, "Few Soldiers Assigned to Domestic Violence Care Finish Programs," *Fay* (North Carolina) *Observer*, September 29, 2010, http://www.fayobserver.com/articles/2010/09/29/1028491?sac=Mil.

36. Lucy Salcido Carter, *Doing the Work and Measuring the Progress: A Report on the December 2009 Experts Roundtable* (San Francisco, CA: Family Violence Prevention Fund, 2010), 5.

37. Edward W. Gondolf, "Evaluating Batterer Counseling Programs: A Difficult Task Showing Some Effects and Implications," *Aggression and Violent Behavior* 9, no. 6 (2004): 623; Richard M. Tolman and Jeffrey L. Edleson, "Intervening With Men for Violence Prevention," in *Sourcebook on Violence Against Women*, 2nd ed., eds. Claire M. Renzetti, Jeffrey L. Edleson, and Raquel Kennedy Bergen (Thousand Oaks, CA: Sage Publications, 2011), 355.

38. Julia C. Babcock, Charles E. Green, and Chet Robie, "Does Batterer's Treatment Work? A Meta-analytic Review of Domestic Violence Treatment," *Clinical Psychology Review* 23, no. 8 (2004): 1044.

39. Edward W. Gondolf, "A Comparison of Four Batterer Intervention Systems: Do Court Referral, Program Length, and Services Matter?" *Journal of Interpersonal Violence* 14, no. 1 (1999): 53.

40. Buttell and Carney, "Do Batterer Intervention Programs Serve?" 27.

41. DeKeserdy and Schwartz, *Dangerous Exits*, 90–91.

42. Tolman and Edleson, "Intervening With Men for Violence Prevention," 356.

43. Daniel G. Saunders, "Feminist-Cognitive-Behavioral and Process-Psychodynamic Treatments for Men Who Batter: Interaction of Abuser Traits and Treatment Model," *Violence and Victims* 11, no. 4 (1996): 393–414; *but see* Gondolf, "Evaluating Batterer Counseling Programs," 623 (arguing that Duluth type programs seem to be appropriate for all types of men).

44. Abrams, "Sex Wars Redux," 375.

45. Raphael, *Saving Bernice*, 149.

46. Leigh Goodmark, "Achieving Batterer Accountability in the Child Protection System," *Kentucky Law Journal* 93, no. 3 (2004–5): 648.

47. Lehrner and Allen, "Still a Movement," 670.

48. Davies, *When Battered Women Stay*, 3

49. Ibid.

50. Ibid., 8.

51. Trinch, *Latinas' Narratives of Domestic Abuse*, 87–118.

52. Jeannie Suk, "Criminal Law Comes Home," *Yale Law Journal* 116, no. 1 (2006): 8.

53. Goldfarb, "Reconceiving Civil Protection Orders," 1522; Leigh Goodmark, "Law Is the Answer? Do We Know That for Sure?: Questioning the Efficacy of Legal Interventions for Battered Women," *Saint Louis University Public Law Review* 23, no. 1 (2004): 25.

54. *Feltmeier v. Feltmeier*, 798 N.E.2d 75, 82–83 (Ill. 2003).

55. *Pugliese v. Pugliese*, 146 Cal. App. 4th 1444, 1452 (Cal. Ct. App. 2007).

56. Spencer S. Hsu, "Domestic-Partner Violence in United States Fell Sharply," *Washington Post*, December 29, 2006, http://www.washingtonpost.com/wp-dyn/content/article/2006/12/28/AR2006122801170.html; Paul Srubas, "Domestic Violence Increases in Green Bay Area," *Green Bay* (Wisconsin) *Press Gazette*, October 3, 2010, http://www.greenbay-pressgazette.com/fdcp/?1268134466187; Jamal Thalji, "Domestic Violence Murders Rise as Crime Falls in Florida," *St. Petersburg Times*, October 12, 2010, http://license.icopyright.net/user/viewFreeUse.act?fuid=MTAzMTczMzI%3D; Matthew Kemeny, "Increase in Domestic Violence-related Deaths Motivates Advocates," *Patriot-News*, October 15, 2010, http://www.pennlive.com/midstate/index.ssf/2010/10/increase_in_domestic_violence-.html.

57. Hsu, "Domestic-Partner Violence in United States Fell Sharply."

58. Christy A. Visher et al., "Reducing Intimate Partner Violence: An Evaluation of a Comprehensive Justice System-Community Collaboration," *Criminology and Public Policy* 7, no. 4 (2008): 496.

59. Ibid., 519.

60. Tjaden and Thoennes, *Extent, Nature and Consequences*, 49–52.

61. Stark, *Coercive Control*, 63.

62. Judith Lewis Herman, "Justice from the Victim's Perspective," *Violence Against Women* 10, no. 5 (2005): 574.

63. Coker, "Shifting Power for Battered Women," 1043. A study examining Wisconsin's implementation of mandatory arrest showed that arrests of women increased 12 times after inception, as opposed to two times for men. L. Kevin Hamberger and Theresa Potente, "Counseling Heterosexual Women Arrested for Domestic Violence: Implications for Theory and Practice," *Violence and Victims* 9, no. 2 (1994): 126. In Los Angeles, women made up 7 percent of the people arrested for domestic violence in 1987 and 14.3 percent by 1995, after the adoption of the mandatory arrest law. John Johnson, "A New Side to Domestic Violence: Arrests of Women Have Risen Sharply Since Passage of Tougher Laws," *L.A. Times*, April 27, 1996, at A1. See also Susan L. Miller, LeeAnn Iovanni, and Kathleen D. Kelley, "Violence Against Women and the Criminal Justice Response," in *Sourcebook on Violence Against Women*, 2nd ed., eds. Claire M. Renzetti, Jeffrey L. Edleson, and Raquel Kennedy Bergen (Thousand Oaks, CA: Sage Publications, 2011), 269; "Women Three Times More Likely to be Arrested for Domestic Violence," *Guardian UK*, August 28, 2009, http://www.guardian.co.uk/society/2009/aug/28/women-arrested-domestic-violence/print (finding the same trend in UK).

64. Christine Fiore and Kristen O'Shea, "Women in Violent Relationships—Experiences with the Legal and Medical Systems," in *Intimate Partner Violence*, eds. K. A. Kendall-Tacket and S. M. Giacomoni (New Jersey: Civic Research Institute, 2007), 18–11.

65. Ferraro, *Neither Angels Nor Demons*, 56.

66. Martha Albertson Fineman, "Preface," in *The Public Nature of Private Violence: The Discovery of Domestic Abuse*, eds. Martha Albertson Fineman and Roxanne Mykitiuk (New York: Routledge, 1994), xvi.

67. Gruber, "The Feminist War on Crime," 809.

68. Jane M. Spinak, "Reforming Family Court: Getting It Right Between Rhetoric and Reality," *Washington University Journal of Law and Policy* 31, no. 1 (2009): 34.

69. Schechter, *Women and Male Violence*, 177

70. Judy L. Postmus et al., "Women's Experiences of Violence and Seeking Help," *Violence Against Women* 15, no. 7 (2009): 862.

71. Domestic Violence Counts 2009: A 24-Hour Census of Domestic Violence Shelters and Services (Washington, DC: National Network to End Domestic Violence, 2009), 9.

72. Römkens, "Law as a Trojan Horse," 290.

73. Jennifer L. Hartman and Joanne Belknap, "Beyond the Gatekeepers: Court Professionals' Self-Reported Attitudes about and Experiences with Misdemeanor Domestic Violence Cases," *Criminal Justice and Behavior* 30, no. 3 (2003): 363.

74. Bowker, *Beating Wife-Beating*, 104.

75. Mimi Kim, *Innovative Strategies to Address Domestic Violence in Asian and Pacific Islander Communities: Examining Themes, Models, and Interventions* (San Francisco: Asian & Pacific Islander Institute on Domestic Violence, July 2002, revised February 2010), 9.

76. Professor Holly Maguigan makes this point in the context of mandatory criminal justice policies; I have adopted it more broadly here. Holly Maguigan, "Wading Into Professor Schneider's 'Murky Middle Ground' Between Acceptance and Rejection of Criminal Justice Responses to Domestic Violence," *American University Journal of Gender, Social Policy and the Law* 11, no. 2 (2003): 443–44.

CHAPTER 7

1. Websdale, *Rural Woman Battering*, 209.

2. Goldfarb, "Reconceiving Civil Protection Orders," 1525.

3. A District of Columbia judge made this statement to a client of law professor Tamara Kuennen. Goodman and Epstein, *Listening to Battered Women*, 81.

4. See ibid., 93–94.

5. Stark, *Coercive Control*, 380–81.

6. Raymond Paternoster et al., "Do Fair Procedures Matter? The Effect of Procedural Justice on Spouse Assault," *Law and Society Review* 31, no. 1 (1997): 194–95; see also Michael King and Becky Batagol, "Enforcer, Manager, or Leader? The Judicial Role in Family Violence Courts," *International Journal of Law and Psychiatry* 33, no. 5–6 (2010): 408 (surveying research).

7. For a discussion of how to implement procedural justice reforms in domestic violence cases, see generally Deborah Epstein, "Procedural Justice: Tempering the State's Response to Domestic Violence," *William & Mary Law Review* 43, no. 5 (2002).

8. Melissa L. Breger, "Introducing the Construct of the Jury into Family Violence Proceedings and Family Court Jurisprudence," *Michigan Journal of Gender and Law* 13, no. 1 (2006): 3.

9. C. Quince Hopkins, Mary P. Koss, and Karen J. Bachar, "Applying Restorative Justice to Ongoing Intimate Violence: Problems and Possibilities," *Saint Louis University Public Law Review* 23, no. 1 (2004): 294.

10. Kay Pranis, "Restorative Values and Family Violence," in *Restorative Justice and Family Violence*, eds. Heather Strang and John Braithwaite (Cambridge: Cambridge University Press, 2002), 30.

11. James Ptacek and Loretta Frederick, *Restorative Justice and Intimate Partner Violence* (VAWNet Applied Research Forum, 2008), 5–8.

12. Lawrence W. Sherman, "Domestic Violence and Restorative Justice: Answering Key Questions," *Virginia Journal of Social Policy and the Law* 8, no. 1 (2000): 281.

13. Donna Coker, "Restorative Justice, Navajo Peacemaking and Domestic Violence," *Theoretical Criminology* 10, no. 1 (2006): 77.

14. Rashmi Goel, "Sita's Trousseau: Restorative Justice, Domestic Violence, and South Asian Culture," *Violence Against Women* 11, no. 5 (2005): 640.

15. Loretta Frederick and Kristine C. Lizdas, "The Role of Restorative Justice in the Battered Women's Movement," in *Restorative Justice and Violence Against Women*, ed. James Ptacek (New York: Oxford University Press, 2010), 40.

16. C. Quince Hopkins and Mary P. Koss, "Incorporating Feminist Theory and Insights Into a Restorative Justice Response to Sex Offenses," *Violence Against Women* 11, no. 5 (2005): 697.

17. Hopkins, Koss, and Bachar, "Applying Restorative Justice," 307–9.

18. Donna Coker, "Transformative Justice: Anti-Subordination Processes in Cases of Domestic Violence," in *Restorative Justice and Family Violence*, 148.

19. Laurie S. Kohn, "What's So Funny About Peace, Love and Understanding? Restorative Justice as a New Paradigm for Domestic Violence Intervention," *Seton Hall Law Review* 40, no. 2 (2010): 576–93.

20. For a discussion of the possibilities of engaging in the collaborative process in the presence of domestic violence, see Nancy Ver Steegh, "The Uniform Law Act and Intimate Partner Violence: A Roadmap for Collaborative (and Non-Collaborative) Lawyers," *Hofstra Law Review* 38, no. 2 (2009).

21. For a longer discussion of the potential of online mediation, see Sarah Rogers, "Online Dispute Resolution: An Option for Mediation in the Midst of Gendered Violence," *Ohio State Journal on Dispute Resolution* 24, no. 2 (2009): 349–79.

22. Amanda Shea Hart, "Child Inclusive Mediation in Parenting Disputes Where Domestic Violence Is an Issue" (School of Social Work & Human Services, Central Queensland University, Rockhampton, Queensland (Australia), 2008. http://www.ausdispute.unisa.edu.au/apmf/2008/papers/20-Amanda%20Shea%20Hart.pdf.), 5.

23. Ibid.

24. Carolyn Y. Tubbs and Oliver J. Williams, "Shared Parenting After Abuse: Battered Mothers' Perspectives on Parenting After Dissolution of a Relationship," in *Parenting by Men Who Batter: New Directions for Assessment and Intervention*, eds. Jeffrey L. Edleson and Oliver J. Williams (New York: Oxford University Press, 2007), 19–44.

25. Goodmark, "From Property to Personhood," 268.

26. Cuthbert et al., *Battered Mothers Speak Out*, 35.

27. Lundy Bancroft and Jay G. Silverman, *The Batterer as Parent: Addressing the Impact of Domestic Violence on Family Dynamics* (Thousand Oaks, CA: Sage Publications, 2002): 29–36.

28. James Ptacek, *Battered Women in the Courtroom: The Power of Judicial Response* (Boston: Northeastern University Press, 1999), 150.

29. Mindie Lazarus-Black, *Everyday Harm: Domestic Violence, Court Rites, and Cultures of Reconciliation* (Urbana: University of Illinois Press, 2007), 163.

CHAPTER 8

1. Herman, "Justice from the Victim's Perspective," 582.

2. Ibid., 585.

3. Brenda V. Smith, "Battering, Forgiveness and Redemption," *American University Journal of Gender, Social Policy and the Law* 11, no. 2 (2003): 929.

4. Herman, "Justice from the Victim's Perspective," 593.

5. Judge Bennett Burkemper and Nina Balsam, "Examining the Use of Restorative Justice Practices in Domestic Violence Cases," *Saint Louis University Public Law Review* 27, no. 1 (2007): 121; "Observations from Participants," *Domestic Violence Surrogate Dialogue,* http://www.dvsdprogram.com/observations.php.

6. "Observations from Participants."

7. Teresa Godwin Phelps, *Shattered Voices: Language, Violence and the Work of Truth Commissions* (Philadelphia: University of Pennsylvania Press, 2004), 9.

8. Ibid., 109.

9. Ibid., 66.

10. Roslyn Myers, "Truth and Reconciliation Commissions 101: What TRCs Can Teach the United States Justice System About Justice," *Revista Juridica Universidad de Puerto Rico* 78, no. 1 (2009): 101.

11. Phelps, *Shattered Voices,* 42.

12. Myers, "Truth and Reconciliation Commissions 101," 124.

13. James L. Gibson, "On Legitimacy Theory and the Effectiveness of Truth Commissions," *Law and Contemporary Problems* 72, no. 2 (2009): 134.

14. Myers, "Truth and Reconciliation Commissions 101," 120.

15. Tristan Anne Borer, "Gendered War and Gendered Peace: Truth Commissions and Postconflict Gender Violence: Lessons From South Africa," *Violence Against Women* 15, no. 10 (2009): 1169–93.

16. Phelps, *Shattered Voices,* 111.

17. Ibid., 57–58.

18. Myers, "Truth and Reconciliation Commissions 101," 115.

19. Phelps, *Shattered Voices,* 112.

20. Jodi Halpern and Harvey M. Weinstein, "Empathy and Rehumanization After Mass Violence," in *My Neighbor, My Enemy: Justice and Community in the Aftermath of Mass Atrocity,* eds. Eric Stover and Harvey M. Weinstein (Cambridge: Cambridge University Press, 2004), 307.

21. Myers, "Truth and Reconciliation Commissions 101," 121.

22. Law professor Sherrilyn Ifill makes this argument in the context of creating a truth commission to examine lynching in the United States. See Sherrilyn A. Ifill, "Creating a Truth and Reconciliation Commission for Lynching," *Law and Inequality* 21, no. 2 (2003): 263–311.

23. Smith, "Battering, Forgiveness and Redemption," 944.

24. Microfinance could be used as a delivery system for reparations. See generally Anita Bernstein, "Pecuniary Reparations Following National Crisis: A Convergence of Tort Theory, Microfinance and Gender Equality," *University of Pennsylvania Journal of International Law* 31, no. 1 (2009).

25. Carlton Waterhouse, "The Good, the Bad, and the Ugly: Moral Agency and the Role of Victims in Reparations Programs," *University of Pennsylvania Journal of International Law* 31, no. 1 (2009): 269–70.

26. Mimi Kim, *The Community Engagement Continuum: Outreach, Mobilization, Organizing and Accountability to Address Violence against Women in Asian and Pacific Islander Communities* (San Francisco: Asian & Pacific Islander Institute on Domestic Violence, March 2005), 40–42.

27. Ibid., 42.

28. Kim, *Innovative Strategies*, 22.

29. Mary P. Koss, "Blame, Shame and Community: Justice Responses to Violence Against Women," *American Psychologist* 55, no. 11 (2000): 1338.

30. Mimi Kim, "Alternative Interventions to Intimate Violence: Defining Political and Pragmatic Challenges," in *Restorative Justice and Violence Against Women*, ed. James Ptacek (New York: Oxford University Press, 2010), 208.

31. Ibid., 209.

32. Ibid., 195.

33. See, e.g., Peter Schworm and John M. Guilfoil, "Rising Economic Stress Cited in Domestic Violence Increase," *Boston Globe*, February 3, 2010, http:/www.boston.com/news/local/Massachusetts/articles/2010/02/03/rising_economic_stress_cited_in_domestic_violence_increase?mode=PF.

34. Jacquelyn C. Campbell et al., "Risk Factors for Femicide in Abusive Relationships: Results from a Multisite Case Control Study," *American Journal of Public Health* 93, no. 7 (2003): 1092.

35. Barbara J. Hart, "Economics and Domestic Violence," in *Why Doesn't She Just Leave*, eds. Stark and Watturs, 19.

36. Patricia Yollin, "When a Little Means a Lot," *San Francisco Chronicle*, September 30, 2007, at A1.

37. Charlotte E. Lott, "Why Women Matter: The Story of Microcredit," *Journal of Law and Commerce* 27, no. 2 (2009): 223.

38. "Microfinance FAQs," *Acción USA*, http://www.accionusa.org/home/support-u.s.-microfinance/about-accion-usa/microfinance-faq.aspx.

39. Lott, "Why Women Matter," 225.

40. Ibid., 226–27; see also Alex Counts, *Small Loans, Big Dreams: How Nobel Prize Winner Muhammad Yunus and Microfinance Are Changing the World* (Hoboken, NJ: John Wiley and Sons, 2008), 4.

41. Sam Daley-Harris, State of the Microcredit Summit Campaign 2009 (Washington, DC: Microcredit Summit Campaign, 2009), 3.

42. Rana Foroohar, "It's Payback Time: How a Bangladeshi Bank Is Growing in the U.S. by Making Tiny Loans to Groups of Poor Women with Entrepreneurial Dreams," *Newsweek*, July 26, 2010, 45.

43. Counts, *Small Loans, Big Dreams*, 16.

44. "Program Results," *Women's Initiative*, http://www.womensinitiative.org/aboutus/program-results.htm

45. Lott, "Why Women Matter," 229.

46. "Kiva Launches Online Microfinance in the United States," June 10, 2009, http://www.marketwire.com/mw/rel_us_print.jsp?id=1001831&lang=E1; see also Kristina Shevory, "With Squeeze on Credit, Microlending Blossoms," *New York Times*, July 28, 2010, http://www.nytimes.com/2010/07/29/business/smallbusiness/29sbiz.html?_r=1&pagewanted=print.

47. Ellen Snook, Marketing Communications Director of Women's Initiative, email message to author, July 21, 2010.

48. Regina Varolli, "Kentucky Microloans Build Battered Women's Credit," *Women's e-News*, May 16, 2010, http://www.womensenews.org/print/8110. Verizon has also began providing start-up funding to women "who have escaped the cycle of domestic violence and are ready to put their skills to work to get a small business up and running." "2010 Verizon Wireless Domestic Violence Entrepreneurship Program," *Office for the Prevention of Domestic Violence (New York State)*, accessed December 18, 2010, http://www.opdv.state.ny.us/help/vzwdveapplication6-10.pdf.

49. Counts, *Small Loans, Big Dreams*, 26.

50. Nicholas D. Kristof and Sheryl Wu Dunn, *Half the Sky: Turning Oppression into Opportunity for Women Worldwide* (New York: Alfred A. Knopf, 2009), 185–87.

51. Counts, *Small Loans, Big Dreams*, 346.

52. Sidney Ruth Schuler et al., "Credit Programs, Patriarchy and Men's Violence Against Women in Rural Bangladesh," *Social Science and Medicine* 43, no. 12 (1996): 1737.

53. Susy Cheston and Lisa Kuhn, *Empowering Women Through Microfinance*, 22, http://www.microcreditsummit.org/papers/empowerment.pdf (citing *Working Women's Forum, Social Platform through Social Innovations: A Coalition with Women in the Informal Sector* (Chennai, India: Working Women's Forum, 2000), 22).

54. Sidney Ruth Schuler, Syed M. Hashemi, and Shamsul Huda Badal, "Men's Violence Against Women in Rural Bangladesh: Undermined or Exacerbated by Microcredit Programmes," *Development in Practice* 8, no. 2 (1998): 151–53.

55. Raphael, *Saving Bernice*, 145.

56. Wayne J. Pitts, Eugena Givens, and Susan McNeeley, "The Need for a Holistic Approach to Specialized Domestic Violence Court Programming: Evaluating Offender Rehabilitation Needs and Recidivism," *Juvenile and Family Court Journal* 60, no. 3 (2009): 18.

57. Raphael, *Saving Bernice*, 140–41.

58. "Interview with Richard Gelles," *Power and Control: Domestic Violence in America*, April 20, 2010, http://www.powerandcontrolfilm.com/the-topics/academics/richard-gelles/.

59. Sandra M. Stith et al., "Treating Intimate Partner Violence Within Intact Couple Relationships: Outcomes of Multi-Couple Versus Individual Couple Therapy," *Journal of Marital and Family Therapy* 30, no. 3 (2004): 316.

60. Tubbs and Williams, "Shared Parenting After Abuse," 28.

61. Juan Carlos Areán and Lonna Davis, "Working with Fathers in Batterer Intervention Programs: Lessons from the Fathering After Violence Program," in *Parenting by Men Who Batter*, 118–30.

62. Ricardo Carrillo and Jerry Tello, "Latino Fathers in Recovery," in *Parenting By Men Who Batter*, 135.

63. Kim, *Community Engagement Continuum*, 49.

64. Ruth Busch, "Domestic Violence and Restorative Justice Initiatives: Who Pays If We Get It Wrong?" in *Restorative Justice and Family Violence*, 241.

65. Pranis, "Restorative Values and Confronting Family Violence," 28.

66. Kim, *Community Engagement Continuum*, 39.

67. Trevor Hunnicutt, "Instead of Assault Shelter, Neighbors Open Doors," *Mercury News*, August 22, 2010, http://www.mercurynews.com/breaking-news/ci_15859528?nclick_check=1.

68. Kim, "Alternative Interventions," 195–96.

69. Ibid., 207.

70. Ibid., 196.

71. Erin A. Casey and Blair Beadnell, "The Structure of Male Adolescent Peer Networks and Risk for Intimate Partner Violence Perpetration: Findings from a National Sample," *Journal of Youth and Adolescence* 39, no. 6 (2010): 620–33.

72. Alan D. Berkowitz, *Working with Men to Prevent Violence Against Women: An Overview (Part Two)* (VAWnet Applied Research Forum, 2004), 3–4.

73. Alan D. Berkowitz, *Working with Men to Prevent Violence Against Women: An Overview (Part One)* (VAWnet Applied Research Forum, 2004), 3–4.

74. Berkowitz, *Part Two*, 3.

75. Karin Hopkins, "Update on Hombres Unidos contra la Violencia Familia," *MCN Streamline: The Migrant Health News Source* 14, no. 6 (2008): 3.

76. Ted Bunch, *Ending Men's Violence Against Women* (A Call to Men, 2005), http://www.nrcdv.org/dvam/docs/materials/09-resource-packet/Issue_Articles_Newsletters/EndingViolenceAgainstWomen.pdf.

77. Nigel Adlam, "You're Banned From Footy If You Bash Your Woman," *Northern Territory News* (Australia), February 7, 2009, at 3.

78. Sameer M. Ashar, "Law Clinics and Collective Mobilization," *Clinical Law Review* 14, no. 2 (2008): 390.

Bibliography

36 Ops. Cal. Attorney General 200 (1960).

140 Cong. Rec.H5177-01 (daily ed. June 28, 1994).

140 Cong. Rec. H8957-02 (daily ed. August 21, 1994).

140 Cong. Rec. H8575-01 (daily ed. August 17, 1994).

750 Ill. Comp. Stat. 60/103 (2010).

750 Ill. Comp. Stat. 60/214(b)(1) (2010).

D.C. Code Ann. §16-1005 (c)(11) (2001).

D.C. Code § 42-3505.01(c-1)(2010).

Del. Code Ann. 10 § 1045(1) (2010).

Del. Code Ann. 13 § 711A (2008).

Haw. Rev. Stat. § 586-1 (2010).

In re Joseph L., 939 A.2d 16 (Conn. App. Ct. 2008).

In the Interest of N.S.E., 651 S.E.2d 123 (Ga. 2007).

Ky. Rev. Stat. Ann. § 209.030(8) (West 2010).

Md. Code Ann., Family Law § 7-103(a)(7), (8) (LexisNexis 2010).

Md. Rule 9-205 (b)–(c) (West 2008).

Mich. Comp. Laws § 600.2950(1)(g), (4) (2010).

Mo. Rev. Stat. § 565.074.1(6) (2010).

Nev. Rev. Stat. § 33.018.

N.M. Stat. Ann. § 40-13-2(D) (2010).

N.M. Stat. Ann. § 47-8-33(J) (2010).

Or. Rev. Stat. 90. 449 (2010).

Victims of Trafficking and Violence Protection Act of 2000 § 1513 (a)(2)(A) (2000).

Wash. Rev. Code § 26.09.060 (2010).

Wash. Rev. Code §§ 59.18.575, 59.18.580 (2010).

Borchgrevink v. Borchgrevink, 941 P.2d 132 (Alaska 1997).

Feltmeier v. Feltmeier, 798 N.E.2d 75 (Ill. 2003).

I.J. v. I.S., 744 A.2d 1246 (N.J. Super. Ct. Ch. Div. 1999).

Nicholson v. Williams, 203 F.Supp. 2d 153 (E.D.N.Y. 2002).

People v. Byrd, 855 N.Y.S.2d 505 (N.Y. App. Div. 2008).

People v. Caldarella, No. 07CV174 (Dist. Ct. Colo. 2007).

People v. Covington, 19 P.3d 15 (Colo. 2001).

Pugliese v. Pugliese, 146 Cal. App. 4th 1444 (Cal. Ct. App. 2007).

State v. B.H., 870 A.2d 273 (N.J. 2005)

State v. Borelli, 629 A.2d 1105 (Conn. 1993).

State v. Drew, No. 07AP-467, 2008 WL 2349649 (Ohio Ct. App. Jun. 10, 2008).

State v. Hancock, No. C-030459, 2004 WL 596103 (Ohio Ct. App. Mar. 26, 2004)

State v. Maelega, 907 P.2d 758 (Haw. 1995).

State v. Spraggins, No. 82170, 2003 WL 22971050 (Ohio Ct. App. Dec. 18, 2003).

State v. Worrall, 220 S.W.3d 346 (Mo. Ct. App. 2007).

Town of Castle Rock v. Gonzales, 545 U.S. 748 (2005).

2006 Biennial Report to Congress on the Effectiveness of Grant Programs Under the Violence Against Women Act. U.S. Department of Justice Office on Violence Against Women, 2006.

"2010 Verizon Wireless Domestic Violence Entrepreneurship Program." Office for the Prevention of Domestic Violence (New York State). Accessed December 18, 2010. http://www.opdv.state.ny.us/help/vzwdveapplication6-10.pdf.

Abrams, Kathryn. "From Autonomy to Agency: Feminist Perspectives on Self-Direction." *William & Mary Law Review* 40, no. 3 (1999): 805–46.

——. "Sex Wars Redux: Agency and Coercion in Feminist Legal Theory." *Columbia Law Review* 95, no. 2 (1995): 304–76.

"Abuse in Intimate Relationships—'The Wheel.'" London Abused Women's Centre, accessed October 17, 2010. http://www.lawc.on.ca/PDF_Files_Reports/Power%20and%20Control%20Wheel.pdf.

Adams, Adrienne E., Cris M. Sullivan, Deborah Bybee, and Megan R. Greeson. "Development of the Scale of Economic Abuse." *Violence Against Women* 14, no. 5 (2008): 563–88.

Adkins, Mary. "Moving Out of the 1990s: An Argument for Updating Protocol on Divorce Mediation in Domestic Abuse Cases." *Yale Journal of Law and Feminism* 22, no. 1 (2010): 97–132.

Adlam, Nigel. "You're Banned from Footy If You Bash Your Woman." *Northern Territory News* (Australia), February 7, 2009.

Aiken, Jane, and Katherine Goldwasser. "The Perils of Empowerment." *Cornell Journal of Law and Public Policy* 20, no. 1 (2010): 139–80.

AMA Data on Violence Between Intimates. American Medical Association, 2000. http://www.ama-assn.org/ama/no-index/about-ama/13577.shtml.

Areán, Juan Carlos, and Lonna Davis. "Working with Fathers in Batterer Intervention Programs: Lessons from the Fathering After Violence Program." In *Parenting by Men Who Batter: New Directions for Assessment and Intervention*, 118–30, edited by Jeffrey L. Edleson and Oliver J. Williams. New York: Oxford University Press, 2007.

Ashar, Sameer M. "Law Clinics and Collective Mobilization." *Clinical Law Review* 14, no. 2 (2008): 355–414.

Babcock, Julia C., Charles E. Green, and Chet Robie. "Does Batterer's Treatment Work? A Meta-analytic Review of Domestic Violence Treatment." *Clinical Psychology Review* 23, no. 8 (2004): 1023–53.

Bailey, Allen M., and Carmen Kay Denny. "Attorneys Comment on Mediation and Domestic Violence." *Alaska Bar Rag* 27, no. 4 (2003): 16–17.

Baker, Jeffrey R. "Enjoining Coercion: Squaring Civil Protection Orders with the Reality of Domestic Abuse." *Journal of Law and Family Studies* 11, no. 1 (2008): 35–64.

Baker, Phyllis L. "And I Went Back: Battered Women's Negotiation of Choice." *Journal of Contemporary Ethnography* 26, no. 1 (1997): 55–74.

Bancroft, Lundy, and Jay G. Silverman. *The Batterer as Parent: Addressing the Impact of Domestic Violence on Family Dynamics*. Thousand Oaks, CA: Sage Publications, 2002.

Barnes, Greg. "Few Soldiers Assigned to Domestic Violence Care Finish Programs." *Fay (North Carolina) Observer*, September 29, 2010. http://www.fayobserver.com/articles/2010/09/29/1028491?sac=Mil.

Bartlett, Katharine T. "Family Law and American Culture: Feminism and Family Law." *Family Law Quarterly* 33, no. 3 (1999): 475–500.

Beck, Connie J. A., Michele E. Walsh, and Rose Weston."Analysis of Mediation Agreements of Families Reporting Specific Intimate Partner Abuse." *Family Court Review* 47, no. 3 (2009): 401–15.

Bedell, Natalie. "'Economic Control' Up 40 Percent as Local Domestic Violence Cause." *Falls Church (Virginia) News-Press*, September 22, 2010. http://www.fcnp.com/news/7394-economic-control-up-40-percent-as-local-domestic-violence-cause.html.

Bergner, Raymond M. "Love and Barriers to Love: An Analysis for Psychotherapists and Others." *American Journal of Psychotherapy* 54, no. 1 (2000): 1–17.

Berkowitz, Alan D. *Working with Men to Prevent Violence Against Women: An Overview (Part One)*. VAWnet Applied Research Forum, 2004.

———. *Working with Men to Prevent Violence Against Women: An Overview (Part Two)*. VAWnet Applied Research Forum, 2004.

Bernstein, Anita. "Pecuniary Reparations Following National Crisis: A Convergence of Tort Theory, Microfinance and Gender Equality." *University of Pennsylvania Journal of International Law* 31, no. 1 (2009).

Borer, Tristan Anne. "Gendered War and Gendered Peace: Truth Commissions and Postconflict Gender Violence: Lessons from South Africa." *Violence Against Women* 15, no. 10 (2009): 1169–93.

Bowker, Lee. *Beating Wife-Beating*. Lanham, MD: Lexington Books, 1983.

Breger, Melissa L. "Introducing the Construct of the Jury into Family Violence Proceedings and Family Court Jurisprudence." *Michigan Journal of Gender and Law* 13, no. 1 (2006): 1–38.

Brown, Wendy. *States of Injury: Power and Freedom in Late Modernity*. Princeton, NJ: Princeton University Press, 1995.

Bunch, Ted. Ending Men's Violence Against Women (A Call to Men, 2005). http://www.nrcdv.org/dvam/docs/materials/09-resource-packet/Issue_Articles_Newsletters/EndingViolenceAgainstWomen.pdf.

Burke, Alafair. "Domestic Violence as a Crime of Pattern and Intent: An Alternative Reconceptualization." *George Washington Law Review* 75, no. 3 (2007): 552–612.

Burke, Alafair S. "Rational Actors, Self-Defense, and Duress: Making Sense, Not Syndromes, Out of the Battered Woman." *North Carolina Law Review* 81, no. 1 (2002): 211–316.

Burkemper, Judge Bennett, and Nina Balsam. "Examining the Use of Restorative Justice Practices in Domestic Violence Cases." *Saint Louis University Public Law Review* 27, no. 1 (2007): 121–33.

Busch, Ruth. "Domestic Violence and Restorative Justice Initiatives: Who Pays If We Get It Wrong?" In *Restorative Justice and Family Violence*, 223–48, edited by Heather Strang and John Braithwaite. Cambridge: Cambridge University Press, 2002.

Buttell, Frederick P., and Michelle M. Carney. "Do Batterer Intervention Programs Serve African American and Caucasian Batterers Equally Well? An Investigation of a 26 Week Program." *Research on Social Work Practice* 15, no. 1 (2005): 19–28.

Campbell, Jacquelyn C., Paul Miller, Mary M. Cardwell, and Ruth Ann Belknap. "Relationship Status of Battered Women Over Time." *Journal of Family Violence* 9, no. 2 (1994): 99–111.

Campbell, Jacquelyn C., Daniel Webster, Jane Koziol-McLain, Carolyn Block, Doris Campbell, Mary Ann Curry, et al. "Risk Factors for Femicide in Abusive Relationships: Results from a Multisite Case Control Study." *American Journal of Public Health* 93, no. 7 (2003): 1089–97.

Carrillo, Ricardo, and Jerry Tello. "Latino Fathers in Recovery." In *Parenting by Men Who Batter: New Directions for Assessment and Intervention*, 131–36, edited by Jeffrey L. Edleson and Oliver J. Williams. New York: Oxford University Press, 2007.

Carter, Lucy Salcido. Doing the Work and Measuring the Progress: A Report on the December 2009 Experts Roundtable. San Francisco, CA: Family Violence Prevention Fund, 2010.

Casey, Erin A., and Blair Beadnell. "The Structure of Male Adolescent Peer Networks and Risk for Intimate Partner Violence Perpetration: Findings from a National Sample." *Journal of Youth and Adolescence* 39, no. 6 (2010): 620–33.

Chamallas, Martha. *Introduction to Feminist Legal Theory*. 3rd ed. New York: Aspen Publishers, 2003.

Chang, Jean, Cynthia J. Berg, Linda E. Saltzman, and Joy Herndon. "Homicide: A Leading Cause of Injury Deaths Among Pregnant and Postpartum Women in the United States, 1991–1999." *American Journal of Public Health* 95, no. 3 (2005): 471–77.

Chaudhuri, Molly, and Kathleen Daly. "Do Restraining Orders Help? Battered Women's Experience with Male Violence and Legal Process." In *Domestic Violence: The Changing Criminal Justice Response*, 227–54, edited by Eve S. Buzawa and Carl G. Buzawa. Westport, CT: Auburn House, 1992.

Cheston, Susy, and Lisa Kuhn. Empowering Women Through Microfinance. http://www.microcreditsummit.org/papers/empowerment.pdf.

Christman, John. "Feminism and Autonomy." In *"Nagging" Questions: Feminist Ethics in Everyday Life*, 17–40, edited by Dana E. Bushnell. Lanham, MD: Rowman & Littlefield, 1995.

Clement, Grace. *Care, Autonomy, and Justice: Feminism and the Ethic of Care*. Boulder, CO: Westview Press, 1996.

Coker, Donna. "Restorative Justice, Navajo Peacemaking and Domestic Violence." *Theoretical Criminology* 10, no. 1 (2006): 67–85.

———. "Addressing Domestic Violence Through a Strategy of Economic Rights." *Women's Rights Law Reporter* 24, no. 3 (2003): 187–90.

———. "Transformative Justice: Anti-Subordination Processes in Domestic Violence." In *Restorative Justice and Family Violence*, 128–52, edited by Heather Strang and John Braithwaite. Cambridge: Cambridge University Press, 2002.

———. "Shifting Power for Battered Women: Law, Material Resources, and Poor Women of Color." *UC Davis Law Review* 33, no. 4 (2000): 1009–55.

Colker, Ruth. "Abortion and Violence." *William & Mary Journal of Women and the Law* 1, no. 1 (1994): 93–129.

Coughlin, Anne. "Excusing Women." *California Law Review* 82, no. 1 (1994): 1–93.

Counts, Alex. *Small Loans, Big Dreams: How Nobel Prize Winner Muhammad Yunus and Microfinance Are Changing the World.* Hoboken, NJ: John Wiley and Sons, 2008.

Crenshaw, Kimberlé. "Mapping the Margins: Intersectionality, Identity Politics, and Violence Against Women of Color." *Stanford Law Review* 43, no. 6 (1991): 1241–99.

Cuthbert, Carrie, Kim Slote, Monica Ghosh Driggers, Cynthia J. Mesh, Lundy Bancroft, and Jay Silverman. *Battered Mothers Speak Out: A Human Rights Report on Domestic Violence and Child Custody in the Massachusetts Family Courts.* Wellesley, MA: Wellesley Centers for Women, 2002.

Daly, Jennifer E., Thomas G. Power, and Edward W. Gondolf. "Predictors of Batterer Program Attendance." *Journal of Interpersonal Violence* 16, no. 10 (2001): 971–91.

Daley-Harris, Sam. State of the Microcredit Summit Campaign 2009. Washington, DC: Microcredit Summit Campaign, 2009.

Dasgupta, Shamita Das. "A Framework for Understanding Women's Use of Nonlethal Violence in Intimate Heterosexual Relationships." *Violence Against Women* 8, no. 11 (2002): 1364–89.

———. "Just Like Men? A Critical View of Violence by Women." In *Coordinating Community Responses to Domestic Violence: Lessons from Duluth and Beyond*, 105–222, edited by Melanie F. Shepard and Ellen L. Pence. Thousand Oaks, CA: Sage Publications, 1999.

Davies, Jill. When Battered Women Stay . . . Advocacy Beyond Leaving. Harrisburg, PA: National Resources Center on Domestic Violence, 2008.

Davila, Yolanda R. "Influence of Abuse on Condom Negotiation Among Mexican-American Women Involved in Abusive Relationships." *Journal Association of Nurses in AIDS Care* 13, no. 6 (2002): 46–56.

Davis, Alice Karyl. "Unlocking the Door by Giving Her the Key: A Comment on the Adequacy of the U-Visa as a Remedy." *Alabama Law Review* 56, no. 2 (2004): 557–76.

Davis, Angela J. *Arbitrary Justice: The Power of the American Prosecutor.* New York: Oxford University Press, 2007.

Dehan, Nicole, and Zipi Levi. "Spiritual Abuse: An Additional Dimension of Abuse Experienced by Abused Haredi (Ultraorthodox) Jewish Wives." *Violence Against Women* 15, no. 11 (2004): 1294–1310.

DeKeserdy, Walter S., and Martin D. Schwartz. *Dangerous Exits: Escaping Abusive Relationships in Rural America.* New Brunswick, NJ: Rutgers University Press, 2009.

Dempsey, Michelle Madden. *Prosecuting Domestic Violence: A Philosophical Analysis.* Oxford: Oxford University Press, 2009.

Diviney, Charles L., Asha Parekh, and Lenora M. Olson. "Outcomes of Civil Protective Orders: Results from One State." *Journal of Interpersonal Violence* 24, no. 7 (2009): 1209–21.

Domestic Violence Counts 2009: A 24-Hour Census of Domestic Violence Shelters and Services. Washington, DC: National Network to End Domestic Violence, 2009.

Dubois, Ellen C., Mary C. Dunlap, Carol J. Gilligan, Catherine A. MacKinnon, and Carrie J. Menkel-Meadow. "Feminist Discourse, Moral Values, and the Law—A Conversation." *Buffalo Law Review* 34, no. 1 (1984): 11–87.

Durfee, Alesha. "Victim Narratives, Legal Representation, and Domestic Violence Civil Protection Orders." *Feminist Criminology* 4, no. 1 (2009): 7–31.

Dutton, Mary Ann, and Lisa A. Goodman." Coercion in Intimate Partner Violence: Toward a New Conceptualization." *Sex Roles* 52, no. 11/12 (2005): 743–56.

Dutton, Mary Ann, Lisa Goodman, and R. James Schmidt. *Development and Validation of a Coercive Control Measure for Intimate Partner Violence: Final Technical Report, Prepared for National Institute of Justice, Office of Justice Programs.* (Washington, DC: U.S. Department of Justice, 2005.

Epstein, Deborah. "Procedural Justice: Tempering the State's Response to Domestic Violence." *William & Mary Law Review* 43, no. 5 (2002): 1843–1906.

Ewing, Charles Patrick, and Moss Aubrey. "Battered Woman and Public Opinion: Some Realities About the Myths." *Journal of Family Violence* 2, no. 3 (1987): 257–64.

Faigman, David L. "The Battered Woman Syndrome and Self-Defense: A Legal and Empirical Dissent." *Virginia Law Review* 72, no. 3 (1986): 619–47.

Families in Transition: A Follow-Up Study Exploring Family Law Issues in Maryland. Towson, MD: Women's Law Center of Maryland, 2006.

Fedders, Barbara. "Lobbying for Mandatory-Arrest Policies: Race, Class and the Politics of the Battered Women's Movement." *New York University Review of Law and Social Change* 23, no. 2 (1997): 281–300.

Feinberg, Joel. "Autonomy." In *The Inner Citadel: Essays on Individual Autonomy*, 27–53, edited by John Christman. New York: Oxford University Press, 1989.

Ferraro, Kathleen J. *Neither Angels Nor Demons: Women, Crime, and Victimization.* Boston: Northeastern University Press, 2006.

———. "The Words Change But the Melody Lingers: The Persistence of Battered Woman Syndrome in Criminal Cases Involving Battered Women." *Violence Against Women* 9, no. 1 (2003): 110–29.

Fineman, Martha Albertson. "Preface." In *The Public Nature of Private Violence: The Discovery of Domestic Abuse*, xi–xviii, edited by Martha Albertson Fineman and Roxanne Mykitiuk. New York: Routledge, 1994.

Fiore, Christine, and Kristen O'Shea. "Women in Violent Relationships—Experiences with the Legal and Medical Systems." In *Intimate Partner Violence*, 18-1 to 18-31, edited by K. A. Kendall-Tacket and S. M. Giacomoni. New Jersey: Civic Research Institute, 2007.

Fischer, Karla, Neil Vidmar, and Rene Ellis. "The Culture of Battering and the Role of Mediation in Domestic Violence Cases." *SMU Law Review* 46, no. 5 (1993): 2117–74.

Fleury, Ruth E., Cris M. Sullivan, and Deborah I. Bybee. "When Ending the Relationship Does Not End the Violence: Women's Experiences of Violence by Former Partners." *Violence Against Women* 6, no. 12 (2000): 1363–83.

Ford, David. A. "Prosecution as a Victim Power Resource: A Note on Empowering Women in Violent Conjugal Relationships." *Law and Society Review* 25, no. 2 (1991): 313–34.

Foroohar, Rana. "It's Payback Time: How a Bangladeshi Bank Is Growing in the U.S. by Making Tiny Loans to Groups of Poor Women with Entrepreneurial Dreams." *Newsweek*, July 26, 2010, 45.

Frederick, Loretta, and Kristine C. Lizdas. "The Role of Restorative Justice in the Battered Women's Movement." In *Restorative Justice and Violence Against Women*, 39–59, edited by James Ptacek. New York: Oxford University Press, 2010.

Friedman, Marilyn. *Autonomy, Gender, Politics.* New York: Oxford University Press, 2003.

Frye, Victoria, Jennifer Manganello, Jacquelyn C. Campbell, Benita Walton-Moss, and Susan Witt. "The Distribution of and Factors Associated with Intimate Terrorism and Situational Couple Violence Among a Population-Based Sample of Urban Women in the United States." *Journal of Interpersonal Violence* 21, no. 10 (2006): 1286–1313.

Garner, Joel H., and Christopher D. Maxwell. "Prosecution and Conviction Rates for Intimate Partner Violence." *Criminal Justice Review* 34, no. 1 (2009): 44–79.

Gibson, James L. "On Legitimacy Theory and the Effectiveness of Truth Commissions." *Law and Contemporary Problems* 72, no. 2 (2009): 123–41.

Goel, Rashmi. "Sita's Trousseau: Restorative Justice, Domestic Violence, and South Asian Culture." *Violence Against Women* 11, no. 5 (2005): 639–65.

Goldfarb, Sally F. "Reconceiving Civil Protection Orders for Domestic Violence: Can Law Help End the Abuse Without Ending the Relationship?" *Cardozo Law Review* 29, no. 4 (2008): 1487–1551.

Goldscheid, Julie, and Robin Runge. *Employment Law and Domestic Violence: A Practitioner's Guide.* Chicago: American Bar Association, 2009.

Gondolf, Edward W. "Theoretical and Research Support for the Duluth Model: A Reply to Dutton and Corvo." *Aggression and Violent Behavior* 12, no. 6 (2007): 644–57.

———. "Evaluating Batterer Counseling Programs: A Difficult Task Showing Some Effects and Implications." *Aggression and Violent Behavior* 9, no. 6 (2004): 605–31.

———. "Mandatory Court Review and Batterer Program Compliance. *Journal of Interpersonal Violence* 15, no. 4 (2000): 428–37.

———. "A Comparison of Four Batterer Intervention Systems: Do Court Referral, Program Length, and Services Matter?" *Journal of Interpersonal Violence* 14, no. 1 (1999): 41–61.

Gondolf, Edward W., and Ellen R. Fisher. *Battered Women as Survivors: An Alternative to Treating Learned Helplessness.* Lexington, MA: Lexington Books, 1988.

Goodman, Lisa A., and Deborah Epstein. *Listening to Battered Women: A Survivor-Centered Approach to Advocacy, Mental Health, and Justice.* Washington, DC: American Psychological Association, 2008.

Goodmark, Leigh. "When Is a Battered Woman Not a Battered Woman? When She Fights Back." *Yale Journal of Law and Feminism* 20, no. 1 (2008): 75–130.

———. "Achieving Batterer Accountability in the Child Protection System." *Kentucky Law Journal* 93, no. 3 (2004–5): 613–57.

———. "Telling Stories, Saving Lives: The Battered Mothers' Testimony Project, Women's Narratives, and the Law." *Arizona State Law Journal* 37, no. 3 (2005): 710–57.

———. "Law Is the Answer? Do We Know That for Sure?: Questioning the Efficacy of Legal Interventions for Battered Women." *Saint Louis University Public Law Review* 23, no. 1 (2004): 7–48.

———. "From Property to Personhood: What the Legal System Should Do for Children in Family Violence Cases." *West Virginia Law Review* 102, no. 2 (1999): 237–338.

Griffing, Sascha, Deborah Fish Ragin, Robert E. Sage, Lorraine Madry, Lewis E. Bingham, and Beny J. Primm."Domestic Violence Survivors' Self-Identified Reasons for Returning to Abusive Relationships." *Journal of Interpersonal Violence* 17, no. 3 (2002): 306–19.

Griffiths, Morwenna. *Feminisms and the Self: The Web of Identity.* London: Routledge, 1995.

Grillo, Trina. "Anti-Essentialism and Intersectionality: Tools to Dismantle the Master's House." *Berkeley Women's Law Journal* 10, no. 1 (2004): 16–30.

Gruber, Aya. "The Feminist War on Crime." *Iowa Law Review* 92, no. 3 (2007): 741–833.

Halley, Janet. *Split Decisions: How and Why to Take a Break from Feminism.* Princeton, NJ: Princeton University Press, 2006.

Halpern, Jodi, and Harvey M. Weinstein. "Empathy and Rehumanization After Mass Violence." In *My Neighbor, My Enemy: Justice and Community in the Aftermath of Mass Atrocity,* 303–22, edited by Eric Stover and Harvey M. Weinstein. Cambridge: Cambridge University Press, 2004.

Hamberger, L. Kevin, and Theresa Potente. "Counseling Heterosexual Women Arrested for Domestic Violence: Implications for Theory and Practice." *Violence and Victims* 9, no. 2 (1994): 125–37.

Hanna, Cheryl. "The Paradox of Progress: Translating Evan Stark's Coercive Control into Legal Doctrine for Abused Women." *Violence Against Women* 15, no. 12 (2009): 1458–76.

———. "No Right to Choose: Mandated Victim Participation in Domestic Violence Prosecutions." *Harvard Law Review* 109, no. 8 (1996): 1849–1910.

Harrell, Adele, and Barbara E. Smith. "Effects of Restraining Orders on Domestic Violence Victims." In *Do Arrests and Restraining Orders Work,* 214–42, edited by Eve S. Buzawa and Carl G. Buzawa. Thousand Oaks, CA: Sage Publications, 1996.

Harris, Angela P. "Race and Essentialism in Feminist Legal Theory." *Stanford Law Review* 42, no. 3 (1990): 581–616.

Hart, Amanda Shea. "Child Inclusive Mediation in Parenting Disputes Where Domestic Violence Is an Issue." School of Social Work and Human Services, Central Queensland University, Rockhampton, Queensland (Australia), 2008. http://www.ausdispute.unisa. edu.au/apmf/2008/papers/20-Amanda%20Shea%20Hart.pdf.

Hart, Barbara J. "Economics and Domestic Violence." In *Why Doesn't She Just Leave: Real Women, Real Stories. A New Perspective on Domestic Violence,* 19–22, edited by Heather Stark and Emilee Watturs. Woodinville, WA: MidPacifik Publishing, 2008.

———. "Arrest: What's the Big Deal?" *William & Mary Journal of Women and the Law* 3, no. 1 (1997): 207–21.

Hart, William L., John Ashcroft, Dr. Ann Burgess, Newman Flanagan, Ursula Meese, Catherine Milton, Dr. Clyde Narramore, Ruben Ortega, and Fraces Seward. *Attorney General's Task Force on Family Violence: Final Report.* Washington, DC: U.S. Department of Justice, 1984.

Hartman, Jennifer L., and Joanne Belknap. "Beyond the Gatekeepers: Court Professionals' Self-Reported Attitudes about and Experiences with Misdemeanor Domestic Violence Cases." *Criminal Justice and Behavior* 30, no. 3 (2003): 349–73.

Heckert, D. Alex, and Edward W. Gondolf. "Battered Women's Perceptions of Risk Versus Risk Factors and Instruments in Predicting Repeat Assault." *Journal of Interpersonal Violence* 19, no. 7 (2004): 778–800.

Henry, Michele. "Pregnant Woman 'Never Calling the Police Again.'" *Toronto Star,* April 8, 2008. http://www.thestar.com/printArticle/411222.

Herman, Judith Lewis. "Justice from the Victim's Perspective." *Violence Against Women* 10, no. 5 (2005): 571–602.

Hilberman, Elaine. "Overview: The 'Wife-Beater's Wife' Reconsidered." *American Journal of Psychiatry* 137, no. 11 (1980): 1336–47.

Hirschel, David, Eve Buzawa, April Pattavina, and Don Faggiani. "Domestic Violence and Mandatory Arrest Laws: To What Extent Do They Influence Police Arrest Decisions." *Journal of Law and Criminology* 98, no. 1 (2007): 255–98.

Holtzworth-Munroe, Amy, Jeffrey C. Meehan, Katherine Herron, Uzma Rehman, and Gregory L. Stuart. "Testing the Holtzworth-Munroe and Stuart Typology." *Journal of Consulting and Clinical Psychology* 68, no. 6 (2000): 1000–1019.

Holtzworth-Munroe, Amy, and Gregory L. Stuart. "Typologies of Male Batterers: Three Subtypes and the Differences Among Them." *Psychological Bull*etin 116, no. 3 (1994): 476–97.

hooks, bell. *Feminist Theory: From Margin to Center.* 2nd ed. Cambridge, MA: South End Press, 2000.

Hopkins, C. Quince, and Mary P. Koss. "Incorporating Feminist Theory and Insights into a Restorative Justice Response to Sex Offenses." *Violence Against Women* 11, no. 5 (2005): 693–723.

Hopkins, C. Quince, Mary P. Koss, and Karen J. Bachar. "Applying Restorative Justice to Ongoing Intimate Violence: Problems and Possibilities." *Saint Louis University Public Law Review* 23, no. 1 (2004): 289–311.

Hopkins, Karin. "Update on Hombres Unidos contra la Violencia Familia." *MCN Streamline: The Migrant Health News Source* 14, no. 6 (2008).

Hsu, Spencer S. "Domestic-Partner Violence in United States Fell Sharply." *Washington Post*, December 29, 2006. http://www.washingtonpost.com/wp-dyn/content/article/2006/12/28/AR2006122801170.html.

Hunnicutt, Trevor. "Instead of Assault Shelter, Neighbors Open Doors." *Mercury News*, August 22, 2010. http://www.mercurynews.com/breaking-news/ci_15859528?nclick_check=1.

Huss, Matthew T., and Jennifer Langhinrichsen-Rohling. "Assessing the Generalization of Psychopathy in a Clinical Sample of Domestic Violence Perpetrators." *Law and Human Behavior* 30, no. 5 (2006): 571–86.

Hyman, Ariella. Mandatory Reporting of Domestic Violence by Health Care Providers: A Policy Paper. San Francisco: Family Violence Prevention Fund, 1997.

Ifill, Sherrilyn A. "Creating a Truth and Reconciliation Commission for Lynching." *Law and Inequality* 21, no. 2 (2003): 263–311.

Ingram, Maia, Deborah Jean McClelland, Jessica Martin, Montserrat F. Caballero, Maria Theresa Mayorga, and Katie Gillespie. "Experiences of Immigrant Women Who Self-Petition Under the Violence Against Women Act." *Violence Against Women* 16, no. 8 (2010): 858–80.

"Interview with Cathryn Curley." *Power and Control: Domestic Violence in America*, April 20, 2010. http://www.powerandcontrolfilm.com/the-topics/founders/cathryn-curley/.

"Interview with Ellen Pence." *Power and Control: Domestic Violence in America*, April 20, 2010. http://www.powerandcontrolfilm.com/the-topics/founders/ellen-pence/.

"Interview with Richard Gelles." *Power and Control: Domestic Violence in America*, April 20, 2010. http://www.powerandcontrolfilm.com/the-topics/academics/richard-gelles/.

Isensee, Laura, Kelly House, Laura Morel, and Luisa Yanez. "Gunman's Rage Over Estranged Wife Leaves 5 Dead at Hialeah Restaurant: Gerardo Regalado, 38, of Coral Gables, Took His Own Life Just Blocks Away from the Shootings, Police Say." *Miami Herald*, June 8, 2010. http://www.sun-sentinel.com/sports/fl-hialeah-restaurant-shootings-20100607,0,5238568,print.story.

Jamieson, Beth Kiyoko. *Real Choices: Feminism, Freedom, and the Limits of Law.* State College: Pennsylvania State University Press, 2001.

Johnson, Holly. "The Cessation of Assaults on Wives: A Study of Domestic Violence Against Women." *Journal of Comparative Family Studies* 34, no. 1 (2003): 75–91.

Johnson, John. "A New Side to Domestic Violence: Arrests of Women Have Risen Sharply Since Passage of Tougher Laws." *L.A. Times*, April 27, 1996.

Johnson, Margaret E. "Balancing Liberty, Dignity and Safety: The Impact of Domestic Violence Lethality Screening." *Cardozo Law Review* 32, no. 2 (2010): 519–80.

———. "Redefining Harm, Reimagining Remedies and Reclaiming Domestic Violence Law." *UC Davis Law Review* 42, no. 4 (2009): 1107–64.

Johnson, Michael P. *A Typology of Domestic Violence: Intimate Terrorism, Violent Resistance, and Situational Couple Violence.* Boston: Northeastern University Press, 2008.

Jones, Ruth. "Guardianship for Coercively Controlled Battered Women: Breaking the Control of the Abuser." *Georgetown Law Journal* 88, no. 4 (2000): 605–57.

Kandel, Minouche. "Women Who Kill Their Batterers Are Getting Battered in Court." *Ms.* (July/August 1993): 88–89.

Kemeny, Matthew. "Increase in Domestic Violence-related Deaths Motivates Advocates." *Patriot-News*, October 15, 2010. http://www.pennlive.com/midstate/index.ssf/2010/10/increase_in_domestic_violence-.html.

Kim, Mimi. "Alternative Interventions to Intimate Violence: Defining Political and Pragmatic Challenges." In *Restorative Justice and Violence Against Women*, 193–217, edited by James Ptacek. New York: Oxford University Press, 2010.

———. *Innovative Strategies to Address Domestic Violence in Asian and Pacific Islander Communities: Examining Themes, Models, and Interventions.* San Francisco: Asian & Pacific Islander Institute on Domestic Violence, July 2002, revised February, 2010.

———. *The Community Engagement Continuum: Outreach, Mobilization, Organizing and Accountability to Address Violence against Women in Asian and Pacific Islander Communities.* San Francisco: Asian & Pacific Islander Institute on Domestic Violence, March 2005.

King, Michael, and Becky Batagol. "Enforcer, Manager, or Leader? The Judicial Role in Family Violence Courts." *International Journal of Law and Psychiatry* 33, no. 5–6 (2010): 406–16.

"Kiva Launches Online Microfinance in the United States." June 10, 2009. http://www.marketwire.com/mw/rel_us_print.jsp?id=1001831&lang=E1.

Kliff, Sarah. "Coerced Reproduction: Experts Are Studying a Phenomenon that Brings a Whole New Meaning to the Term 'Unwanted Pregnancy.'" *Newsweek*, January 26, 2010. http://www.newsweek.com/id/232542/output/print.

Kohn, Laurie S. "What's So Funny About Peace, Love and Understanding? Restorative Justice as a New Paradigm for Domestic Violence Intervention." *Seton Hall Law Review* 40, no. 2 (2010): 517–95.

Koss, Mary P. "Blame, Shame and Community: Justice Responses to Violence Against Women." *American Psychologist* 55, no. 11 (2000): 1332–43.

Krieger, Sarah. "The Dangers of Mediation in Domestic Violence Cases." *Cardozo Women's Law Journal* 8, no. 2 (2002): 235–59.

Kristof, Nicholas D., and Sheryl Wu Dunn. *Half the Sky: Turning Oppression into Opportunity for Women Worldwide.* New York: Alfred A. Knopf, 2009.

Kuennen, Tamara L. "Analyzing the Impact of Coercion on Domestic Violence Victims: How Much Is Too Much?" *Berkeley Journal of Gender Law and Justice* 22, no. 1 (2007): 2–30.

Kurz, Demie. "Separation, Divorce, and Woman Abuse." *Violence Against Women* 2, no. 1 (1996): 63–81.

Lamb, Sharon. "Constructing the Victim: Popular Images and Lasting Labels." In *New Versions of Victims: Feminists Struggle with the Concept*, 108–38, edited by Sharon Lamb. New York: New York University Press, 1999.

Laney, Garrine P. *Violence Against Women Act: History and Federal Funding*. Washington, DC: Congressional Research Service, 2005.

Lazarus-Black, Mindie. *Everyday Harm: Domestic Violence, Court Rites, and Cultures of Reconciliation*. Urbana: University of Illinois Press, 2007.

Le Breton, Suzanne. "Man Sentenced After Fifth Domestic Violence Conviction." *St. Tammany News*, May 19, 2010. http://www.thesttammanynews.com/articles.2010/05/19/news/doc4bf315981614c395906231.prt.

Lee, Donna H. "Next Steps: Intimate Partner Violence Against Asian American Women." Discussion draft, CUNY School of Law, Flushing, NY, 2009.

Lehrner, Amy, and Nicole E. Allen. "Still a Movement After All These Years?: Current Tensions in the Domestic Violence Movement." *Violence Against Women* 15, no. 6 (2009): 656–77.

Lemon, Nancy K. D. "Statutes Creating Rebuttable Presumptions Against Custody to Batterers: How Effective Are They?" *William Mitchell Law Review* 28, no. 2 (2001): 601–76.

Lempert, Lora Bex. "Women's Strategies for Survival: Developing Agency in Abusive Relationships." *Journal of Family Violence* 11, no. 3 (1996): 269–89.

Levit, Nancy. "Feminism for Men: Legal Ideology and the Construction of Maleness." *University of California Los Angeles Law Review* 43, no. 4 (1996): 1037–1116.

Littleton, Christine A. "Women's Experience and the Problem of Transition: Perspectives on Male Battering of Women." *University of Chicago Legal Forum* 1989, (1989): 23–57.

Logan, TK, Lisa Shannon, Robert Walker, and Teri Marie Faragher. "Protective Orders: Questions and Conundrums." *Trauma, Violence and Abuse* 7, no. 3 (2006): 175–205.

Lollar, Michael. "Economy, Technology Feed Rising Domestic Violence Rates." (Memphis, Tennessee) Commercial Appeal, October 11, 2010. http://www.commercialappeal.com/news/2010/oct/10/economy-technology-feed-rising-domestic-02/.

Long, Jennifer Gentile. "Prosecuting Intimate Partner Sexual Assault." *Prosecutor* 42, no. 2 (2008); http://www.wcsap.org/advocacy/PDF/CONNECTIONS_IPSV.pdf.

Lott, Charlotte E. "Why Women Matter: The Story of Microcredit." *Journal of Law and Commerce* 27, no. 2 (2009): 219–30.

MacKinnon, Catharine A. *Toward a Feminist Theory of the State*. Cambridge, MA: Harvard University Press, 1989.

———. *Feminism Unmodified: Discourses on Life and Law*. Cambridge, MA: Harvard University Press, 1987.

———. "Feminism, Marxism, Method, and the State: An Agenda for Theory." *Signs: Journal of Women in Culture and Society* 7, no. 3 (1982): 515–44.

Maguigan, Holly. "Wading onto Professor Schneider's 'Murky Middle Ground' Between Acceptance and Rejection of Criminal Justice Responses to Domestic Violence." *American University Journal of Gender, Social Policy and the Law* 11, no. 2 (2003): 427–45.

Mahoney, Martha R. "Whiteness and Women, in Practice and Theory: A Response to Catharine MacKinnon." *Yale Journal of Law and Feminism* 5, no. 2 (1993): 217–51.

————. "Legal Images of Battered Women: Redefining the Issue of Separation." *Michigan Law Review* 90, no. 1 (1991): 1–94.

Malecha, Ann, Judith McFarlane, Julia Gist, Kathy Watson, Elizabeth Batten, Iva Hall, and Sheila Smith. "Applying for and Dropping a Protection Order: A Study with 150 Women." *Criminal Justice Policy Review* 14, no. 4 (2003): 486–504.

McDermott, M. Joan, and James Garofalo. "When Advocacy for Domestic Violence Victims Backfires: Types and Sources of Victim Disempowerment." *Violence Against Women* 10, no. 11 (2004): 1245–66.

McFarlane, Mia M. "Mandatory Reporting of Domestic Violence: An Inappropriate Response for New York Health Care Professionals." *Buffalo Public Interest Law Journal* 17, no. 1 (1999): 1–41.

McMenamin, Jennifer. "Abuse Victim, Children to Return Home After Appeal." *Baltimore Sun.* October 24, 2008, http://articles.baltimoresun.com/2008-10-24/news/0810230170_1_bisnath-lamdin-judge.

Meier, Joan S. "Domestic Violence, Child Custody, and Child Protection: Understanding Judicial Resistance and Imagining the Solutions." *American University Journal of Gender, Social Policy and the Law* 11, no. 2 (2003): 657–730.

Mendelson, Margot. "The Legal Production of Identities: A Narrative Analysis of Conversations with Battered Undocumented Women." *Berkeley Women's Law Journal* 19, no. 1 (2004): 138–216.

Meyers, Diana T. *Self, Society, and Personal Choice.* New York: Columbia University Press, 1989.

Miccio, G. Kristian. "If Not Now, When? Individual and Collective Responsibility for Male Intimate Violence." *Washington and Lee Journal of Civil Rights and Social Justice* 15, no. 2 (2009): 405–50.

————. "A House Divided: Mandatory Arrest, Domestic Violence, and the Conservatization of the Battered Women's Movement." *Houston Law Review* 42, no. 2 (2005): 237–323.

Michalski, Joseph H. "Explaining Intimate Partner Violence: The Sociological Limitations of Victimization Studies." *Sociological Forum* 20, no. 4 (2005): 613–40.

"Microfinance FAQs." *Acción USA.* http://www.accionusa.org/home/support-u.s.-microfinance/about-accion-usa/microfinance-faq.aspx.

Miller, Elizabeth, Michele R. Decker, Heather L. McCauley, Daniel J. Tancredi, Rebecca R. Levenson, Jeffrey Waldman, Phyllis Shoenwald, and Jay G. Silverman. "Pregnancy Coercion, Intimate Partner Violence and Unintended Pregnancy." *Contraception 2010,* no. 4 (2010): 1–2.

Miller, Susan L., LeeAnn Iovanni, and Kathleen D. Kelley. "Violence Against Women and the Criminal Justice Response." In *Sourcebook on Violence Against Women,* 2nd ed., 267–88, edited by Claire M. Renzetti, Jeffrey L. Edleson, and Raquel Kennedy Bergen. Thousand Oaks, CA: Sage Publications, 2011.

Mills, Linda G. *Insult to Injury: Rethinking Our Responses to Intimate Abuse.* Princeton, NJ: Princeton University Press, 2003.

Moore, Shelby A. D. "Battered Woman Syndrome: Selling the Shadow to Support the Substance." *Howard Law Journal* 38, no. 2 (1995): 297–352.

Morrison, Adele M. "Changing the Domestic Violence (Dis)Course: Moving from White Victim to Multi-Cultural Survivor." *UC Davis Law Review* 39, no. 3 (2006): 1061–1118.

———. "Queering Domestic Violence to 'Straighten Out' Criminal Law: What Might Happen When Queer Theory and Practice Meet Criminal Law's Conventional Responses to Domestic Violence." *Southern California Review of Law and Women's Studies* 13, no. 1 (2003): 81–162.

Muhlhauser, Tara Lea, and Douglas D. Knowlton. "Mediation in the Presence of Domestic Violence: Is It the Light at the End of the Tunnel or Is a Train On the Track?" *North Dakota Law Review* 70, no. 2 (1994): 255–68.

Murphy, Jane C. "Engaging with the State: The Growing Reliance on Judges and Lawyers to Protect Battered Women." *American University Journal of Gender, Social Policy, and Law* 11, no. 2 (2003): 499–521.

———. "Lawyering for Social Change: The Power of the Narrative in Domestic Violence Law Reform." *Hofstra Law Review* 21, no. 4 (1993): 1243–93.

Murphy, Jane C., and Robert Rubinson. "Domestic Violence and Mediation: Responding to the Challenges of Crafting Effective Screens." *Family Law Quarterly* 39, no. 1 (2005): 53–85.

Myers, Roslyn. "Truth and Reconciliation Commissions 101: What TRCs Can Teach the United States Justice System About Justice." *Revista Juridica Universidad de Puerto Rico* 78, no. 1 (2009): 95–128.

Nelson, Lynn Ingrid. "Community Solutions to Domestic Violence Must Address Cultural Roots and Beliefs." *Assembling the Pieces* 3, no. 2 (2002).

"Observations from Participants." Domestic Violence Surrogate Dialogue. http://www.dvsdprogram.com/observations.php.

Office on Violence Against Women. The American Recovery and Reinvestment Act of 2009: A Message from OVW Acting Director Catherine Pierce, March 2009, 6.

Ops. Kentucky Attorney General 83-187 (1983).

Orloff, Leslye E., Mary Ann Dutton, Giselle Aguilar Haas, and Nawal Ammar. "Battered Immigrant Women's Willingness to Call for Help and Police Response." *UCLA Women's Law Journal* 13, no. 1 (2003): 43–100.

Osthoff, Sue. "But, Gertrude, I Beg to Differ, a Hit Is Not a Hit Is Not a Hit: When Battered Women Are Arrested for Assaulting Their Partners." *Violence Against Women* 8, no. 12 (2002): 1521–44.

Owen, Mary, and Steve Schmadeke. "Police: Attorney Beat Wife Outside Joliet Courtroom." *Chicago Tribune*, November 20, 2010. http://www.chicagotribune.com/news/local/southsouthwest/ct-met-joliet-lawyer-beating-1121-20101120.0.2346242.story.

Owens, David. "West Hartford Man Arrested Three Times on Domestic Violence Charges." *Hartford Courant*, June 1, 2010. http://www.courant.com/news/domestic-violence/hc-westhartford-arrested-tree-times-020100531,0,1352850,print.story.

Panchanadeswaran, Subadra, Laura Ting, Jessica G. Burke, Patricia O'Campo, Karen A. McDonnell, and Andrea Gielen. "Profiling Abusive Men Based on Women's Self-Reports: Findings from a Sample of Urban Low-Income Minority Women." *Violence Against Women* 16, no. 3 (2010): 313–27.

Paternoster, Raymond, Robert Brame, Ronet Bachman, and Lawrence W. Sherman. "Do Fair Procedures Matter? The Effect of Procedural Justice on Spouse Assault." *Law and Society Review* 31, no. 1 (1997): 163–200.

Pence, Ellen. "Some Thoughts on Philosophy." In *Coordinating Community Responses to Domestic Violence: Lessons from Duluth and Beyond*. Thousand Oaks, CA: Sage Publications, 1999.

Pence, Ellen, and Shamita Das Dasgupta. *Re-Examining "Battering": Are All Acts of Violence Against Intimate Partners the Same?* Duluth, MN: Praxis International, 2006.

Phelps, Teresa Godwin. *Shattered Voices: Language, Violence and the Work of Truth Commissions.* Philadelphia: University of Pennsylvania Press, 2004.

Piepzna-Samarasinha, Leah Lakshmi. "What It Feels Like When It Finally Comes: Surviving Incest in Real Life." In *Yes Means Yes: Visions of Female Sexual Power and a World Without Rape*, 93–106, edited by Jaclyn Friedman and Jessica Valenti. Berkeley, CA: Seal Press, 2008.

Pierce, Catherine. *The American Recovery and Reinvestment Act of 2009: A Message from OVW Acting Director Catherine Pierce.* Washington, DC: Office on Violence Against Women, 2009.

Pierre, Robert E., and Clarence Williams. "Woman Had Lived in Fear of Former Boyfriend: DC Victim Slain After Calling Police." *Washington Post*, November 25, 2008. http://www.washingtonpost.com/wp-dyn/content/article/2008/11/24/AR2008112402763.html.

Pitts, Wayne J., Eugena Givens, and Susan McNeeley. "The Need for a Holistic Approach to Specialized Domestic Violence Court Programming: Evaluating Offender Rehabilitation Needs and Recidivism." *Juvenile and Family Court Journal* 60, no. 3 (2009): 1–21.

Pleck, Elizabeth. *Domestic Tyranny: The Making of American Social Policy against Family Violence from Colonial Times to the Present.* New York: Oxford University Press, 1987.

Postmus, Judy L., Margaret Severson, Marianne Berry, and Jeong Ah Yoo. "Women's Experiences of Violence and Seeking Help." *Violence Against Women* 15, no. 7 (2009): 852–68.

Power and Control Wheel (edited version), available online at www.lawc.on.ca/images/power-control-wheel.jpg.

Powers, Laurie E., Paula Renker, Susan Robinson-Whelen, Mary Oschwald, Rosemary Hughes, Paul Swank, and Mary Ann Curry. "Interpersonal Violence and Women with Disabilities: Analysis of Safety Promoting Behaviors." *Violence Against Women* 15, no. 9 (2009): 1040–69.

Pranis, Kay. "Restorative Values and Family Violence." In *Restorative Justice and Family Violence*, 23–41, edited by Heather Strang and John Braithwaite. Cambridge: Cambridge University Press, 2002.

"Program Results." Women's Initiative, http://www.womensinitiative.org/aboutus/program-results.htm.

Pruitt, Lisa R. "Place Matters: Domestic Violence and Rural Difference." *Wisconsin Journal of Law, Gender and Society* 23, no. 2 (2008): 347–416.

———. "Toward a Feminist Theory of the Rural." *Utah Law Review 2007*, no. 2 (2007): 421–88.

Ptacek, James. *Battered Women in the Courtroom: The Power of Judicial Response.* Boston: Northeastern University Press, 1999.

Ptacek, James, and Loretta Frederick. *Restorative Justice and Intimate Partner Violence.* VAWNet Applied Research Forum, 2008.

Randall, Melanie. "Domestic Violence and the Construction of 'Ideal Victims': Assaulted Women's 'Image Problems' in Law." *Saint Louis University Public Law Review* 23, no. 1 (2004): 107–54.

Raphael, Jody. "Battering Through the Lens of Class." *American University Journal of Gender, Social Policy and the Law* 11, no. 2 (2003): 367–75.

————. *Saving Bernice: Battered Women, Welfare and Poverty*. Boston: Northeastern University Press, 2000.

Rasche, Christine E. "Early Models for Contemporary Thought on Domestic Violence and Women Who Kill Their Mates: A Review of the Literature from 1895 to 1970." *Women and Criminal Justice* 1, no. 2 (1990): 31–53.

Rebovich, Donald J. "Prosecution Response to Domestic Violence: Results of a Survey of Large Jurisdictions." In *Do Arrests and Restraining Orders Work?* 176–91, edited by Eve S. Buzawa and Carl G. Buzawa. Thousand Oaks, CA: Sage Publications, 1996.

Rennison, Callie Marie, and Sarah Welchans. *Intimate Partner Violence*. Washington, DC: U.S. Department of Justice, 2001.

Renzetti, Claire M. "Economic Issues and Intimate Partner Violence." In *Sourcebook on Violence Against Women*, 2nd ed., 171–88, edited by Claire M. Renzetti, Jeffrey L. Edleson, and Raquel Kennedy Bergen. Thousand Oaks, CA: Sage Publications, 2011.

————. *Economic Stress and Domestic Violence*. VAWNet Applied Research Forum, 2009.

Richie, Beth E. "A Black Feminist Reflection on the Antiviolence Movement." In *Domestic Violence at the Margins: Readings on Race, Class, Gender and Culture*, 50–55, edited by Natalie J. Sokoloff and Christina Pratt. New Brunswick, NJ: Rutgers University Press, 2005.

————. *Compelled to Crime: The Gender Entrapment of Battered Black Women*. New York: Routledge, 1996.

Rogers, Sarah. "Online Dispute Resolution: An Option for Mediation in the Midst of Gendered Violence." *Ohio State Journal on Dispute Resolution* 24, no. 2 (2009): 349–79.

Römkens, Renée. "Protecting Prosecution: Exploring the Powers of Law in an Intervention Program for Domestic Violence." *Violence Against Women* 12, no. 2 (2006): 160–86.

————. "Law as a Trojan Horse: Unintended Consequences of Rights-Based Interventions to Support Battered Women." *Yale Journal of Law and Feminism* 13, no. 2 (2001): 265–90.

Saunders, Daniel G. "Feminist-Cognitive-Behavioral and Process-Psychodynamic Treatments for Men Who Batter: Interactions of Abuser Traits and Treatment Model." *Violence and Victims* 4, no. 4 (1996): 393–414.

Schechter, Susan. *Women and Male Violence: The Visions and Struggles of the Battered Women's Movement*. Boston: South End Press, 1982.

Schneider, Elizabeth M. *Battered Women and Feminist Lawmaking*. New Haven, CT: Yale University Press, 2000.

————. "Particularity and Generality: Challenges of Feminist Theory and Practice in Work on Woman-Abuse." *New York University Law Review* 67, no. 3 (1992): 520–68.

————. "The Violence of Privacy." *Connecticut Law Review* 23, no. 4 (1991): 973–99.

Schuler, Sidney Ruth, Syed M. Hashemi, and Shamsul Huda Badal. "Men's Violence Against Women in Rural Bangladesh: Undermined or Exacerbated by Microcredit Programmes?" *Development in Practice* 8, no. 2 (1998): 148–57.

Schuler, Sidney Ruth, Syed M. Hashemi, Ann P. Riley, and Shireen Akhter. "Credit Programs, Patriarchy and Men's Violence Against Women in Rural Bangladesh." *Social Science and Medicine* 43, no. 12 (1996): 1729–42.

Schworm, Peter, and John M. Guilfoil. "Rising Economic Stress Cited in Domestic Violence Increase." *Boston Globe*. February 3, 2010. http:/ www.boston.com/news/local/Massachusetts/articles/2010/02/03/ rising_economic_stress_cited_in_domestic_violence_increase?mode=PF.

Scott, Susan, Judge. "Panel Discussion: Advocating for Victims of Domestic Violence." *Women's Rights Law Reports* 20, no. 1 (1999): 73–84.

Shainess, Natalie. "Vulnerability to Violence: Masochism as Process." *American Journal of Psychotherapy* 33, no. 2 (1979): 174–89.

Shepard, Melanie F., and Ellen L. Pence. "An Introduction: Developing a Coordinated Community Response." In *Coordinating Community Responses to Domestic Violence: Lessons from Duluth and Beyond*, 3–23, edited by Melanie F. Shepard and Ellen L. Pence. Thousand Oaks, CA: Sage Publications, 1999.

Sherman, Lawrence W. "Domestic Violence and Restorative Justice: Answering Key Questions." *Virginia Journal of Social Policy and the Law* 8, no. 1 (2000): 263–89.

Sherman, Lawrence, Douglas A. Smith, Janell D. Schmidt, and Dennis P. Rogan. "Crime, Punishment, and Stake in Conformity: Legal and Informal Control of Domestic Violence." *American Sociological Review* 57, no. 5 (1992): 680–90.

Shevory, Kristina. "With Squeeze on Credit, Microlending Blossoms." *New York Times*, July 28, 2010. http://www.nytimes.com/2010/07/29/business/smallbusiness/29sbiz.html?_r=1&pagewanted=print.

Smith, Andrea. "Beyond Restorative Justice: Radical Organizing Against Violence." In *Restorative Justice and Violence Against Women*, 255–78, edited by James Ptacek. New York: Oxford University Press, 2010.

Smith, Brenda V. "Battering, Forgiveness and Redemption." *American University Journal of Gender, Social Policy and the Law* 11, no. 2 (2003): 921–62.

Snell, John E., Richard J. Rosenwald, and Ames Robey. "The Wifebeater's Wife: A Study of Family Interaction." *Archives of General Psychiatry* 11, no. 2 (1964): 107–12.

Spinak, Jane M. "Reforming Family Court: Getting It Right Between Rhetoric and Reality." *Washington University Journal of Law and Policy* 31, no. 1 (2009): 11–38.

Spivak, Gayatri Chakravorty. "Subaltern Studies: Deconstructing Historiography." In *Selected Subaltern Studies*, 3–32, edited by Ranajit Guha and Gayatri Chakravorty Spivak. New York: Oxford University Press, 1988.

Srubas, Paul. "Domestic Violence Increases in Green Bay Area." *Green Bay* (Wisconsin) *Press Gazette*, October 3, 2010. http://www.greenbaypressgazette.com/fdcp/?1268134466187.

Stark, Evan. *Coercive Control: How Men Entrap Women in Personal Life*. Oxford: Oxford University Press, 2007.

———. "Framing and Reframing Battered Women." In *Domestic Violence: The Changing Criminal Justice Response*, 271–92, edited by Eve S. Buzawa and Carl G. Buzawa. Westport, CT: Auburn House, 1992.

Stark, Heather, and Emilee Watturs. *Why Doesn't She Just Leave: Real Women, Real Stories. A New Perspective on Domestic Violence*. Woodinville, WA: MidPacifik Publishing, 2008.

Stith, Sandra M., Karen H. Rosen, Eric E. McCollum, and Cynthia J. Thomsen. "Treating Intimate Partner Violence Within Intact Couple Relationships: Outcomes of Multi-Couple Versus Individual Couple Therapy." *Journal of Marital and Family Therapy* 30, no. 3 (2004): 305–18.

Stover, Carla Smith, Miriam Berkman, Rani Desai, and Steven Marans. "The Efficacy of a Police-Advisory Intervention for Victims of Domestic Violence: 12 Month Follow-Up Data." *Violence Against Women* 16, no. 4 (2010): 410–25.

Strauss, Misha. "The Role of Recognition in the Formation of Self-Understanding." In *Recognition, Responsibility, and Rights: Feminist Ethics and Social Theory*, 37–52, edited by Robin N. Fiore and Hilde Lindemann Nelson. Lanham, MD: Rowman & Littlefield, 2003.

Suk, Jeannie. *At Home in the Law: How the Domestic Violence Revolution Is Transforming Privacy*. New Haven, CT: Yale University Press, 2009.

———. "Criminal Law Comes Home." *Yale Law Journal* 116, no. 1 (2006): 2–70.

Tarr, Nina W. "Employment and Economic Security for Victims of Domestic Abuse." *Southern California Review of Law and Social Justice* 16, no. 2 (2007): 371–427.

Taylor, Rae, and Erin L. Nabors. "Pink or Blue . . . Black and Blue? Examining Pregnancy as a Predictor of Intimate Partner Violence and Femicide." *Violence Against Women* 15, no. 11 (2009): 1273–93.

Thalji, Jamal. "Domestic Violence Murders Rise as Crime Falls in Florida." *St. Petersburg Times*, October 12, 2010. http://license.icopyright.net/user/viewFreeUse.act?fuid=MTAzMTczMzI1%3D.

Thiel de Bocanegra, Heike, Daria P. Rostovtseva, Satin Khera, and Nita Godhwani. "Birth Control Sabotage and Forced Sex: Experiences Reported by Women in Domestic Violence Shelters." *Violence Against Women* 16, no. 5 (2010): 601–12.

Thoennes, Nancy, Peter Salem, and Jessica Pearson. "Mediation and Domestic Violence: Current Policies and Practices." *Family and Conciliation Courts Review* 33, no. 1 (1995): 6–29.

Tjaden, Patricia, and Nancy Thoennes. *Extent, Nature and Consequences of Intimate Partner Violence: Findings from the National Violence Against Women Survey*. Washington, DC: National Institute of Justice, 2000.

———. *Prevalence, Incidence and Consequences of Violence Against Women: Findings From the National Violence Against Women Survey*. Washington, DC: National Institute of Justice Centers for Disease Control and Prevention, 1998.

Tolman, Richard M. "The Validation of the Psychological Maltreatment of Women Inventory." *Violence and Victims* 14, no. 1 (1999): 25–35.

Tolman, Richard M., and Jeffrey L. Edleson. "Intervening with Men for Violence Prevention." In *Sourcebook on Violence Against Women*, 2nd ed., 351–67, edited by Claire M. Renzetti, Jeffrey L. Edleson, and Raquel Kennedy Bergen. Thousand Oaks, CA: Sage Publications, 2011.

Transcript of Trial, *State v. Shanahan*, No. FECR006475 (Iowa Dist. Ct. Shelby County Apr. 28, 2004).

Trinch, Shonna L. *Latinas' Narratives of Domestic Abuse: Discrepant Versions of Violence*. Amsterdam: John Benjamins Publishing, 2003.

Tubbs, Carolyn Y., and Oliver J. Williams. "Shared Parenting After Abuse: Battered Mothers' Perspectives on Parenting After Dissolution of a Relationship." In *Parenting by Men Who Batter: New Directions for Assessment and Intervention*, 19–44, edited by Jeffrey L. Edleson and Oliver J. Williams. New York: Oxford University Press, 2007.

Tuerkheimer, Deborah. "Recognizing and Remedying the Harm of Battering: A Call to Criminalize Domestic Violence." *Journal of Criminal Law and Criminology* 94, no. 4 (2004): 959–1032.

Twohey, Megan. "One Woman's Struggle to Escape Abuse." *Chicago Tribune*, November 11, 2008. http://www.chicagotribune.com/news/local/chi-regan_tuenov11,0,3909502,print.story.

United States Department of Justice Office on Violence Against Women, 2006 Biennial Report to Congress on the Effectiveness of Grant Programs Under the Violence Against Women Act 143, 144.

Varolli, Regina. "Kentucky Microloans Build Battered Women's Credit." *Women's e-News*, May 16, 2010.http://www.womensenews.org/print/8110.

Vedantam, Shankar. "Call For Help Leads to Possible Deportation for Hyattsville Mother." *Washington Post*, November 1, 2010. http://www.washingtonpost.com/wp-dyn/content/article/2010/11/01/AR2010110103073_pf.html.

Ver Steegh, Nancy. "The Uniform Law Act and Intimate Partner Violence: A Roadmap for Collaborative (and Non-Collaborative) Lawyers." *Hofstra Law Review* 38, no. 2 (2009): 699–756.

Visher, Christy A., Adele Harrell, Lisa Newmark, and Jennifer Yahner. "Reducing Intimate Partner Violence: An Evaluation of a Comprehensive Justice System–Community Collaboration." *Criminology and Public Policy* 7, no. 4 (2008): 495–523.

Waites, Elizabeth A. "Female Masochism and the Enforced Restriction of Choice." *Victimology: An International Journal* 2, no. 3–4 (1977–78): 535–44.

Walker Lenore E. *The Battered Woman*. New York: Harper Perennial, 1979.

Walker, Lenore E. A. *The Battered Woman Syndrome*. 3rd ed. New York: Springer Publishing, 2009.

———. "Politics, Psychology and the Battered Woman's Movement." *Journal of Trauma Practice* 1, no. 1 (2002): 81–102.

———. *The Battered Woman Syndrome*. New York: Springer Publishing, 1984.

Wan, Angela Moe. "Battered Women in the Restraining Order Process: Observations on a Court Advocacy Program." *Violence Against Women* 6, no. 6 (2000): 606–32.

Waterhouse, Carlton. "The Good, the Bad, and the Ugly: Moral Agency and the Role of Victims in Reparations Programs." *University of Pennsylvania Journal of International Law* 31, no. 1 (2009): 257–94.

Weaver, Hilary N. "The Colonial Context of Violence: Reflections on Violence in the Lives of Native American Women." *Journal of Interpersonal Violence* 24, no. 9 (2009): 1552–63.

Websdale, Neil. *Rural Woman Battering and the Justice System: An Ethnography*. Thousand Oaks, CA: Sage Publications, 1998.

Weiner, Merle H. "The Potential and Challenges of Transnational Litigation for Feminists Concerned About Domestic Violence Here and Abroad." *American University Journal of Gender, Social Policy, and Law* 11, no. 2 (2003): 749–800.

———. "From Dollars to Sense: A Critique of Government Funding for the Battered Women's Shelter Movement." *Law and Inequality: A Journal of Theory and Practice* 9, no. 2 (1991): 185–277.

Weissman, Deborah M. "Gender-Based Violence as Judicial Anomaly: Between 'The Truly National and the Truly Local.'" *Boston College Law Review* 42, no. 5 (2001): 1081–1159.

Weisz, A., R. Tolman, and Daniel Saunders. "Assessing the Risk of Severe Domestic Violence: The Importance of Survivors' Predictions." *Journal of Interpersonal Violence* 15, no. 1 (2000): 75–90.

Wendell, Susan. "Oppression and Victimization: Choice and Responsibility." In *"Nagging" Questions: Feminist Ethics in Everyday Life*, 41–76, edited by Dana E. Bushnell. Lanham, MD: Rowman & Littlefield, 1995.

White, Rebecca L., and James J. Postl. "Domestic Violence Spikes Amid Financial Stress." *Houston Chronicle*, October 16, 2010. http://www.chron.com/disp/story.mpl/editorial/outlook/7250193.html.

Williams, Susan H., and David C. Williams. "A Feminist Theory of Malebashing." *Michigan Journal of Gender and the Law* 4, no. 1 (1996): 35–127.

"Women Three Times More Likely to be Arrested for Domestic Violence." *Guardian UK*, August 28, 2009, http://www.guardian.co.uk/society/2009/aug/28/women-arrested-domestic-violence/print.

Yllo, Kersti. "Through a Feminist Lens: Gender, Diversity, and Violence: Extending the Feminist Framework." In *Current Controversies on Family Violence*, 19–34, edited by Donileen R. Loseke, Richard J. Gelles, and Mary M. Cavanaugh. Thousand Oaks, CA: Sage Publications, 2005.

Yollin, Patricia. "When a Little Means a Lot." *San Francisco Chronicle*, September 30, 2007, at A1.

Zeoli, April M., Hannah Brenner, and Alexis Norris. "A Summary and Analysis of Warrantless Arrest Statutes for Domestic Violence in the United States." *Journal of Interpersonal Violence* 26 (forthcoming).

Zoellner, Lori A., Norah C. Feeny, Jennifer Alvarez, Christina Wattington, Melanie L. O'Neill, Ruth Zager, and Edna B. Foa. "Factors Associated with Completion of the Restraining Order Process in Female Victims of Partner Violence." *Journal of Interpersonal Violence* 15, no. 10 (2000): 1081–99.

Zorza, Joan. "Protecting the Children in Custody Disputes When One Parent Abuses the Other." *Clearinghouse Review* 29, no. 12 (1996).

Index

About the Author

LEIGH GOODMARK is Associate Professor of Law, Director of Clinical Education, and Co-Director of the Center on Applied Feminism at the University of Baltimore School of Law.